YOGA THERAPY
for CHILDREN
with AUTISM and
SPECIAL NEEDS

A Norton Professional Book

YOGA THERAPY
for CHILDREN
with AUTISM and
SPECIAL NEEDS

Louise Goldberg

W. W. Norton & Company

New York • London

For information about permission to reproduce selections from this book, write to
Permissions, W. W. Norton & Company, Inc., 500 Fifth Avenue, New York, NY 10110

For information about special discounts for bulk purchases, please contact
W. W. Norton Special Sales at specialsales@wwnorton.com or 800-233-4830

Manufacturing by Walsworth
Book design by Molly Heron
Production manager: Leeann Graham

Library of Congress Cataloging-in-Publication Data

Goldberg, Louise, 1950–
 Yoga therapy for children with autism and special needs / Louise Goldberg.
 — First edition.
     pages cm
 "A Norton professional book."
 Includes bibliographical references and index.
 ISBN 978-0-393-70785-4 (hardcover)
1. Hatha yoga for children—Therapeutic use. 2. Autistic children—Health and hygiene.
3. Children with disabilities—Health and hygiene. I. Title.
 RJ133.7.G65 2013
 618.92'85882062—dc23
                          2013005798

W. W. Norton & Company, Inc., 500 Fifth Avenue, New York, N.Y. 10110
                    www.wwnorton.com
W. W. Norton & Company Ltd., Castle House, 75/76 Wells Street, London W1T 3QT

1 2 3 4 5 6 7 8 9 0

To my husband Rich Foss
my partner in all things

Contents

Acknowledgments

THE CHILDREN IN these photos are of varied backgrounds. Some are on the autism spectrum, some have varied special needs, and some are from general education classes with no special needs. My thanks to all of these children and their families for granting me permission to share their talents.

The names and details of the children described in this book have been changed to protect their privacy.

I am indebted to my photographer and friend Ed Zeiss for his extraordinary eye, his patience and gentleness with the children, and his willingness to always go the extra mile.

Thank you to the fine group at W. W. Norton: Thank you to my editor Deborah Malmud for envisioning this book and for her valuable assistance in organizing and structuring the material. Sophie Hagen coached me through every phase of the production process—from cover to cover. I am grateful for her talents, kindness, and care. Thanks to Jackie Estrada for her thorough copyediting and to Ben Yarling for his diligence in answering my many questions.

I'd like to thank my teachers, students, family, and friends for their gracious support and encouragement throughout the writing process. I am grateful to my yoga community, especially my longtime friend and teacher JoAnn Evans. Her knowledge of asana and love for Vedanta philosophy infuse my teaching. Thanks to my dear teacher and friend Eunice Wellington for her inspiration and to my first teachers: Carole Goya, Swami Vishnudevananda, and Pearl Van Aalst.

My gratitude to the students and faculty of the Yoga Center of Deerfield

Beach, Florida, my spiritual home, and especially to Dotty Zevin, for her unflagging support.

Thanks to my friends and family who propped me up when I needed it: my sister Roberta Callaghan, who knew when to listen and when to "let me go"; Karen Deerwester, author and teacher, for helping me craft a vision and stay on course, and inspiring me with her own work; acupuncturist Steve Templin, who proofread my stress chapter and talked endlessly with me about heart rate variability and coherence; Debby Reynolds, Brenda Martin, Joni and Pat Clare, Marty O'Neill, Eileen Templin, Howard and Anita Goldberg, Siri Goldberg, Rachel Rosenblum, Fred and Debbie Foss, and Dave Foss. Thanks to you all for knowing when to talk and when to leave me alone.

Thanks to my partners in S.T.O.P. and Relax©, Your Special Needs Toolbox—Debra Collins, Daniela Morales, and Sally Miller—for pooling their talents to bring a visual yoga-based curriculum to children in schools around the world.

My gratitude to the Broward Schools, starting with John Smith, retired principal, who introduced the yoga ESE program in 1981, and to Sally Creswell, retired curriculum coordinator, who continued the project with autism education in 2000. Thank you to the autism cluster at Coconut Creek Elementary School, especially to autism coach Barb Hennessey, classroom teacher Cheryl Loomis, and the entire cluster faculty, Principal Kathy Good, the extraordinary children, and their families.

I am grateful to Roger Cole, Amy Weintraub, Steven Porges, Chris Streeter, and the many yoga teachers, therapists, educators, researchers, and professors who so generously took time from their busy schedules to share their insights and respond to my queries.

Thanks to Al Rego, Stacy Layer, Maria DeJesus, and the staff, families, and children at the Miami Children's Hospital-Dan Marino Center for the support and opportunity to teach yoga at the day camp for the past decade.

I am indebted to the International Association of Yoga Therapists, particularly Tricia Lamb for her assistance with my article in 2004, and to John Kepner and Matt Taylor for their guidance in the process of yoga therapy.

Thanks to mathematician Brian Clare for his statistical analysis of the study published in the *IJYT* in 2004.

My thanks for contributions made by Marie Birchansky, Linda Becker, Linda Citron, Sharon Gelbaum Dolinsky, Dan Ewing, Sonia Kay, Sara Levin, and the many students, clients, and colleagues who graciously supported my preoccupation with this book.

I am grateful to my son, Mark Goldberg-Foss, musician, historian, poet, for his inquiring mind, good humor, and the inspiration of his creative quest.

To my husband and partner Rich Foss, for his unwavering support, for reading, rereading, editing, encouraging, laughing, commiserating, clarifying, listening, and supporting me through every phase of this process. How fortunate I am to have you in my life.

And to our dog Ralph, who puts all things in perspective.

Finally, I want to thank my parents, Abe and Annette Goldberg, who instilled in each of their children and grandchildren a belief in ourselves and in the natural goodness of others. How I wish they were here to share this moment.

Introduction

MY FIRST YOGA class was held in a locker room in January 1979. It was supposed to be in the gym at the small south Florida college, but there was a scheduling conflict and we got bumped by the weightlifters.

I must confess that I'm not much of a fan of locker rooms; I don't like the smell of dirty socks and sweat. Lined up on the floor between the lockers, I couldn't even see my teacher's face as she weaved her way through the oddly shaped room. Still, as I lay on the cold, hard floor, I could hear the rhythmic tones of her voice guiding me into unusual positions. I heard her gentle reminders to breathe, breathe, breathe. The smell and feel of the locker room fell away; I was home.

Late that spring, my mother and I went to our favorite deli in Massachusetts for a corned beef sandwich—my last, ever—before I boarded the bus to Montreal. From there I traveled north to the Sivananda Yoga Camp in the Laurentian Mountains, where I pitched my pup tent on the mountainside. I had come for three weeks and stayed for three months. The following summer I traveled to Europe to study at the Sivananda Centers in London, Paris, and Geneva. I returned to the ashram in Canada to take my Yoga Teacher Training course in the summer of 1981.

The yogic life, as instructed by Swami Vishnudevananda at the Sivananda Yoga Vedanta Centers, is an ascetic, disciplined existence, with equal attention paid to "proper exercise, proper breathing, proper relaxation, proper diet, positive thinking (deep philosophy) and meditation" (1960, p. xi). The teacher certification required a month-long commitment to the ashram life and intense study of the science of yoga. The wake-up bell at 5:30 each morning signaled the call to meditation, followed by Sanskrit chant. There were two-hour hatha yoga classes twice daily on the bare wooden deck outside—no cushions or props. Each day included hours of instruction on the principles of yoga, posture (*asana*) and breathing (*pranayama*), the philosophy of *The Bhagavad Gita,* anatomy and physiology, ancient cleansing practices (*kriyas*), and Sanskrit chant. I ate two vegan meals per day and practiced karma yoga to keep the ashram clean and organized. Late each evening after meditation, I trekked back up the mountain and crawled into my sleeping bag. That summer was the beginning of a lifetime of study and practice in becoming a yoga teacher.

Returning to south Florida, where I had become an adjunct member of the English Department at Broward College, I began teaching yoga in the Physical Education Department. While the students in my composition classes strived to complete the perfect sentence, my yoga students across campus learned to quiet their minds. My English students left class as tense and preoccupied as they had arrived; my yoga students left class humming and serene. That disparity didn't seem fair (Goldberg, 2004a).

One test day, seeing my English students' knotted brows, I shared a simple abdominal breathing exercise. Despite their initial eye rolling and quizzical looks, the students' faces began to relax. Gradually I added neck rotations and shoulder shrugs on writing days. Watching my students' breathing deepen and their bodies release tension after just a few minutes of yoga made me realize how easily it could be introduced into conventional classrooms.

In 1982 my teacher and friend Carole Goya and I began teaching yoga to children K–12 with emotional behavior disorders at a state hospital in the Broward County Public Schools. I had been an educator for a decade by that time, first teaching English at the middle and high school levels, and then becoming a reading specialist for middle school children with varied learning disabilities. Still, nothing had prepared me for the challenges of teaching yoga to children with emotional behavioral disorders, low functioning autism, and other severe emotional and neurological disorders.

As one accustomed to the effectiveness of language, I was surprised to discover the limitations of words in conveying what I wanted to teach in yoga. I learned to rely on touch and movement, pace and rhythm, the quality of my voice and my breathing. There were times that Carole and I looked helplessly at one another; the children were tangled around our arms, our legs, or each other. But there were also moments of stillness, an unfamiliar calm.

The classroom teachers and administrators were as amazed as we were at the moments of quiet in yoga. So many of the children's problems—being withdrawn, insecure, anxious, hyperactive, dissociated from others and their own bodies—seemed to be addressed through yoga posture and breathing. Opening the chest, grounding the feet and hands, deepening the breath, focusing on one point, and interacting with others occurred naturally through the practice. I began to see children change.

As a licensed massage therapist, I started incorporating touch in my work. I discovered the calming effects of steady pressure or a reassuring hand for many children. These tools provided another form of communicating with children with special needs that is often less confusing than words. To help educators and therapists implement yoga-based programs for varied needs, I began a certification program in Creative Relaxation, Yoga Therapy for Children with Autism and Special Needs.

Yoga therapy is a wonderful medium for teaching children many skills. It is fun, it is balancing for all kinds of bodies, and it fosters imagination. Yoga therapy teaches self-control and self-calming and promotes ethical interaction with others. It enhances self-esteem and the skills needed to attend and be still. Children learn to inhabit their bodies with greater efficiency and awareness.

Most children are natural yogis. They love to move and play and bend their bodies into varied shapes and forms. Yoga therapy levels the field between adults and children. Getting down on hands and knees, we share the child's physical perspective. Yoga therapy speaks the universal language of touch, helping children learn to receive and use touch for body awareness and calming. Yoga lends itself to a visual curriculum, with postures inspired from nature or familiar objects. Finally, yoga fosters creativity. Children become dogs, cats, trees, and butterflies. Even as their bodies follow our instructions, their imaginations soar!

Yoga therapy offers tools for improving physical strength, flexibility, and balance; increasing self-confidence and self-awareness; learning to process sensory information; practicing methods for calming and focusing the mind; and fostering imagination. Sharing an ancient philosophy in a noncompetitive, supportive environment is a gift that serves a child into adulthood. Yoga therapy feels good to youngsters, and it is fun. That makes it a delight for the therapist, as well.

What You Will Find in the Pages Ahead

This book begins with an overview of everything you need before beginning instruction. Chapter 1 begins with a brief history of yoga and distinguishes it from yoga therapy. The chapter introduces methods of providing yoga therapy to children with special needs. The second chapter describes the assessment process, including gathering medical history and background information, tools for developing a therapeutic plan, and a system of assessing its effectiveness. (Appendix 2 summarizes this process.) Chapter 3 provides a description of the special needs that will be explored and discusses properties of yoga therapy that suit it to a child with each condition. The fourth chapter outlines physical, emotional, and sensory benefits of yoga therapy, including relief from stress, connection building, and increased self-awareness. In Chapter 5, Ten Golden Rules offer guidelines for interacting with children with special needs.

Part I (Chapters 6–9), a rationale, explores current research that underscores the efficacy of a movement-based yoga therapy program. Chapter 6 examines the effects of stress on children's health and their capacity to learn. It explores the role of the limbic and vagal systems in the stress response and the impact on children in whom these systems may be compromised.

The benefits of exercise to enhance health and learning, inspiring much research in recent years, is the topic of Chapter 7. The energizing, playful, and calming properties of yoga therapy relative to ADHD and ASD are of particular note. Chapter 8 considers yoga's effectiveness for stress relief and includes current research supporting yoga's efficacy at elevating GABA levels and calming children throughout their day. The process of relaxation—through posture, breathing, and the mind—is explored in Chapter 9. That chapter covers the role of touch, progressive relaxation, and meditation and is packed with examples and teaching techniques to make the experience of relaxation accessible to special children.

The process of yoga therapy is the subject of Part II (Chapters 10–13). Chapter 10 guides you in creating a sacred space for students, regardless of the limitations of your practice area. You will learn techniques for creating a mood using your voice and demeanor, rules for consistency and safety, and suggestions for minimizing distractions and maintaining control. Chapter 11 teaches methods for meeting children where they are, drawing them out as well as reining them in through your manner and communication style. Using techniques such as imitation, contracts, and familiar language engages the child while making yoga therapy fun.

As Chapter 12 explains, a structured environment, the use of visual supports, simplifying instruction, and consistent routines are all part of the process of empowering children with tools for success. In addition, the chapter explores the use of schedules, familiar routines, and transitional cues and provides guidance for averting meltdowns. Chapter 13 contains methods for enhancing the child's independence through self-control and awareness of his or her levels of stress. It includes tools to help children learn to control their volume and to develop independence through the use of touch pressure, cues for relaxation, and personalized yoga breaks.

Application, the final section of the book (Chapters 14–20), arms you with postures and lessons for the application of the rationale and principles you have learned. Chapter 14 prepares you with information about using Chapter 15's posture catalog and specific guidelines for teaching. Chapter 15 contains 60 illustrated postures with descriptions, benefits, and contraindications. The instructions are provided in child-friendly language with variations and adaptations for special needs.

Chapter 16 distinguishes characteristics of yoga therapy in schools from other settings, with lessons for children at their desks or standing in line. It includes routines for mitigating test anxiety and keeping the school day peaceful. Chapter 17 contains a model for your curriculum, with gradations of challenge based on your initial assessment of the child's abilities. Chapter 18 presents postures and sequences that correspond to specific benefits of yoga therapy. This section includes lessons for sensory integration, energizing and calming, parent-child partnering, and guided relaxation. Chapter 19 is all about breathing, providing postures and routines to enhance breath awareness, strengthen the muscles of respiration, and elongate exhalation. Finally, Chapter 20 teaches chants, songs, and games to promote language and motor skills and social engagement.

I am certain that you will find sharing yoga therapy with children a most gratifying path. My hope is that the tools you take from this book will enhance your practice and be of service to the children with whom you have the privilege of working.

YOGA THERAPY
for CHILDREN
with AUTISM and
SPECIAL NEEDS

OVERVIEW

BEFORE YOU BEGIN YOGA THERAPY

CHAPTER 1

YOGA AND YOGA THERAPY

A Curriculum for Calm

ALL CHILDREN ARE special. And each is different from the next. Ask any parent or educator.

But one quality that most children share is the disinclination to sit quietly in one place for hours at a time.

Yet this is the premise of our education system.

Throughout their day, teachers ask their students to be quiet, sit still, listen, pay attention, and settle down. Exasperated parents ask their kids why they can't control themselves. If only the children could take a deep breath and relax for one minute!

And this is sound advice.

But where in a child's day does he learn these skills? How does he learn to attend, be still, and calm down? Where in the school day is the instruction for relaxation?

Yoga therapy teaches children how to control their bodies, how to breathe, how to focus, and how to relax. It provides instruction, practice, and reward. Yoga therapy is, in fact, a curriculum for calm.

What Is Yoga?

When people think of yoga, they imagine headstands, intricate back bending, and contorted twists. With all the emphasis on postures, many would be surprised to learn that yoga is a system for attaining "undisturbed calmness of mind," according to the *Yoga Sutras*, as translated by Prabhavananda and Isherwood (1981, p. 66, v.1:33). This guidebook summarizes the science and philosophy of yoga, a tradition that had been passed orally from master to student for at least 5000 years before an Indian scholar named Patanjali, the presumed author of the *Yoga Sutras,* organized and recorded these Sanskrit teachings approximately 2000 years ago (Feuerstein, 1998).

For millennia, people have practiced the sequential steps or rungs (*ashtanga*) outlined in these 196 short verses. The second sutra is still part of the oral tradition for 21st-century yoga teachers—*Yoga chitta vrtti nirodah:* "Yoga is the control of thought-waves in the mind" (Prabhavananda & Isherwood, 1981, p. 15).

The *Yoga Sutras* described a yoga posture (*asana*) as "seated in a position which is firm but relaxed" (Prabhavananda & Isherwood, 1981, p. 79). In fact, preparing the body to sit in stillness was the emphasis of ancient instruction. The varied postures used in most classes today were collected in the *Hatha Yoga Pradipika*, a manual written in the mid-14th century, according to Georg Feuerstein (1997). *Yoga* is a Sanskrit word meaning yoke or union; *hatha* means force or "forceful" (Feuerstein, p. 118). Hatha yoga brings union to mind and spirit through disciplined refinement of the body.

Yoga postures are one of eight limbs included in Patanjali's *Yoga Sutras*. The text offers a sequential approach to inner stillness that begins with ethical codes of conduct, postures, and breathing practices (*pranayama*). Only after extensive practice is the student advised to commence the more challenging work of withdrawing from the distractions of the world around him. Concentration and meditation are considered further advanced rungs on the hierarchy of yoga. The ultimate state is union, "when all the 'whirls' or 'fluctuations' of the ordinary waking state are fully restricted" (Feuerstein, 1998, p. 335).

Clearly, yoga is more than a series of exercises. Its teachings offer a code of living in harmony among others and within oneself, tools to improve and maintain one's health, and a system to quiet and focus the mind. In addition to posture, breathing, and meditation, techniques for yoga instruction include chanting mantra (sound or words), hand positions (*mudra*), ritual, and self-discipline. According to the IAYT (International Association of Yoga Therapists), "yoga is a scientific system of self-investigation, self-transformation, and self-realization . . . that . . . includes all aspects of body; breath; and mind, intellect, and emotions" (2012, p. 4).

Yoga Therapy

There is a distinction between yoga and yoga therapy:

> Yoga therapy is the appropriate application of these teachings and practices in a therapeutic context in order to . . . engage the client/student's energy in the direction of desired goals. The goals of yoga therapy include eliminating, reducing, or managing symptoms that cause suffering; improving function; helping to prevent the occurrence or reoccurrence of underlying causes of illness; and moving toward improved health and wellbeing. Yoga therapy also helps clients/students change their relationship to and identification with their condition . . . The efficacy of yoga therapy is supported by an increasing body of research evidence, which contributes to the growing understanding and acceptance of its value as a therapeutic discipline." (International Association of Yoga Therapy, 2012, p. 4)

Becoming a yoga therapist requires extensive experience, study, and practice with specialized populations. The IAYT recommends 800 additional hours of education for Registered Yoga Teachers (RYT) who already have 200 hours of training. Yoga therapists must be conversant with the benefits and contraindications of postures. B. K. S. Iyengar cautions that choosing poses that are unsuitable for an individual's condition can "adversely affect his or her health" (2001, p. 238).

The terms *yoga* and *yoga therapy* are used throughout this book. There are times that they may be used interchangeably. Many of the benefits of yoga therapy are also benefits of yoga in general. Many teachers believe that all yoga is therapeutic. But there are also individuals who apply the "no pain, no gain" principle to yoga, separating the postures from the philosophy of *ahimsa*, do no harm. Although beneficial for many, this is not therapeutic yoga.

Individualizing the program and bringing specific goals to each session make yoga therapeutic. Although you may apply the principles of yoga therapy in your instruction, there are distinctions between teaching yoga and providing yoga therapy for those with special needs.

YOGA THERAPY FOR CHILDREN

Whereas adults generally seek yoga therapy, it's the parent or school that arranges it for a child. For that reason, it's especially important to engage the child by making yoga therapy a playful activity. Laughing and having fun can be more important than precision of form.

Sadly, for some children there is little laughter; the goal instead is to reduce suffering. If a child experiences relief or comfort in a position, his breathing may become rhythmic and his mind less agitated. He may view his body in a more positive way. Providing opportunities to experience success in posture can change how a child feels about himself. These are appropriate goals of yoga therapy for children with special needs.

YOGA CLASSES VERSUS YOGA THERAPY

General yoga classes include an equal number of postures for strength, flexibility, and balance. Poses are chosen to work each area of the body and move the spine through a full range of motion. Classes generally include music, play, a variety of postures, interaction with peers, and brief or extended periods of quiet relaxation. If the teacher comports herself appropriately and takes care in selecting her routines, children will be successful in observing the rules for class, following verbal instructions, and replicating the postures that are modeled. Clearly, a great deal of effort and guidance is required by the teacher to make this happen, but it is within the realm of possibility.

For yoga therapy, it's useful to obtain extensive information about the child's history and predispositions. Knowing the child's preferences, learning style, strengths, and limitations informs every yoga therapy session. Visual guides, for example, may be necessary for a child with ASD (autism spectrum disorder) to follow directions. While a child with ADHD (attention deficit hyperactivity disorder) may respond to detailed instruction in a posture, the same information could frustrate a child with developmental delays. Long, focused periods of quiet breathing or the use of background music may calm one child and agitate another. Individualizing instruction is essential.

The structure of the classes will differ, as well. Drawing from yoga's vast well of resources—ethical teachings, posture, breathing, inward focus, concentration, mudra, and mantra—the yoga therapist selects a limited number of challenges to address at one time. For example, yoga therapy offers diverse tools for building strength. If a child has low body tone, you can help him increase stamina by teaching breathing or chanting techniques. You may introduce postures that strengthen one area of his body at a time. The child with limited mobility might imagine himself a strong warrior in a story about strength of mind overcoming physical prowess. Perhaps the child can master a hand position or make the sound of an animal represented by the pose. These accomplishments help strengthen his self-esteem and increase his resolve to continue his practice.

Yoga therapy is highly individualized, which means establishing goals and objectives to determine its efficacy. Success in yoga therapy, however, is measured by the process as well as the outcome. For example, a child may perform a posture awkwardly, if at all, but he may smile or make eye contact while attempting the pose. In this instance, the child's responsiveness is the measure of success, rather than the achievement of a specific pose.

YOGA THERAPY FOR GROUPS

Addressing specific needs in yoga therapy is most effective when working with individuals. With careful organization, however, you can group children by ability, adjusting instruction to match the challenges of the participants. You will need at least one skilled assistant, so one of you can conduct the class and model the poses, while the other supports individual students.

Working with groups of diverse abilities also has its benefits, providing opportunities to improve social interaction and communication skills in a natural setting. It is less costly for parents and institutions, so that more children can receive instruction. By practicing yoga therapy with school groups, children learn to implement self-regulating techniques in the classroom with the support of their peers. Providing instruction to families brings tools for relaxation into their homes.

Integrating Yoga with Other Therapies

Yoga is also therapeutic when used as an adjunct to an existing form of therapy such as physical, occupational, speech, or behavioral. Educators also use yoga techniques to enhance the learning environment. Rather than being the goal of such sessions, yoga interventions are used as a means.

Some of these individuals may be yoga teachers, so this marriage of therapies is seamless. Through training and practice, however, non-yoga teachers can also learn to implement aspects of yoga in their work with children with special needs. Having a personal yoga practice is advisable, but some individuals start off helping children and then discover the benefits of yoga for themselves. This book will explore many ways to implement yoga as a therapeutic tool for therapists and educators to augment their programs.

Moving Forward

Clearly, this book will not make you a yoga therapist or an expert on special needs. Working within your own area of expertise, however, you will find ways to implement therapeutic aspects of yoga into your programs. If you are a yoga teacher, this book will expand your knowledge of teaching children with special needs. If you are a yoga therapist, you will appreciate the research, posture adaptations, and specialized lesson plans. If you are a therapist or educator, you will learn the benefits of yoga therapy for specific challenges and tools for using them in your office or classroom.

Yoga therapy reflects the qualities taught in traditional yoga literature—balance, discipline, equanimity, seeing oneself in others and others in oneself. The task of the therapist is not to impose the philosophy and practices of yoga but rather to exemplify them, to create an atmosphere of safety and support, to provide a mirror for each child to see himself as a sacred being.

CHAPTER 2

ASSESSMENT PROCESS

"Let not thy motive be the fruit of action. Act . . . without attachment . . . in success and failure. Even-mindedness is yoga."

—M. K. GANDHI

Ongoing Anecdotal Assessment

Whereas yoga in its purest form is purposefully goal-less, contemporary therapy and education are usually assessed in terms of goals, objectives, and achievement. This presents a contradiction for many yoga practitioners. To be effective, yoga therapy should include specific objectives in measurable terms. However, no assessment or objective can provide the full measure of a child.

An important distinction between therapeutic yoga and other forms of therapy, according to speech-language pathologist Molly Lannon Kenny, founder of Integrated Movement Therapy, is that "if your objective is not achieved, it doesn't mean the instruction was a failure" (personal communication, August 9, 2012).

Yoga develops self-transformation and awareness; many of the changes that occur will be subtle. It's essential to become a skillful witness by refining your capacity for observation and inner quiet. Yoga therapy is as much about being fully present with the child and creating a harmonious interchange as it is about any other specific outcome.

Keep records and notes of improvements and changes that you observe, no matter how subtle. This anecdotal data will be useful in adjusting objectives and validating progress. Throughout this book, you will learn methods to build trust and make a connection with children with special needs. Progress in those areas, though difficult to quantify, is perhaps the most important assessment of your program.

Preliminary Assessment

When working with children, your first responsibility is their safety. You need to know if any position or activity could cause them harm. Collect as much information as possible from the child's parents, school, teachers, and therapists. In addition to interviews, use the Parent Questionnaire in Appendix 1, which can be adapted for other professionals. Initially, you will need a parent's written permission and the child's medical history. Information about his cognitive, physical, emotional, and behavioral challenges, as well as learning style, is important in determining your instructional approach.

This information will help you determine whether to work with the child privately or with other children. It's important that children are grouped in a way that is conducive to learning together and interacting safely.

Yoga Therapy Assessment

When you meet with the child, observe his physical limitations or discomfort. Does he respond to your words or gestures? Notice if he watches you when you speak. Can he imitate what you do? How close to him do you need to be to catch his attention, and how long can you keep it? Does he seem interested in what you are doing? Is he aggressive or anxious?

Determine if the child can sit comfortably in a chair. Can he sit on the floor cross-legged, on his feet with knees tucked beneath him, or with his legs straight in front of him? Can he sit up independently or does he need assistance?

What do you notice about his breathing? Is it fast and shallow? Rhythmic and deep? In the belly or chest? Through his nose or mouth? Does his respiration speed up when he moves quickly and slow down when he stops? Can he follow instructions about breathing in and out?

Are there physical conditions from his medical history that prohibit movements such as forward or backward bending, twisting, lowering the head below the heart, or putting weight on a joint? Does he seem uncomfortable?

Implementation

After this process of assessment, you will determine whether you are the appropriate therapist for this child. Do you feel confident in your ability to address his needs while keeping him, other children around him, and yourself safe? Do you believe you can be of service to him? If so, it's time to get started.

Determine a mode of instruction— what you have to do to engage the child's attention and get a response. The duration of each session will depend on how long he can focus and participate. How frequently can you meet? Juggle the ideal with what is practical for the family or institution.

To develop a therapeutic plan of postures, you will need to assess the child's ability, level of independence, and comfort in each of the foundational postures. These are the starting positions for every subsequent pose you will teach. Refer to the Benefits of Yoga (Chapter 4) to establish your goals and to the results of your Assessment of Foundational Postures (Appendix 2) to determine objectives.

Familiarize yourself with the child's medical history and the benefits and precautions for each posture (Chapter 15). Based on all of this information, you will select your first lessons (see Chapter 17). To enhance your curriculum, choose postures, lessons, breathing techniques, songs, and games from Chapters 15 to 20. Determine the frequency of reassessment, based on the child's response to yoga therapy. To measure the effectiveness of your program, include anecdotal data as well as specific postures and routines that have been successfully implemented. Remember, children will continually gain new skills, so reassess periodically.

Start with those things the child can do easily, and add challenges gradually in future sessions. If any posture does not seem right for the child, omit it. Trust your own observations and intuition.

CHAPTER 3

SPECIAL NEEDS

Y OGA THERAPY AFFORDS children an opportunity to play and learn in an environment that embraces their uniqueness and supports their strengths. To develop a therapeutic plan that addresses the diverse qualities of each child, it's useful to have a greater understanding of his or her condition. Of course, there are no "cookie cutter" children, nor is there any one approach that will guarantee success.

Physical Disabilities

A physical impairment is defined by the Americans with Disabilities Act (1990) as "any physiological disorder or condition, cosmetic disfigurement, or anatomical loss affecting one or more of the following body systems: neurological, musculoskeletal, special sense organs, respiratory (including speech organs), cardiovascular, reproductive, digestive, genitourinary, hemic and lymphatic, skin, and endocrine."

Children with physical disabilities have multifaceted challenges. Although many of these problems are inherent to the child's physical condition, they can be aggravated by how other children respond to them. Feeling left out or different can be painful.

Noncompetitive yoga therapy provides all children with the opportunity to be part of a group. Working with children with limited mobility invites a creative approach to your teaching. You will see many variations in the posture catalog and final chapters for children with various physical challenges. Use these variations for private sessions and then move the child into a group class if appropriate. Postures that work specific areas of the body, breathing practices, chanting, and progressive relaxation are often suitable for children with diverse physical disabilities.

Yoga therapy invites children into a world of possibilities. By practicing mental focus, self-calming, and mindfulness, a child may find a source of strength he had not known. Matthew Sanford is a yoga teacher who specializes in adapting postures for those with physical disabilities. Matthew is paraplegic; his story of healing inspires and informs: "I have never seen anyone truly become more aware of his or her body without also becoming more compassionate" (2006). Feeling disconnected from our bodies, he explains, can lead to self-destructive behaviors. "Each day, as I practice connecting my mind and my body, I am able to feel a more compassionate path" (2008).

Yoga is a valuable tool for children with visual and auditory impairments because it is multimodal. It combines verbal instruction with demonstration, auditory and visual cues, and hands-on assistance. Because vision affects the vestibular system, eliminate unsupported balance postures from your lessons with children who have visual impairments. Standing poses may also require additional assistance and support. Have the child practice poses with his back on a wall or seated in a chair. Team the child with a visually able partner and remain close to the child. Match hearing-impaired children with a partner in group classes, or provide one-to-one instruction. Use visual cues and demonstration as instructional tools. Position yourself close to the child to maintain his attention and facilitate his participation.

Many children enjoy partnering with a child with special needs. Children with challenges of their own often rise to the occasion when given the opportunity to help another child. That is the advantage of mixed classes—both the child with disabilities and his assistant feel "special."

Down Syndrome

According to A.D.A.M. Medical Encyclopedia (2012), Down syndrome is a genetic condition caused by an extra chromosome. There are recognizable physical attributes, but other symptoms vary widely among individuals. Poor muscle tone, poor strength, high body fat, cognitive delays, and slow physical development are common. Some individuals with Down syndrome may have heart defects, gastrointestinal issues, constipation, hearing or vision problems, tendencies toward hip dislocation, and hypothyroidism. "Children may also have delayed mental and social development. Common problems may include impulsive behavior, poor judgment, short attention span, and slow learning" (A.D.A.M. Medical Encyclopedia, 2012).

In *Yoga for the Special Child* (1998), Sonia Sumar discusses atlanto-cervical instability and its contraindications in postures with neck flexion, extension, or rotation. She provides detailed sequences for varying developmental stages. Sonia's book and the inspiration of her own daughter provide an excellent resource, especially when working with infants and young children with Down syndrome.

If a child has language deficits, use visual cues, such as posture illustrations and modeling. Excessive challenge may frustrate a child, resulting in loss of interest or in giving up. Children with Down syndrome are often responsive to praise and affection.

Strength poses are very important. Start with the child seated to gradually strengthen the upper body; use prone postures to develop back strength. Balance is often a challenge, so begin with hands and knees balance poses and provide support. Begin standing postures using a wall or chair. Avoid postures that put excessive weight on unstable, hyperextended joints.

Flexibility is usually more comfortable for the child, so mix strength poses with flexion to maintain enthusiasm and attention. Children are often responsive to partner postures, songs and chant, and games.

Children may have difficulty breathing through the nose; redirect the child to nasal breathing whenever possible. If the child has difficulty keeping his mouth closed, use "Breathing Routine to Strengthen Muscles of the Mouth" on page 255.

Emotional Behavioral Disorders

Children with behavior disorders/emotional disturbance or emotional behavioral disorder (EBD) may be aggressive, disruptive, noncompliant, withdrawn, anxious, or depressed (Smith, 2007).

Recommendations to enhance learning, according to the Council for Exceptional Children (2011), include a "structured environment where students experience a high degree of success; rules and routines are predictable; and students are consistently rewarded for appropriate behavior." Recommended modalities for teaching social skills include "modeling, discussion, and rehearsal . . . to help students increase control over their behavior and improve their relations with others. In addition, supportive therapies involving music, art, exercise, and relaxation techniques . . . are sometimes employed to improve self-understanding, self-esteem, and self-control."

Children with emotional behavioral disorders are especially vulnerable to stress. Their world is often marked by fear and uncertainty, difficulty in interacting appropriately with others, poor impulse control, contempt for their bodies, and anxiety about change. Their behavior often adversely affects their school performance.

The noncompetitive nature of yoga and the many variations in the poses create opportunities for every child to feel successful. As children learn ways to control their movements, they become more accepting of their physical bodies. Using students as models is highly motivating; partnering creates a connection among peers. Teaching children how to monitor their breathing and coaching them in ways to release tension provide tools for independent self-calming.

Feeling safe and accepted is essential for children with EBD. Yoga therapy creates a non-threatening space. Many children respond to imagery in posture, extended guided relaxation, and the rhythm of energetic or soothing flows. The combination of deep breathing and calming postures de-escalates high levels of physical tension.

Shifting between active and slow postures and noisy and quiet routines is important for children with EBD. You may choose from the full catalog of postures and lessons. Provide children with an experience of being in control. Offer choices whenever possible while maintaining structure. Be respectful of physical boundaries.

Autism Spectrum Disorder (ASD)

Autism spectrum disorder (ASD) also includes Asperger's disorder and pervasive developmental disorder not otherwise specified.

Autism is a neurobiological disorder of development that causes discrepancies or differences in the way information is processed, affecting the ability to

- Understand and use language to interact and communicate with people
- Understand and relate in typical ways to people, events and objects in environment
- Understand and respond to sensory stimuli—pain, hearing, etc.
- Learn and think in the same way as typically developing children

The effects of autism on learning and functioning can range from mild to severe. These . . . differences can cause confusion, frustration, and anxiety that is expressed in a variety of unexpected ways, such as withdrawing, engaging in unusual repetitive behaviors, and occasionally, in extreme situations, by aggression and/or self-injury. (Janzen, 1996, pp. 5–6)

Autism is a spectrum disorder, an umbrella that categorizes a huge range of abilities. There are children on the spectrum who require assistance in many aspects of daily care and those who do not appear to respond to language. There are individuals with autism who excel intellectually and artistically—writers, teachers, inventors, painters, musicians, scientists, and engineers.

The American Psychiatric Association's *Diagnostic and Statistical Manual of Mental Disorders* (DSM-IV) (2000) specifies that there are individuals with autism who demonstrate "no clinically significant . . . delay in language . . . [or] cognitive development, . . . age appropriate self-help skills, adaptive behavior (other than social interaction), and curiosity about the environment" (p. 77).

An estimated 1 in 88 American children has an autism spectrum disorder, according to the U.S. Centers for Disease Control and Prevention (2012a). The Autism Society of America (2012) explains, "Children do not 'outgrow' autism, but studies show that early diagnosis and intervention lead to significantly improved outcomes."

Even the most accomplished individuals with autism may struggle with social interactions, nuanced communication, or other subtle forms of language. They are often literal and respond better to concrete language, visual cues, and illustrations. They may appear indifferent or listen without affect when communicating with others. It is sometimes uncomfortable for children on the spectrum to make or keep eye contact.

Schedules and contracts mitigate anxiety; children know what to expect and how it will transpire. When you are working with verbal individuals who enjoy learning facts and data, teaching anatomical details and benefits of postures can be motivating.

Some children may have trouble following directions. Sifting through the distractions of sounds, movements, and sights around them can derail their attention. They may become fixated on an object or topic that is of intense personal interest. Children may echo your words or phrases without attaching meaning to them. Some children may remember every detail of your instructions for a posture yet cannot process that information into movement.

Many individuals will respond to physical prompts such as pointing or tapping their hand or foot. Some, however, are extremely sensitive to touch. Auditory sensitivities can make sounds such as singing painful to one child, while another may not appear to notice auditory input. A third child may light up at the sound of your voice. Over- or underresponsiveness to varied sensory input is characteristic of many individuals on the spectrum.

Children with autism may not be aware of the impact of their words or behaviors on others. Lying or placating another's feelings is uncommon. They may lack the skills to pretend or play with peers. Some have the capacity to store and access memories for long periods and to concentrate fully on areas of interest to them. They may be perfectionists. Children with ASD often resist change but thrive on consistency and routine. Stress often exacerbates repetitive or odd behaviors.

Clearly, there is no single approach to teaching individuals within this wide range of behaviors and aptitudes. You will find numerous examples throughout this book of yoga therapy adapted to the diverse needs of children on the autism spectrum.

Attention Deficit Hyperactivity Disorder (ADHD)

Attention Deficit Hyperactivity Disorder affects many children within the exceptional community, as well as general education students. The characteristics of ADHD, according to the DSM-IV, include inattention, hyperactivity, and impulsivity. Individuals may have difficulty focusing on a specific task, curbing their talking, sitting still, or doing one thing at a time. They tend to fidget and are easily distracted. Waiting their turn, listening to and following instructions, and completing and organizing assignments are also challenging. Many of these qualities are also prevalent among children with emotional disorders and within the autism spectrum.

According to the National Institute of Mental Health (2008), ADHD is not in itself a specific learning disability, but it can interfere with concentration and attention. A child may have trouble mastering language or academic skills such as reading or math. Children with ADHD may also have oppositional defiant disorder. They may be stubborn and rebellious or have outbursts of temper. Sometimes this behavior progresses to more serious conduct disorders. ADHD may be associated with anxiety and depression.

As indicated by a study of 125 children with ADHD conducted in 2010, children with ADHD are four times more likely to experience depression than others their age (Chronis-Tuscano et al., 2010). Depression can disrupt sleep, appetite, and the ability to think and deal with everyday tasks.

Children with ADHD benefit from having instructions repeated often, breaking skills down into small tasks, creating their own schedules, learning to sequence tasks appropriately, and being rewarded on task completion (Weinstein, 1994). Following consistent routines, maintaining a quiet environment, and providing short breaks between tasks often improve behavior and productivity (Weinstein).

Yoga is a particularly beneficial therapy for those with ADHD. Instructions are simplified into sequential tasks. There are basic starting positions, or foundational postures, on which all lessons are built. The teaching methodology combines visual, auditory, kinesthetic, and tactile modes, involving all areas of the child's attention. The environment is quiet; children master one skill at a time; there are designated times for relaxation.

Yoga therapy provides a routine, starting and ending each class the same way. Children learn to wait their turn; physical boundaries are clearly established. They have opportunities to be quiet and noisy, to be active and still.

Children with ADHD are frequently penalized for their behavior; yoga therapy provides many opportunities to receive praise and experience success. In school or therapy, having yoga breaks may derail potential upsets. Teaching children to self-regulate through posture and breathing may provide them with an outlet for frustration or a moment to recalculate impulsive responses.

Sensory Processing Disorder (SPD)

Children with SPD are frequently misdiagnosed as having other conditions, according to Lucy Miller (2006). She explains that a child with autism who appears withdrawn may have "sensory under-responsivity" (p. 149); a child with ADHD who is always on the move may be "sensory seeking" (p. 181). But there are children with these same sensory challenges who do not have autism or ADHD. Miller cautions that SPD is a distinct condition and that incorrect diagnoses may lead to inappropriate therapies.

Miller points out, however, that "40 to 85 percent of children who have other disabilities (e.g., ADHD, autism . . .) have sensory processing problems as well" (p. 283).

According to the SPD Foundation (2012), children with SPD may overreact to stimulation; be extremely sensitive to smells, noise, or touch; be fidgety and distracted, clumsy, or in constant motion; lack language fluency; be slow moving or slow to learn new tasks; be sedentary; or have difficulty making friends.

Because of the prevalence of sensory processing problems among children with special needs, a great deal of attention is given to these challenges throughout this book. You will find a discussion in the next chapter of specific benefits of yoga for sensory processing disorders. In addition, Chapter 18 includes therapeutic yoga postures and activities for children with SPD.

CHAPTER 4

BENEFITS OF YOGA THERAPY FOR CHILDREN WITH SPECIAL NEEDS

YOGA IS A movement therapy that teaches children how to quiet and focus their minds. It builds strength, flexibility, and balance and improves a child's capacity to perceive and interact within the world; breathing techniques calm the mind and still the body. Through mindfulness and one-pointedness, the child develops self-awareness. Creative play, yoga games, and partner interaction make yoga therapy fun. Children stretch their imaginations as they stretch their bodies. Yoga is noncompetitive; partnering in poses and sharing thoughts create a sense of community and elevate self-esteem.

Creating an environment that is quiet and spare prevents overloading the sensory-defensive child. Yoga therapy is not dependent on language skills or cognitive abilities. The duration of the session, choice of postures, and extent of interaction with others is tailored to the individual. Yoga therapy offers routine and structure, as well as novelty and play. It is a therapy that meets children wherever they are.

Stress Relief and Relaxation

Through posture and breathing, yoga relieves stress and induces relaxation. Yoga has been shown to elevate GABA levels (Streeter et al., 2007, 2010) and increase parasympathetic nervous system activity (Robin, 2009). With practice, many children experience calm and learn to self-regulate.

Anxiety exacerbates many factors relevant to special needs. Stress relief and relaxation are explored in Chapters 8 and 9.

Energizing

There's a growing body of research on the effectiveness of physical activity in improving success in school, social interactions, and overall health. Chapter 7 examines the energizing benefits of exercise, including yoga, for children.

Mindfulness

Yoga is different from other forms of exercise because it directs awareness to the body, breath, and feelings in each posture. A moving meditation, yoga therapy provides an opportunity to connect with a deeper sense of self. It teaches a child to observe his body—how it feels when he moves, when he is still, when he breathes, when he is agitated or calm. These are aspects of mindfulness.

In *Foundations of Mindfulness* the Buddha taught mindfulness of the body through observing the breath and physical posture and mindfulness of the feelings by attending to sensations within the body and mind. Mindfulness of the mind comes through awareness of distractions, such as anger, worry, and desire. To redirect a scattered mind, the Buddha offered these strategies: fully attending to each area of the body and the practices of loving kindness and mindful breathing (Jotika & Dhamminda, 1986).

Yoga therapy uses each of these techniques. Children learn to recognize and release tension in different parts of their bodies through movement, breath, and stillness. Instruction in posture teaches them where and how to focus. Anchoring the mind in the rhythm of the breath helps redirect wandering attention. Finally, your unconditional presence and acceptance of each child teaches loving kindness through example.

Giving a child your full attention can be transformative. Acupuncture physician Steven Templin of Bio-Energetic Focusing explains: "Calm, embodied presence translates into a biological signal. Studies suggest that when the therapist is focused and serene, he can evoke a calming effect on others in the same room" (personal communication, October 3, 2012).

Psychiatrist and educator Dan Siegel defines mindfulness as "being fully present in our awareness" (2007, p. 4). Siegel emphasizes that "being aware, being conscientious, with kindness and love . . . is the essential state of mind of a parent (or teacher or clinician) to promote well-being in children" (p. 3).

Connection with Others in a Natural Setting

PLAY

Having fun with movement is an important benefit of yoga therapy. Play, according to Brown and Vaughan, makes animals "smarter and more adaptable." The researchers explain that playing teaches children to empathize and get along with others and is essential to "creativity and innovation," to learning "how the world works, and how friends interact" (2009, pp. 5–6).

Most children welcome the opportunity to laugh and be silly. Play offers a release from the demands of school and therapy. By making yoga practice playful and implementing elements of it in a child's day, you promote stress-free learning.

Some children, however, don't know how to play or pretend. In yoga therapy, you have the opportunity to model playful, creative behaviors. Watching you, a child can learn when to laugh or what it means to "be" a cat or dog. Creating a safe environment, you can teach a child how to release tension from her face, how to curve her lips into a smile.

Play provides an outlet available to children of varied abilities. A child with limited mobility, for example, can pretend that she is loping through the forest or soaring overhead. She can participate with other children or have a private adventure with you. With creative play, there are no limitations.

SOCIAL INTERACTION THROUGH PLAY

Many children smile and laugh spontaneously while participating in their favorite postures and games. They develop additional social skills such as listening to others and waiting their turn. They may lead the group or request a posture to share. In yoga games, they follow instructions and imitate movements; these are important social skills for children on the autism spectrum or with diverse challenges.

Playing sometimes blurs the lines of acceptable and unacceptable behaviors for children. They may test the edges of another child's tolerance or your patience. Yoga therapy uses rules to create safe boundaries while playing. Delineating each child's space and where one's hands and feet are permitted clarifies appropriate interaction with peers.

How children play affects others' responses to them. Choosing partners within groups requires negotiation and compromise. Children learn to seek out partners whom they like and trust. If a child is a little rough with his partner, the other child will not choose to be his partner again. This is a natural consequence of how children play.

SPEECH AND LANGUAGE DEVELOPMENT

Children with special needs often lack the tools to explain what they want or how they feel, which can lead to feelings of frustration and isolation. Playful interaction in a comfortable environment can stimulate communication and social exchanges. Research suggests a correlation between "imitation and play skills" and the development of language skills when using a "naturalistic behavioral approach" with children on the autism spectrum (Ingersoll & Schreibman, 2006, p. 488).

Yoga therapy offers many ways to improve and motivate speech in a natural environment. According to pediatric speech pathologist and yoga therapist Nancy Williams, "Using simple chants . . . eliminates semantic attachment to the words . . . 'OM' is one of the earliest and easiest vowel-consonant combinations and is close to the child's earliest vocabulary of 'mom' or 'mama'" (2010, p. 170).

Play and social interaction, as described, often motivate children to express themselves through words, gestures, or facial expression. Replicating animal sounds and movements makes communication fun and interactive. Relational concepts such as "up" and "down" become meaningful to children as they adjust their limbs in postures.

The use of visual cues, gestures, hand positions, and modeling engages children who are nonverbal or language delayed. They may participate by using their bodies to express language. Using postures named for common animals and familiar objects often increases a child's vocabulary.

Finally, yoga breathing strengthens the diaphragm and improves lung capacity. Deep breathing and physical activity relieve stress, inviting opportunities for spontaneous communication in a more relaxed state.

SELF-ESTEEM

Children with special needs often experience exclusion by their peers. The noncompetitive, inclusive qualities of yoga create a sense of community; there are no winners or losers, no penalties for doing things differently from others. A child with special needs may be willing to try something new when he is having fun and being supported.

When children interact without fear of failure, their confidence grows. Receiving praise and acceptance elevates self-esteem.

CONNECTION WITH THE THERAPIST

Children with special needs may feel keenly aware of their differences. In yoga therapy, you have the opportunity to build trust and connection.

Through your own mindfulness practice, you learn to observe subtle changes. Seeing the hint of a smile while in posture, you know that the child is engaged. You notice a glimmer of recognition when you name a posture, which shows language readiness. Her eyes follow you when you do a pose, which is the beginning of imitation.

Acknowledge these subtle forms of communication. Let the child know that you understand. This builds trust and increases her sense of belonging. Being with a child, making a connection, cultivates your capacity to teach and hers to learn.

Strength

Many children with special needs benefit from strengthening exercises. Children with ASD are often low toned (Ming, Brimacombe, & Wagner, 2007), a characteristic also common among children with Down syndrome (Sumar, 1998). According to the Centers for Disease Control (2012b), sedentary lifestyles and childhood obesity present additional challenges for many reluctant exercisers.

Yoga therapy affords many tools for building strength. Stress relief fortifies the immune system, increasing energy reserves and stamina. Breathing exercises strengthen the diaphragm muscle. Children learn to use their own body weight to build strength; they practice postures that isolate and contract specific muscles. Developing this ability builds new pathways in the brain. Being able to perform movements that they could not do before motivates children, strengthening their resolve and sense of accomplishment.

Yoga therapy builds strong bones (Sparrowe & Walden, 2004), and it strengthens and lubricates joints (Fishman & Saltonstall, 2008). With a stronger body, a child can sit up straighter in class, affecting how his teachers perceive him. He can walk with greater ease, affecting how his peers perceive him. Developing the large postural muscles makes it easier for a child to stand erect—and to stand up for himself.

Flexibility

Finding a suitable variation in posture for each child—without straining, without bouncing, without holding the breath—increases muscular flexibility. While holding a position comfortably increases flexibility, forced stretching does not.

The first resistance when stretching is caused by the stretch reflex, which actually tightens the muscle, explains yoga anatomist David Coulter (2001). Holding the position for 30 seconds activates the Golgi tendon reflex, allowing the tight muscles to begin to lengthen. Pain, trembling, and weakness are messages from the nervous system that a stretch is too forceful. Stretching and releasing, adding brief holds, invite increased flexibility.

As the body becomes more agile, there is greater ease when moving in and out of postures. By releasing tension from her joints and muscles, a child finds an openness in her body that she may not have experienced before. As her body becomes less rigid, her response to others softens, too. A more flexible body is a more relaxed body, and a more relaxed body means a more relaxed mind.

Balance

In addition to helping children improve their vestibular function (discussed later in this chapter), yoga is a system that is balancing in and of itself. Unlike most other physical exercise systems, there is no one-sided dominance in yoga practice. Using both sides of the body ensures that opposing muscle groups are strengthened and stretched equally. Postures move the spine through a vast range of motions—forward and backward bending, rotations, and lateral flexion.

In yoga therapy children use their limbs together and independently. Crawling postures and bilateral movements (using both sides of the body) are believed to balance the right and left hemispheres of the brain. Brain Gym, a system of simple exercises designed to "repattern" the brain, originates from "ancient disciplines such as yoga . . . and enhance[s] whole brain learning" (Dennison & Dennison, 1986, pp. i–ii).

Yoga postures regulate the blood supply to the endocrine system, which balances the release of hormones (Weintraub, 2012). Yoga triggers the sympathetic nervous system in active poses and the parasympathetic in quieting poses, creating balance within the autonomic nervous system (McCall, 2007). "Yoga involves the equal exertion of all parts of the body and does not overstrain any one part" (Iyengar, 2001, p. 19).

Sensory Processing

Sensory integration is the ability of the brain to receive, organize, and use sensory input in order to participate effectively and satisfactorily in the world. It affects how an individual perceives his body and the world outside, his capacity to learn new skills and develop adaptive behaviors, and how he moves, thinks, acts, feels, and relates to others (Ayres, 1995; Kranowitz, 2005).

Motor skills, including proprioception, bilateral movements, postural control, balance, and motor planning, are often challenging for children with ASD and other special needs. There is much evidence that improving motor skills also improves language and social skills (Daichman, Cueli-Dutil, & Tuchman, 2002).

PROPRIOCEPTION

Proprioception is the information that comes from the muscles, tendons, and joints, enabling the brain to recognize positions such as flexion, extension, compression, and stretching within joints, as well as contraction and lengthening of muscles (Ayres, 1995). Through proprioception, the brain determines where the body is in space and how it is moving, which contributes to the ability to coordinate movements using both sides of the body. Postures that push and pull also increase this awareness.

Yoga therapy improves proprioception. Postures flex and extend, compress and stretch the joints and their surrounding muscles. To carry out a posture, a child learns where his hands, feet, and other body parts are and how to move them.

Proprioception is especially challenged by inversions. Discerning how to move or adjust the limbs while upside down requires a great deal of information processing.

VESTIBULAR SENSE

The vestibular system detects balance and movement, as well as the position of the head, eyes, and body relative to the earth. It affects the sense of equilibrium, muscle tone, vision, hearing, and emotional security (Kranowitz, 2005). "Vestibular dysfunction may lead to gravitational insecurity, decreased motor planning, decreased bilateral coordination, decreased balance and decreased body awareness" (Daichman, Cueli-Dutil, & Tuchman, 2002).

The vestibular receptors, located in the inner ear, respond when a person moves quickly in a circular direction. These receptors help maintain balance by coordinating motions of the eyes and head. The vestibular system also activates postural reflexes throughout the body to keep it in balance (Coulter, 2001). A. J. Ayres points out that many children with autism seek the sensation of spinning, without experiencing the typical dizziness response, suggesting that "some vestibular input is not being registered" (1995, p. 126).

There are many opportunities to strengthen the vestibular system through yoga therapy. Moving through a flow of standing yoga postures or supporting oneself on one foot requires balance. Most individuals find that their balance improves when they use their eyes to focus on an unmoving point, such as a spot on the floor. Coordinating the motion of the eyes and head helps the child maintain his equilibrium during slow, steady motion. Postures where the child follows the movement of his own hands improve the visual sense, part of the vestibular system.

Practicing balance postures may be beneficial to children with deficits in the visual-motor channel (Robin, 2009). According to an article in the *New Scientist*, a British team of educators who developed an experimental approach using balance exercises reported significant improvement among children with dyslexia (Young, 2001).

Movements that stimulate the vestibular system include rolling, rocking, spinning, elevating the head from a prone position, and balancing (Kranowitz, 2005). In Chapters 18–20, you will find yoga postures and games involving these motions.

SENSORY AWARENESS THROUGH TOUCH PRESSURE

Some children are so sensitive to touch that the feeling of a label inside their shirt or the seam of their socks distracts them beyond functioning. Others may not respond to touch unless it is deep and prolonged. Interestingly, "the autistic child senses input from his muscles and joints better than he does through his eyes and ears," according to A. J. Ayres. "Very heavy touch-pressure is the kind of tactile stimulation that often produces a positive response in the autistic child . . . He wants to feel something, but perhaps only very strong sensations register in his brain. Some of these children act as though their bodies felt uncomfortable much of the time, and the hard pressure made them feel better" (1995, p. 125).

This could offer an explanation for pinching oneself or lying under heavy objects. Temple Grandin's (2006) squeeze machine, which compressed her entire body, brought her great relief from anxiety and the overstimulation of the world around her.

Touch sensitivity also suits many children with sensory challenges to yoga therapy. In prone postures requiring an upper body lift, the child experiences the strong contact of his skin touching the ground, the full extension within his limbs and spine, and the intense pressure of his belly against the floor (Coulter, 2001). Such strenuous postures may enhance an individual's body awareness through his or her sense of touch.

Of equal importance, the yoga practice of stillness in posture may offer a respite from constant sensory input. Coulter continues: "Touch receptors . . . stop sending signals to the central nervous system after a few seconds of stillness" (p. 50). When a child holds a pose, the chaotic messages of discomfort and distraction from within his body may be temporarily interrupted (Coulter, 2001).

Perhaps head banging or other self-injurious or repetitive stereotypical behaviors are the best methods available to some individuals for relieving the body from its constant hypersensitivity. This capacity of the central nervous system to adapt to touch pressure and stillness in posture may offer a reprieve for children with extreme sensitivities to touch.

GRAVITATIONAL SECURITY

Gravitational insecurity is anxiety and fear of falling during movements of the head or body. It is often related to poor vestibular and proprioceptive senses (Ayres, 1995). Yoga therapy helps a child feel grounded through his joints, muscles, and skin. In seated postures, he feels the contact of his hips and legs on the floor. Standing on his hands and feet in a semi-inversion, he experiences the pressure through his palms and soles.

Yoga therapy eases a child into position changes. Learning to shift the weight from leg to leg or arm to arm is less unnerving from hands-and-knees poses. The inversion process for children with gravitational insecurity may begin by raising just one foot or leg—or toe—while the rest of the body remains securely on the floor.

By using cushions or blankets beneath his head or leaning his back on a wall or chair, a child may gradually become comfortable releasing the weight of his head. Feeling supported on the ground facilitates relaxation.

MOTOR PLANNING

Also called *praxis,* motor planning is the brain's ability to create, organize and complete a sequence of unfamiliar body movements (Ayres, 1995). Yoga therapy improves motor planning by breaking postures down into their smallest components. The visual cues and tactile prompts used in yoga therapy are helpful motor-planning tools for children on the autism spectrum.

Bilateral motions require motor planning. Coordinating the movements of both sides of the body, crawling, and moving the limbs across the midline "wake up" the brain. Used in many yoga therapy postures, these movements are believed to enhance communication between different areas of the brain and improve learning (Dennison & Dennison, 1986).

Imitating animals (Kranowitz, 2005) by crawling, sliding, squatting, or hopping, as well as follow-the-leader games, requires motor planning (see Chapters 18–20).

CHAPTER 5

TEN GOLDEN RULES

BEFORE IMPLEMENTING THE benefits of yoga therapy in your program, here are ten guidelines for working with exceptional children (Goldberg, 2011):

1. See the whole child
2. Make yoga therapy fun
3. Ahimsa: Do no harm
4. Maintain your enthusiasm
5. Teach what you are comfortable doing
6. Take nothing personally
7. Satya: Be yourself
8. Plan to be surprised
9. Know when to walk away
10. Keep it positive

1. See the Whole Child

It is your responsibility to learn everything you can about the children with whom you work. Speak to family, teachers, and physicians if possible. Gather information about the child's medical and psychological history. Seizures, joint instability, recent injuries, fears, behavioral patterns, sources of anxiety—all are significant when developing your therapeutic plan for the child.

But that's not the whole child. It's not just Samantha with atlanto-cervical instability, or Andrew who obsesses about time, or Ben whose flailing arms must be avoided. A child is neither this problem nor that diagnosis. Being informed is not the same as being limited by what others have experienced.

My teacher, Swami Vishnudevananda, used to express this philosophy in a song: "I am not this body; I am not this mind; this body is not mine; this mind is not mine." He taught that the way a person looks and acts and thinks is ever changing and unpredictable. It is not reality. Like his teacher Swami Sivananda, he believed that seeing the "blessed immortal soul" within each child was the task of the yoga teacher and yoga therapist.

Children with special needs experience a great deal of frustration and misunderstanding—their own and from those around them. They need a place where they are accepted without reservation and where allowances are made for their challenges. This acceptance is not the same as excusing behaviors and choices that are within the realm of control for the child. Rather, it means that the child does not have to apologize for who she is or fear ridicule for who she is not.

Providing yoga therapy does not presume that a child needs to be fixed. It means meeting the child where she is without judgment. Be attentive to what makes her laugh or withdraw. Learn her strengths and challenges. Make a connection with the child, even if it's simply to breathe together. This is the heart of yoga therapy.

2. Make Yoga Therapy Fun

Barking like a dog, hissing like a snake, and hopping like a frog make yoga a therapy that children enjoy. They sing with their partners and fly like their favorite superhero. Because yoga is a therapy that's fun, children are more willing to participate. They want to come again and are willing to try a little more.

Getting down on all fours and wagging your doggie tail, it's natural to laugh with your students. Pretending with the child helps him see you as a partner in his therapy. Through laughter and play, you create a light-hearted mood. Even a child who cannot emulate your behavior perceives this energetic shift.

Incorporating yoga into other therapies makes them feel less like work. After completing a demanding task, let the child choose his favorite pose. He might enjoy ending his session with a game or song.

Spending so much time in therapy often makes special-needs children feel different from other members of their family and other kids. Yoga, on the other hand, is an activity that lots of people enjoy. Children may have friends who take yoga classes or a parent who practices at home. They see yoga on television and in movies. When a child with special needs goes to yoga, he doesn't feel like he's doing therapy. He's doing something that lots of folks do because it's fun and feels good.

3. Ahimsa: Do No Harm

Mahatma Gandhi used the Sanskrit term *ahimsa* as his creed: Avoid physical or mental violence toward oneself or another. In every yoga therapy session, it is essential that the child be safe and that no harm come to either of you. Safety requires your full attention, control of the environment, and self-awareness. If for any reason you are not able to assure a child's safety, change the circumstances of the experience: Find an assistant, choose different postures, or refer the child elsewhere.

Know your limits and the child's limits. Choose postures and routines that you can teach competently. Always refer to the child's medical history for conditions that might preclude certain positions. By starting with postures a child can do comfortably, you engender confidence and trust. Increase challenges slowly; avoid frustrating or pressuring the child.

Be aware of the effects of what you say and how you say it, where your body is in relationship to the child, your facial expression, the tone and volume of your voice, and your posture and stance. Use touch judiciously, or not at all.

There is a great deal of physical handling of children with special needs. Generally, it is for the safety of the child or those around him, but sometimes people become forgetful or rough in these circumstances. If a child is noncompliant, never wrestle him into a pose. Certainly, it's faster to pick up a child and put him where you want him. But unless the child is a threat to you or others, give him the chance to learn at his own pace.

It's easy to forget that children who do not speak or respond can still be fully aware. Talking about a child as if she is absent is harmful to the child and to those around her. Don't forget that there's a person inside every child—one that you may not yet know (or may never know), but one with the same sensibilities that many children have. To keep that awareness alive in both you and the child, maintain an ever-respectful attitude when working with all children.

4. Maintain Your Enthusiasm

Enthusiasm can't be feigned, but it can be mustered. When working with children, it's important to summon up the child within yourself. Having fun, being thrilled by what you are doing and what those around you are doing—these are the qualities to which children respond.

The Buddha, when asked how he was different from those around him, responded, "I am awake." This quality is essential when offering yoga therapy. No matter how often I "light" a student's candle and rush back to blow out the flame, I act as if I've never done anything so fascinating before! Enthusiasm is infectious, as is the lack thereof, particularly with children.

When I was an English teacher, I discovered the necessity for enthusiasm. On days when I showed a video to all of my classes, it was easy to be interested when I watched it the first or even second time. After that, I could have happily spent the time doing anything else. But I discovered that if I began to grade papers instead of watching, my students also found something else to do. When I sat rapt and appeared fascinated, my students were far more likely to remain attentive. It was apparent that I couldn't expect them to perceive the value of something that seemed unimportant to me.

For the five minutes or five hours that you use yoga therapy, summon your enthusiasm for yoga, your love for the kids, your belief in their capacity to change, your interest in sharing alternative therapies. If you cannot call up these feelings, shorten the duration or frequency of your program. It's like baking bread: If you leave out the yeast, it won't rise. Enthusiasm provides the oomph in your teaching.

5. Teach What You Are Comfortable Doing

Give yourself permission to incorporate those aspects of yoga therapy that feel right to you. Choose only postures that you can teach safely and confidently, especially if you are not an experienced yoga teacher. Your comfort is communicated directly to the student without your saying a word. Children sense uncertainty and make it their own.

Even for yoga teachers, there will be postures and sequences that are not appropriate in some circumstances. With large groups in classrooms crowded with desks, children's arms and legs may overlap their assigned spaces. Unless you can be close enough to help each child in challenging postures, simplify your lesson. If control is a concern, eliminate transitioning from one starting position to another to prevent potential chaos. Therapists seeing children in small offices may select seated routines.

You can always add more, but it's important to present yoga therapy in a manner that is suitable for your environment, program, and training.

6. Take Nothing Personally

Children, particularly those on the autism spectrum, frequently lack nuance. They often express their feelings without an awareness of the impact on others. It's an honesty that is endearing and trying. If a child sees a blemish on my face, he thinks nothing of shouting out, "Miss Louise, what is that big red spot right next to your nose?" Or, on bad hair days, "Why is your hair sticking out like that?"

It's not uncommon for a child who sees me entering the room to shout, "Oh, no! Not yoga!" Yet that same child may run up to me after class or the next time and say, "I love yoga!" And he really does mean what he says, in each instance.

This lack of guile is also what makes children especially delightful. Remember, it's not about *you*.

It is your task in yoga therapy to appreciate children's curiosity or powers of observation without identifying with their commentary. Maintaining your equilibrium begins with detachment from reaction. Even if the children mean no harm, they will notice when they make you squirm, and this response can inadvertently perpetuate an otherwise offhand behavior.

My response: "Yes, I do have a red spot next to my nose." And, "Curly hair sticks out sometimes." Or, "It's yoga time." No emotion. No condemnation. No attachment.

7. Satya: Be Yourself

Children have an uncanny capacity to sense artificiality or dishonesty. It is essential to speak the truth (*satya*), because they will know if you do not. Don't tell a child that he has done something well if you don't believe it. And don't pretend that you like everything he does.

There are times when you will be upset or fatigued. If a child senses this, he may feel responsible. Children sometimes make this leap of self-blame because their world revolves around themselves. You don't want to burden children, but there are times when it's appropriate to let them know you are having a tough day. Take this opportunity to model appropriate and honest ways to reveal your feelings.

"I'm really tired today. I need to sit and take some deep breaths." Let the child see you breathing in and out. He may join you or not, but let him know that this is something you need to do for yourself. After you are done, explain, "That usually makes me feel better. Thanks for your patience."

If you are displeased with a child's behavior, express yourself honestly and kindly. Identify the problem: "Ethan, remember the rules. Stay on your own mat." Tell the child how to resolve it: "Please get off Alex's mat and sit here on yours." You may need to take his hand to guide him to his seat. Acknowledge appropriate responses: "I like the way Marion and Finley are sitting on their own mats. Nice job!" If you do this without anger or blame, you make it easier for a child to comply. Here you also teach children ways to express their displeasure or ask for what they want without causing harm.

8. Plan to Be Surprised

There is only one thing you can be sure of when working with children, especially those with special needs: They will surprise you. Build this anticipation of uncertainty into your curriculum. What was accomplished yesterday may appear impossible today, and does not lend itself to predictions about tomorrow.

It is essential to plan and create lessons, but don't set yourself up for frustration by assuming outcomes. Allow yourself to come to the children each day with the potential to be surprised in the best possible way.

Manage your expectations. Disappointment is palpable and exhausting to both you and the child. Be careful not to evaluate yourself or the child based on the activities of any one day or on the success or challenges of the child. In this way, you'll be less likely to take on responsibilities and expectations that diminish you and do nothing for those in your charge.

People talk about how rewarding it is to work with children. This is true, but the rewards must come from within. It is not the responsibility of the child to make a therapist or teacher feel successful. They or their parents may thank you some day or they may not. In any event, the therapist must nourish her emotional needs outside of the therapeutic setting so that she is fully able to attend to the extraordinary needs of the child.

Children need understanding, not fixing. Your job is to observe and learn and try again. And know that you'll likely be surprised tomorrow.

9. Know When to Walk Away

Anger, hurt, frustration will come. Sometimes even the most patient adult needs a "breather." Teach children how to release tension by letting them see you do it. Alter your breathing. Do a simple twist or chest opener. Explain why you are doing the pose, and help children observe the difference in you when you "step back in." By being honest about your own needs and removing yourself either physically or emotionally from a potentially explosive environment, you demonstrate effective self-control and avoid doing harm.

Resist the temptation to blame or doubt yourself or others when things don't go well. Everyone experiences setbacks. This is where Golden Rule 6 applies: Take nothing personally.

None of us is the ideal therapist for all children. Sometimes it's simply not a good match, or the demands of the child exceed our capacity or experience. Part of every educator and therapist's arsenal should be a list of qualified individuals who specialize in areas that she or he does not. Never hesitate to refer a child to someone else. If you can't serve that child after making a reasonable effort, it becomes a disservice to you and to the child to force the partnership.

Whether or not you can help a child does not reflect your success or failure as a therapist or educator. Nor does it mean that the child is unable to learn. It simply means that you have not, at this moment, found a way "in" with that child. What's important is the effort you put in and your capacity to detach from the outcome.

Yoga has been defined in *The Bhagavad Gita* as "skill in action" (Easwaran, 2007, p. 95). Engaging your energy when it is useful and surrendering effort when it is not by appropriately referring a child elsewhere is an example of yoga therapy.

10. Keep It Positive

Your best tool for correction and guidance is to reinforce positive behaviors. If a child can sit for only a moment, reward that accomplishment. If the students are running amok and one child remains on his mat, praise him for following directions. If a screaming child has a moment of quiet, acknowledge the moment.

Never belittle a student for his postures; find something positive to say about whatever form a child takes. Avoid using yoga therapy as a punishment. When removing a disruptive child from a group, do not send him off to "do yoga." Throughout this book, you will find techniques to alter and derail meltdowns, but that is very different from making yoga therapy a penalty for undesirable behavior.

When teaching children with special needs, I am very busy searching for ways to acknowledge every positive effort on their part. "Nice sitting . . . Good listening . . . I like the way you are following directions . . . Great job staying on your mat . . ." This is my continual patter. And of course, I only say it if it's true.

Praise does not have to be noisy. Your quiet acceptance of a child can be expressed through your body language. Entering a child's space gently, without demand, also creates a positive experience for the child.

The Bhagavad Gita teaches that no effort is ever wasted (Easwaran, 2007). That is our refrain in yoga therapy for children with special needs.

RATIONALE:
THE BRAIN,
LEARNING,
AND RELAXATION

CHAPTER 6

STRESS AND THE BRAIN

SCHOOLS CAN BE chaotic, noisy places: Bells clang, children shout, teachers yell, loudspeakers bellow. Overhead fluorescent lights hum and glare. Children are herded from class to class, while adults determine where they sit, when they speak, and what they do.

Many kids are whisked from school to activities every day. Others spend long hours in aftercare, often getting home after dark. At home, children are bombarded with stimulation from TV, computers, text messages, video games, and iPads. Children's lives are often highly structured and overloaded with "too much stuff, too many choices, too much information, and too much speed" (Payne & Ross, 2010, p. 5).

Excessive stimulation means fewer opportunities to play and relax, to daydream and imagine, all of which affect anxiety levels, sleep, and behavior. As observed by school social worker Rich Foss, who has worked with children and families for over 30 years:

When you enter an elementary school classroom, you'll see a list of class rules: "Raise your hand. Stay in your seat. Speak only with permission." These rules make the classroom manageable; it would be anarchy without them.

But what teachers and parents often don't realize is that every one of these requests is completely contrary to the nature of a young child. Children don't sit. They jump and dance and roll and climb and run. They're not quiet. They laugh and scream and giggle and sing and make noises. And when we require children to obey these rules for lengthy periods without a break, we force children to deny their instincts and suppress their very nature. (personal communication, November 2, 2011)

Yet there is scarcely a place where children can run and play—not in the halls at school, not even at recess. That is, if they have recess. New schools are often built without playgrounds to lower costs. What's even more surprising is that many overscheduled kids don't know what to do at recess: A charter school in Chicago had to hire a "recess coach" to teach children how to play dodgeball and tag (Ahmed-Ullah, 2011).

Increased emphasis on high-stakes testing and grades contributes to increased pressure in school. Recess, field trips, class parties, physical education, and the arts are viewed in many schools as an interruption of time deemed more valuable for test preparation. This pressure to succeed in school, often exerted by parents, starts at an early age. Even though scientific research points to better learning when children are in more playful, happier, and less-demanding environments, "The trend in early education is to move from a play-based curriculum to a more school-like environment of directed learning"—starting in preschool (Tullis, 2011, p. 37)!

Subduing the impulses to play and staying on task are challenging for many children, particularly those with special needs. Yet these constraints are essential for success in school and many other areas of children's lives. Excessive stimulation and demands, lack of control, and fewer outlets for release lead to high levels of stress for many children with special needs.

What Is Stress?

Hans Selye described stress as the "response of the body to any demand made upon it." He explained that any change in routine, whether "pleasant or unpleasant, . . . elicits essentially the same biological response" (1974, p. 13). Children's lives are full of unfamiliar demands. Learning something new, interacting with others, and adjusting to a different teacher all require taking risks and discarding familiar routines.

For those with special needs, the alarms that trigger stress may be even less predictable than they are for other children. Changes in the daily schedule at school or something unexpected in a lunchbox can lead to meltdowns. These behaviors are more frequent among children who have not developed impulse control or who live in a chronic state of agitation.

RESPONSE TO STRESS

The body responds to the environment via the nervous system. The peripheral nervous system collects information from the environment and sends it to the brain for processing. Signals from the brain travel through the spinal cord back to the periphery with commands about how to proceed. If the news is bad, the autonomic nervous system shifts into stress mode.

The autonomic nervous system maintains a sort of checks-and-balances function in our bodies. When we are stressed, the sympathetic nervous system dominates, accelerating heart rate, respiration, and blood flow to the limbs. This is *allostasis*, the internal system that "helps the body stay stable . . . and provides enough energy to cope with any challenge" (McEwen, 2001, p. 7). The body is flooded with hormones required to meet and survive the threat—fight, flight, or freeze. For intense, brief bouts with danger, these changes facilitate survival.

When the crisis passes, hormonal signals cancel the stress response and parasympathetic dominance of the nervous system resumes: Immune function, digestion, respiration, heart rate, and blood pressure return to normal levels. This is *homeostasis*.

Although we are far less likely to be hunted down by charging lions than our forebears, our bodies are relatively unchanged in the manner in which we respond to dangers—real or imagined (Selye, 1974). My yoga teacher Swami

Vishnudevandana described a barefoot walk outside a quiet Indian village. An elderly man notices a snake, coiled to attack just a few feet ahead. His heart racing, he lifts his walking stick to strike. With newfound strength, he pummels the snake, only to discover that the "snake" is in fact a coil of rope. Exhausted, he heaves a sigh of relief and continues on his way.

Believing that the rope was a snake, the man suffered exactly as he would have if the threat had been real. Our perceptions, often primitive and inaccurate, activate our nervous system.

THE LIMBIC SYSTEM

The stress response emanates from the brain. Two components of the limbic system are key players in the process of stress and learning: the amygdala and the hippocampus. The amygdala is the brain's "panic button," reacting instantaneously to fear or other strong emotions. It initiates the stress cycle, bypassing the prefrontal cortex (McEwen, 2001). The amygdala signals the hippocampus to begin recording memories and alerts the prefrontal cortex to assess the threat (Rately, 2008).

This collaboration of the amygdala and hippocampus is the reason traumatic events are often seared into our memories. The hippocampus plays an important role in the formation of new memories and helps organize all kinds of input from our lives (McEwen, 2001). It has the capacity to generate new cells (*neurogenesis*) throughout a person's lifetime (Gage, 2003; McGuire, 2000). Conversely, the hippocampus is affected by prolonged periods of stress, actually shrinking and reducing the capacity to retain new information (Sapolsky, 2003; Vythilingam et al., 2002).

THE STRESS RESPONSE

Frederick, a slender second-grader on the autism spectrum, walked into school one spring morning to discover that his teacher was not sitting at her usual place. Instead, a stranger greeted him that day. He threw down his bookbag, overturned his desk, and ran from the room. Pushing his way through the crowded hallway, he found his way to the school office, something he had not done before. Frederick cried until his mother arrived to take him home, exhausted. What had happened?

When Frederick saw the substitute, his body reacted by creating *allostatic load:* he "stressed out" (McEwen, 2001). First, Frederick's amygdala sounded the alarm to the adrenal glands. The neurotransmitter norepinephrine triggered the adrenals to release a deluge of epinephrine (also known as adrenaline), preparing his body for fight or flight. His heart rate and blood pressure increased; an extra supply of blood rushed to his arms and legs, increasing his strength. The neurotransmitter dopamine, which "sharpens and focuses the mind" (Rately, 2008, p. 64), helped him find his own way to the office.

PROLONGED STRESS: HPA AXIS AND CORTISOL

Signals travel from the amygdala to the hypothalamus to the pituitary, activating the hypothalamic-pituitary-adrenal (HPA) axis (McEwen, 2001). The adrenals send a second wave of stress hormones: cortisol, a glucocorticoid. Among its tasks is converting muscle to fat and leaching minerals from bone. The heart, brain, and large muscles remain in a state of heightened alert while the HPA axis instructs the immune, digestive, and reproductive systems to shut down until the crisis has passed.

When all is well, cortisol has another function: It sends a message to the hypothalamus that it is safe to shut off the stress circuit, and the body begins to relax. Sometimes, however, the switch gets stuck in the "on" position, and the body doesn't know that it's time to slow down.

FRUSTRATION AND STRESS

Hans Selye (1974) believed that stress brought on by frustration was far more harmful than any other form. Research by Robert Sapolsky demonstrates this: "Stress is exacerbated if there is no outlet for frustration, no sense of control, no social support and no impression that something better will follow" (2003, p. 89).

Sapolsky also found that fewer stress hormones are released in response to an unpleasant situation if a person believes he can change his circumstances. The simple belief that one has control over the source of stress will lessen its impact.

This may be one of the reasons that preparing a child for a change in routine helps mitigate its impact. After the upset with Frederick, the school began calling his family on mornings that he would have a sub. His teacher devised a picture book to describe the changes on substitute days, and his mother used it to prepare him at home. Although he was not happy, his reaction became far more manageable for all involved.

When individuals are repeatedly placed in situations without any sense of control, or are expected to perform tasks that are too demanding, their bodies habituate to this level of chronic stress, "with or without apparent cause" (Sapolsky, 2003, p. 88). Continual activation of the fight-or-flight response by the amygdala can lead to uncontrollable outbursts or aggressive behaviors: "Anxiety seems to wreak havoc in the . . . amygdala, [which is] . . . central to aggression, underlying the fact that aggression can be rooted in fear" (p. 88).

THE COSTS OF PROLONGED STRESS

Chronic stress can impair the body's ability to switch off the stress responses, even during periods of calm. Long-term stress compromises many aspects of a child's health, affecting behavior, sleep, school attendance, and school performance. High levels of cortisol over extended periods of time lower immunity, making children more prone to colds, infections, and illness (McEwen, 2001). Prolonged stress can affect behavior, cognition, and mental health (Lupien et al. 2009) and may lead to depression (Streeter et al, 2012). Excessive levels of cortisol have been shown to decrease the size of the hippocampus and increase the reactivity of the amygdala (Bremner et al., 2008). These components of the limbic system are "crucial . . . in 'higher' thought functions such as learning and memory" (McEwen, 2001, p. 26).

The diversion of the body's resources from digestion, growth, and immune function is especially significant and potentially long-lasting in children, affecting their sleep, school attendance and performance, and overall sense of well-being. In a 2007 study, Schilling and colleagues reported "the very strong association between childhood adversity and . . . antisocial behavior, and drug use during the early transition to adulthood." Audrey Tyrka of Brown University and her colleagues have conducted research suggesting that extreme stress due to childhood trauma "was linked to alterations in HPA axis" (2012, p. 7).

Learning, Stress, and the Brain

In her book *How Your Child Learns Best* (2008), physician and elementary school teacher Judy Willis explains that the way a child's brain responds to incoming information determines how much of it he will remember. The reticular activating system, the brain's "sensory switchboard," acts as the first filter in selecting which data gains admission to the "thinking brain."

A child's emotional state at the time that she receives information has a significant influence on her capacity to retain that information. The amygdala, which triggers "nonthinking reactions" such as fight-or-flight, is the second filter. When the amygdala is in a "safe state and emotions are positive, information is passed on to the reflective, memory-making, and thinking networks in the brain" (Willis, 2008, p. 4). That's when learning takes place.

The chemical neurotransmitter dopamine helps information pass through both of these filters. "When learning is associated with pleasure, dopamine is released. This surge increases focus, helping the brain stay attentive" (Willis, 2008, p. 7).

Remember that the brain's primary job is survival, and it responds to external stimuli (Selye, 1974) in the same way that our ancestors did: fight, flight, or freeze. When information bypasses the thinking brain because of high levels of anxiety, one child may perceive a threat where none is apparent to others. His response—charging at a classmate, running from a teacher, or withdrawing under a desk—may seem inappropriate. Nonetheless, these extreme behaviors make sense when we understand the neural processes that motivate them.

Sympathetic control of the nervous system—stress mode—is meant to be a temporary interruption, with all systems rebalanced once the danger has passed. When stress is continual, the person acclimates to the stress response (Rately, 2008); with each repetition of the pattern, the process becomes more automatic.

This same principle affects learning. Willis describes the "neuroplasticity" of the brain, which is under continual reconstruction, adding new pathways, refining old ones, and eliminating unused ones, in response to experiences. New memories are formed by "linking new information onto existing memory networks," making the learning process faster and more efficient. "Learning promotes learning" (Willis, 2008, p. 13). Each repetition of an action increases and accelerates neural connections, making it easier to perform a task.

A small amount of challenge stimulates the release of the neurotransmitter dopamine and feels good: "More dopamine can lead to a feeling of well-being in situations of moderate . . . stress [with] a . . . high likelihood of success" (Sapolsky, 2003, p. 93). When a child begins to grow fatigued or frustrated from a task, however, she enters a "state of depletion of neurotransmitters; she can become fidgety, distracted, and unfocused" (Willis, 2008, p. 23).

Willis suggests providing "brain rest" before excessive stress inhibits the child's ability to take in new information. She calls this "amygdala hyperactivity," a state of "burnout [where] new memories can't be stored efficiently" (2008, p. 23). If the task or material is complex, Willis believes children may need brain rests every 15 minutes. "When a child is not alert and focused, no amount of rep- etition will drive the information into his memory storage banks" (p. 23). Willis suggests movement and stretching, among other restful activities, to interrupt periods of high demand. Yoga therapy is well suited to this purpose.

Along with scheduled relaxation periods, many children learn to reduce stress by slowing down their pace, asking questions, or expressing frustration. Individuals with autism, however, may be lacking in these abilities. "Most people automatically know when their stress is so high that they must get out of a situa- tion quickly, and they automatically know how to reduce that stress . . . But those with autism must be taught positive ways to escape overwhelming stress before they lose control," explains autism educator Janet Janzen: "Taking a break to relieve stress is a positive skill that is taught and reinforced in order to prevent a behavior problem. This break is very different from a time-out that occurs after losing control" (1996, pp. 358–359).

VAGAL INFLUENCE

Neuroscientist Stephen Porges's fascinating research on the autonomic nervous system may explain why children with autism spectrum disorder are particularly susceptible to high levels of stress. He notes the significance of the vagus, not just one nerve but "an intricate neural pathway" spanning the brain- stem through the abdomen (McEwen, 2001). The vagus nerve affects such func- tions as speaking, swallowing, respiration, heart rate, and digestion (Tortora & Grabowski, 1996).

Porges explains: "The vagal afferents exert a powerful regulatory influence on several systems—including . . . pain thresholds, the HPA axis, and the immune system—that are dysfunctional in autism" (2005, pp 75–76). This apparent deficit may affect the body's capacity to contain the stress response.

When the autonomic nervous system gets the all-clear sign from the brain after stressful situations, it shifts from sympathetic to parasympathetic dominance. The sensory nerves of the vagus, according to Porges, inhibit "the HPA axis and reduce cortisol secretion, . . . slow heart rate, lower blood pressure, and reduce arousal to promote calm" (p. 75).

A healthy autonomic nervous system contains a control mechanism that Porges calls the "polyvagal brake." It works just like the brake on your car when you are cruising downhill. To accelerate, you ease up on the brake; by keeping the brake on, you maintain control. "The effective polyvagal brake lets up just enough to activate the sympathetic nervous system when needed, while preventing the body from full fight-or-flight mode at every stressful juncture," explains Bruce McEwen. "A person without a vagal brake lives in an unending state of emergency" (2001, p. 74).

Porges discusses another autonomic response controlled by the vagus nerve, the social engagement system. This system controls the face and larynx, "enabling complex facial gestures and vocalizations associated with social communication." It regulates the ability to "extract . . . the human voice from background noise . . . and head turning muscles" that permit routine "social gestures" (2005, pp. 68–69). As Porges points out, these characteristics often function poorly among those with autism spectrum disorder.

By smiling or choosing her words carefully, a child may avert the ire of a teacher or an impending quarrel with a classmate. The capacities to recognize a friendly voice, to distinguish between a shriek of laughter and one of pain, and to ask for clarification are all part of the social engagement system. These serve to deter immediate arousal of the HPA axis (Porges, 2005). By listening and asking questions, a child can determine whether a threat is significant enough to sound the internal alarms, avoiding domination by the limbic system or emotional brain.

Porges explores the significance of the polyvagal theory relative to "social and defensive behaviors." It is the vagus that enables an individual to switch between engaging with others and summoning the stress response, as needed, and "to promote self-soothing behaviors and calm behavioral states. These behaviors are obviously compromised in autism" (p. 68).

Porges discusses rocking and other self-soothing behaviors common to many on the spectrum. These, he suggests, are instinctive ways to lower the cortisol levels in their systems. Yoga therapy includes many postures that rock, rotate, roll, and invert the body, triggering the calming centers of the brain. Such poses are especially important for children whose systems may lack the ability to regulate their stress response.

Respiration and the Autonomic Nervous System

Every time you breathe, your body makes a slight adjustment via the autonomic nervous system. The inhalation is "energizing and sympathetic," whereas the exhalation "is calming and parasympathetic" (Robin, 2009, p. 619). The heart rate accelerates slightly with each inhalation, as the vagal brake exerts less inhibition of the sympathetic nervous system. With each exhalation, the vagal tone increases, slowing the heart rate, reflecting parasympathetic nervous system dominance. This irregularity between heartbeats is known as heart rate variability (HRV), or respiratory sinus arrhythmia (Porges, 2005). Greater variations in the rhythms correspond to a more responsive autonomic nervous system, a general sign of good health (Robin, 2009). Controlled by the autonomic nervous system, these changes occur without our awareness or conscious participation.

However, respiration is an autonomic function that can be altered voluntarily. What's more, changing the rate of your breathing, independent of any other activity, can change how you feel. Let's experiment.

Start to take quick, shallow breaths through your mouth, letting your upper chest heave. Notice how quickly you observe changes in your body. Your muscular tension increases, and you will likely feel anxious and uncomfortable. By accelerating your rate of respiration, you trigger the sympathetic nervous system.

Now slow it down, breathing deeply through your nostrils, noticing the full expansion of your abdomen with the inhalation and its slow, even descent with the exhalation. Feel the wave of calm that washes over you. When you slow the rate of respiration, you trigger the parasympathetic nervous system.

When your system is stressed, your breathing becomes fast and shallow. As your heart rate accelerates, the body begins releasing stress hormones. "All of the sympathetic reactions are bound together, so that if one of them is excited, all are excited," explains yoga scholar Mel Robin (2009, p. 181). The reactions of the sympathetic nervous system are not interconnected in this same way. "Consequently, if one particular body function can be turned from sympathetic to parasympathetic, it can have the effect of turning off all or most sympathetic functions!" (p. 181). By significantly slowing the breathing, for example, you may begin a calming cascade. Coulter (2001) notes that increasing the duration of the exhalation to twice that of the inhalation shifts the nervous system to para-sympathetic dominance, promoting healing and overall well-being.

Elongating the exhalation does not work during extreme agitation or activity (Coulter, 2001), so there's no point in trying to teach a child in the midst of a tantrum to slow down his breath. Nonetheless, by offering tools to deepen the breathing during structured class or therapeutic sessions, you will help him activate parasympathetic dominance of the nervous system. This is something he can feel in his body, especially if he practices it regularly during quiet times in his day.

This became apparent when teaching a group of fourth- and fifth-graders on the autism spectrum. One child who was prone to aggressive outbursts had an upset during the final class of an eight-week yoga therapy program at his school. Prone to allergies, he began a fit of sneezing. His volume escalated and his breathing became fast and jagged. His classmates braced themselves for the expected explosion.

In the midst of his sneezing episode, I redirected him to slow his breathing. He began counting quietly, holding up one finger for each breath, something he had practiced many times, but that required his full attention. We continued through a series of familiar calming poses, focusing on slow steady breathing and chest openers. Within five minutes the sneezing episode had passed and the child was engaged in a partner activity that involved gentle rocking back and forth.

Although there is no certain way to avert the path of a nervous system careening into fight-or-flight mode, yoga therapy provides tools for change. Teaching children to slow themselves down through movement and breathing has helped derail or abbreviate countless meltdowns.

CHAPTER 7

BENEFITS OF EXERCISE

STRESS IS NOT always bad. Sympathetic activation develops pathways in the brain to meet new challenges. It is only in excess that stress becomes harmful (McEwen, 2001). In fact, you get many of the same benefits from short bursts of stress as from exercise.

The boost of energy and brain power from the release of stress hormones sometimes turns individuals with ADHD into "stress junkies," according to John Rately (2008, p. 65). Procrastinating with homework or picking a fight with a friend pushes their nervous system into fight or flight, releasing neurotransmitters that help keep them on task. "Norepinephrine arouses attention, and dopamine sharpens and focuses it" (p. 64). Fortunately, there are alternatives to creating crises.

Rately explains that an exercise regimen helps many individuals improve their focus, without the emotional wear and tear brought on by excessive stressful episodes. "An overactive cerebellum contributes to fidgetiness in ADHD kids," and medications that rebalance the cerebellum elevate the levels of dopamine and norepinephrine. Physical exercise, as long as it is not extreme, releases these same neurotransmitters without overloading the body with cortisol (p. 159).

Rately discovered that patients with ADHD with an established exercise regimen experienced fewer extremes in their reactions to stress—less road rage, fewer screaming fits. "Exercise helps regulate the amygdala, which in the context of ADHD blunts the hair trigger responsiveness of a lot of patients' experience" (p. 159).

A balanced exercise regimen also contributes to improved productivity. Stimulation, novelty, and exercise enhance learning by increasing the number of cells in the hippocampus and improving memory and reasoning ability (Gage, 2003). When followed with rest, exercise is considered a beneficial form of stress that "promotes adaptation and growth, preserves brain function," and prepares the brain to address future challenges (Sattellmair & Rately, 2009, p. 366).

A review of the literature on physical activity and academic outcomes among school-aged children concluded, "Physical activities programs help children develop social skills, improve mental health, and reduce risk-taking behaviors . . . There is evidence to suggest that short-term cognitive benefits of physical activity during the school day adequately compensate for time spent away from other academic areas" (Taras, 2005, p. 218).

According to John Medina, "exercise aids all areas of executive function: concentration, impulse control, foresight, and problem solving" (2012). Among the other benefits, "children and adolescents who are fit . . . are less likely to be disruptive in the classroom, have higher self-esteem, less depression, less anxiety . . . Exercise improves children" (2008, p. 18).

Charles Hillman and other researchers at the University of Illinois, Urbana, have studied the impact of aerobic exercise and fitness on schoolchildren, noting that those who exercise have higher math and reading scores on standardized tests (Hillman, Erickson, & Kramer, 2008). Fitness appears to improve executive function—planning, scheduling, and switching between tasks—in addition to the ability to stay focused while in a highly stimulating environment (Hillman et al., 2006).

Yoga as Aerobic Exercise

The research about the efficacy of yoga to improve cardiovascular health is inconclusive, in part because of the variety in postures and teaching styles (Hagins, Moore, & Rundle, 2007). Physician Tim McCall asserts that yoga, "if done vigorously enough, can raise the heart rate into the aerobic range" (2007, p. 339). Mel Robin has noted increased heart rate and blood pressure in rigorous yoga poses and routines (2009). A 2007 study showed that continuous posture flows such as Sun Salutations can elevate an adult's heart rate into the aerobic range, comparable to walking 4.2 mph, whereas a typical class with seated, standing, and floor postures was comparable to a more moderate 3.5 mph of treadmill walking (Hagins et al., 2007).

Although yoga may be used as aerobic exercise, that is not its primary purpose. Yoga therapy strives to strengthen bodies and minds while continuing to oxygenate the muscles, organs, and tissues. Health psychologist and yoga therapist Kelly McGonigal explains: "If you do aerobics, which has no direct breathing or mindfulness component, the physical challenge can trigger a full-fledged stress response in the body. But when physical demands are met with mindfulness and steady breathing, as they are in yoga, the nervous system . . . maintains activation . . . without going into full-fledged fight-or-flight mode." McGonigal points out that by embodying "steadiness and ease" in posture, "you're enabling your autonomic nervous system to imprint that response and . . . return to it during everyday stress" (2008, p. 122).

Yoga for Reluctant Exercisers

Most school-aged kids spend about 50 hours a week sitting in front of computers, using phones, or watching television, "the equivalent of a full-time job" (Walsh, 2011, p. 111). How do you get kids off the couch?

Based on systematic review, "yoga may be an option for children to increase physical activity and fitness. In particular, yoga may be a gateway for adopting a healthy, active lifestyle for sedentary children who are intimidated by more vigorous forms of exercise" (Birdee et al., 2009, p. 217). Introducing yoga therapy with gentle postures might entice a reluctant exerciser. Yoga games that seem more like play than therapy may also get children moving.

Play

When children run, jump, hop, and hang upside down, they are triggering important changes within their bodies and brains. John Rately (2009) explains

that as the heart rate and respiration accelerate, the brain releases a growth factor called brain-derived neurotrophic factor (BDNF). Like "Miracle Gro," it stimulates neuron production in the brain and strengthens new connections. Active
play apparently promotes learning.

Most children love to play. In fact, they need to play. Play allows "the social brain
to develop," according to neuroscientist Jaak Panksepp; "the urge to play is a neurological drive" (2008, p. 69). His vast research suggests that play reduces impulsivity, promotes socialization skills, and is essential for normal cognitive development.

Panksepp proposes that depriving children of opportunities for play and
the excessive use of medications that reduce the impulse to play may be coun-
terproductive. "Our past work with animal models has also demonstrated that
play 'therapy' reduces impulsive behaviors resembling ADHD" (p. 69). He specu-
lates that by suppressing the urge to play, "symptoms of ADHD will more easily
emerge in social situations, such as classrooms," and that "abundant physical
play might . . . be therapeutic for children diagnosed with ADHD" (p. 69).

Yoga and ADHD

In a systematic review of yoga's benefits for youth, researchers acknowledged a potential benefit of yoga for ADHD symptoms (Birdee et al, 2009).
DSM-IV characterizes ADHD as difficulty in attending, sitting still, and controlling impulses. Yoga is a therapeutic model that addresses these very skills. It
increases attention by capturing the imagination, generates stillness by releasing
tension, and teaches self-control through breath awareness. This is empowering
to children who may rarely feel in control of their actions or thoughts.

Education therapist Rebecca Barker studied a seven-year-old boy diagnosed with ADHD. The combination of yoga using the S.T.O.P. and Relax curriculum (Goldberg et al., 2006/2010) with mindfulness training "proved to be
a successful intervention" (2009, p. 10). The child reported feeling calmer; his
mother observed improved anger management and better focus. Barker noted
his success in generalizing self-calming techniques at home and during school
recess when he "felt hyper." According to the child, the breathing exercises
"totally worked" (p. 12).

Oklahoma psychologist Clint Lewis recommends yoga for kids with ADHD,
who benefit from the "physical and emotional awareness that come through

the practice. Becoming attuned to their emotions, especially with young men, increases their ability to talk about their feelings and to control their behaviors. They make different decisions, so are less likely to poke the kid in the next seat. Yoga breathing and mindful muscle relaxation are helpful to many of the young people I work with" (personal communication, June 1, 2012).

Improving Focus

In a study in 2004, scientists examined the effect of jogging on school performance. Joggers improved their scores on complex computer tests, but once the exercise regimen ended, so did the improvements (Harada, Okagawa, & Kubota, 2004). "These results suggest . . . that the level of fitness was not as important as a steady increase in the oxygen supply to the brain," explains molecular biologist John Medina (2008, p. 25); "an increase in oxygen is always accompanied by an uptick in mental sharpness" (2012). The regular practice of yoga improves lung capacity and increases oxygen intake (McCall, 2007). Postures that open the chest "help maintain the elasticity of lung tissue" (Iyengar, 2001, p. 223).

Complex exercises such as acrobatics, yoga, tai chi, and martial arts help children improve focus while keeping their interest (Rately, 2008). "Rats . . . who practiced complex motor skills improved levels of brain-derived neurotrophic factor (BDNF) more dramatically, which suggests that growth is happening in the cerebellum" (p. 159).

Children with ADHD are often instructed to focus, to pay attention. The problem is, they may not know how. For some children, being directed to use every muscle—where to place the right hand, the left foot, in which direction to point the toes, where to look with the eyes, how to turn the head, when to breathe in and when to breathe out— provides a rare opportunity to be fully present within the body. When all of their senses are engaged in implementing a yoga posture, they are freed from the usual distractions from their environment. In that moment, they experience the calm that comes with focused attention.

Exercise for Children with ASD

David Walsh encourages a wide variety of exercise for children, including martial arts and yoga. What's important is to get kids moving, without making exercise just another chore or expecting "physical performance beyond their ability or age." Rather than forcing them to join a team, he suggests "a variety of aerobic, strengthening, balancing and flexibility options . . . that emphasize fun, teamwork, and inclusion while downplaying the competitiveness" (2011, p. 115).

Tactile defensiveness makes contact sports such as soccer and football intolerable for some children. Competitive play requires a great deal of social skill, a challenge for many children on the autism spectrum (O'Connor, French, & Henderson, 2000). Children with special needs often experience greater success with cooperative activities. Loud, unstructured activities in gyms or playgrounds can be overwhelming. "Care should be taken to address one sensory modality at a time" (p. 24). Extreme sensitivity may result in outbursts or increased repetitive behaviors. Keeping exercise periods short with planned transitions is helpful for those with attention deficits. Recommended physical activities for children with ASD include "rhythmic, large muscle activities that are continuous in nature" (p. 25).

O'Connor and colleagues emphasize that "participating in structured physical activity programs . . . may lead to a decrease in inappropriate behaviors, an increase in their level of physical fitness, as well as greater enjoyment of physical activities and recreational times" (p. 26) .

There is evidence that exercise can ameliorate stereotypical behaviors, such as rocking or spinning, in individuals with autism. After assessing studies conducted from 1980 to 2007, Petrus and colleagues recommended "including exercise as an intervention when treating children with autism." The research suggests that "exercise produces short-term decreases in stereotypic behaviours," as well as "improvements in . . . academic responses, [and] on-task behaviours" (p. 143).

The key to fitness programs for children with ASD is to "find ways to make movement enjoyable," explains autism fitness educator Eric Chessen (2010). Individuals with autism are often deficient "in their imaginary or free play skills," as well as in gross motor skills such as jumping, bending, and squatting, which contribute to "an increased risk of muscular imbalances, low muscle tone and lack of initiative to engage in free play or movement activities." The good news is that "play is a skill that can be taught using exercise as the components" (p. 44).

There are many ways that yoga therapy is suited to children with ASD. Teaching a student on the spectrum to imitate an animal in a yoga pose, for example, engages him in a playful activity that is common to many children. By simplifying and repeating the motions involved in the posture, you reinforce the behavior. He may mirror you as you demonstrate the skills needed to move his body in a playful way.

Yoga therapy is highly structured, with clear rules, specific starting positions, and a sequential routine. Children begin with foundational postures, gradually building strength and increasing flexibility and balance, at a pace determined by their individual skills. There are consistent beginning and ending activities to help ease transitions.

Movements are rhythmic and repetitive. Motor skills involved range from gross to fine. Yoga therapy is inclusive and noncompetitive, and there are many opportunities to laugh and play. Students are not required to interact with others, although they may participate in partner or peer activities. Neither physical contact nor loud noise is encouraged. Routines can be active and playful, or slow and calming; instructions are adapted to the abilities and challenges of each child.

Conclusion

Research has demonstrated the effectiveness of exercise in improving behavior, performance, and well-being in school-aged children through robust exercise such as jogging, as well as moderate exercise that increases oxygen intake. Stimulation and play also contribute to socialization and brain development.

Yoga is an exercise therapy that encompasses rigorous exercise, moderate exercise, extended respiration to increase oxygen supply, and creative play. It can be performed noisily or quietly and is inclusive and noncompetitive. It works well with groups or individuals and meets the needs of a variety of learning styles and exceptionalities. Its complexity suits children with attention deficits; its structure appeals to those on the autism spectrum. In addition, yoga therapy is exquisitely suited to stress relief, as you'll see in the next chapter.

CHAPTER 8

YOGA FOR STRESS RELIEF

BASED ON A survey of more than 9,000 children in 2007, the National Center for Complementary and Alternative Medicines at the National Institutes of Health discovered that almost 12% had used some form of alternative therapy. Among the top ten therapies identified to treat such conditions as anxiety, stress, and ADHD were deep breathing, yoga, meditation, and progressive relaxation (Barnes, Bloom, & Nahin, 2008).

Yoga continues to be studied as a therapy for relieving stress and its related conditions for young people. Research shows that yoga and meditation reduced performance anxiety in young professional musicians (Khalsa et al., 2009). In a 2012 study comparing high school students after a semester of either standard PE classes or yoga, the differences in the levels of fatigue and anger management were statistically significant for the yoga group (Khalsa et al., 2012).

In an article exploring meditation as a potential therapy for autism, researchers from Memorial Sloan-Kettering Cancer Center note the impact of stress: "Autism is characterized by widespread disruption of the brain networks . . . that results in an imbalanced neurological response to cues from the external world

57

and, particularly, in the way the child responds to stress" (Sequeira & Ahmed, 2012, p. 1). Meditation programs that combine rhythmic movement, mantra chanting, and breathing exercises (Shannahoff-Khalsa, 2010) are proposed as less challenging for children on the autism spectrum (Sequeira & Ahmed, 2012).

Tamar Mendelson and colleagues (2010) studied the effects of yoga and mindfulness with 97 at-risk fourth- and fifth-graders from the Baltimore public schools. The twelve-week program, including postures, breathing, and mindfulness relaxation, demonstrated that yoga is an effective intervention for alleviating stress, particularly in the areas of "rumination, intrusive thoughts, and emotional arousal" (p. 985).

In fall 2011, a fifth-grade class combining varying exceptionalities and general education students received training using the S.T.O.P. and Relax curriculum in yoga-based strategies for self-calming. Children practiced seated postures, abdominal breathing, and relaxation procedures for self-regulation under the direction of the school psychologist and their classroom teacher. After six weeks, their teacher asked them to write about their experiences using these skills. The responses below, in the students' own words, suggest an ability to generalize the yoga-based relaxation techniques in and out of school settings:

Standardized tests: "I was very stressed before the test. But I remembered S.T.O.P. When I was done with the positions I was very relaxed."—B

Relationships: "I know it works because when I get mad at my sister, I use it. Trust me, it works really good."— J

Helping others: "My mom was stressed, so I taught her to S.T.O.P. and that really helped her to calm down."—A

Summing it up: "I don't know how they did it but they made relaxation work."—L (Collins & Goldberg, 2012, p. 358)

In an autism cluster at a Florida elementary school where yoga therapy is included in the curriculum, teachers report seeing students, unprompted, helping classmates with relaxation strategies (Collins & Goldberg, 2012). "Try this," said a child to his friend when he was upset, handing him a visual relaxation cue. Parents also shared stories of stressful moments when their children suggested they take five slow deep breaths.

One mother of a child on the autism spectrum described her daughter's challenges while having dental impressions. Each time the dentist placed the gel-filled impression tray in her mouth, the girl would panic. After three failed attempts, the child held up her hand and signaled for the doctor to give her a moment. Sitting in the dental chair, she independently reviewed the self-calming procedure she had learned in school, and then announced that she was ready. The dentist was successful in taking impressions of her teeth (Goldberg et al., 2010).

The parent of a child with autism who had taken yoga classes told me that after the child's grandmother died, she found her daughter in her room in an unusual position. The girl was lying on the floor supporting her back with her legs up in the air. Since her daughter seemed comforted, her mother did not disturb her. Six months later, while attending a workshop where I described the calming properties of this posture, the mother shared her observation. We both marveled at the intuitive wisdom of her 8-year-old.

Yoga and GABA

Gamma amino butyric acid (GABA) is a neurotransmitter that has a tranquilizing effect on the nervous system and the capacity to override the effects of stress hormones (Tortora & Grabowski, 1996). Normal levels of GABA coincide with feelings of relaxation and comfort; they enhance well-being and learning (Walsh, 2012).

After demonstrating an increase in GABA levels from yoga postures in 2007, Chris Streeter of Boston University School of Medicine and colleagues conducted a second study to determine "whether changes in mood, anxiety, and GABA levels are specific to yoga or related to physical activity" (2010, p. 1145). Compared to a walking group, the yoga subjects "reported greater improvement in mood and greater decreases in anxiety." This was the "first time that a behavioral intervention (i.e., yoga postures) has been associated with a positive correlation between acute increases in thalamic GABA levels and improvements in mood and anxiety scales" (p. 1145).

In 2012 Streeter and colleagues reviewed the anatomical effects of yoga relative to stress-related illnesses. When exploring yoga's efficacy, the researchers "hypothesized that yoga-based practices correct underactivity of the PNS and GABA system in part through stimulation of the vagal nerves, and reduce allostatic load resulting in symptom relief" (p. 571). They noted that the practice of yoga has "been associated with decreased cortisol levels," and that yoga breathing triggers an increase in "parasympathetic tone . . . associated with improved mood and anxiety reduction" (p. 575).

The 2012 review makes an excellent case for implementing yoga therapy when working with chronically stressed children. Imagine the benefits of addressing the symptoms of stress before they escalate! Through yoga therapy, you can teach children to defuse their tension with self-calming techniques that improve their capacity to learn and interact with others.

A 2012 groundbreaking study conducted by occupational therapists Koenig, Buckley-Reen, and Garg examined the impact of a sixteen-week daily yoga intervention for twenty-five elementary school children with autism. The researchers trained classroom teachers to use the Get Ready to Learn curriculum and DVD, a 15- to 20-minute program combining breathing, postures, relaxation, and chanting developed by Anne Buckley-Reen (2009). Based on assessment scales and observation, the "intervention group showed a reduction in behaviors that were identified as maladaptive by teachers, including irritability, lethargy, social withdrawal, hyperactivity, and noncompliance . . . The GRTL program appears to have social validity as well, because teacher feedback forms indicated . . . that the daily routine improved classroom functioning" (p. 544).

The consistent schedule apparently suited children on the autism spectrum, according to Kristie Patten Koenig, lead author of the study. "The students would start moving desks and preparing the room as soon as they heard the introductory music. We found positive changes that lasted throughout the day" (personal communication, October 12, 2012).

CHAPTER 9

THE PROCESS OF RELAXATION

Posture, mind, and breath are interwoven in the process of relaxation. What you are thinking affects how you sit or stand, how you move, and how you breathe. Movement alters the rhythm of your breathing, which affects the autonomic nervous system and hormone output of the body. When you change the rate of respiration—whether through posture or focused control—you also change how the body feels and your state of mind.

Yoga is a system uniquely designed to enhance relaxation. Postures unite steadiness in movements with mental focus. Many of the positions trigger the quieting reflexes of the brain (Cole, 2008). Yoga offers instruction on controlling the process of breathing.

In yoga therapy, children learn to release tension through posture, breathing, and focus of the mind. For the purpose of our discussion, we'll explore each of these factors separately, but you will find that they interconnect and overlap.

Relaxation Through Posture

The body is continually sending information to the brain. A clenching in your gut lets you know that something is wrong. Butterflies in your stomach coincide with excitement or fear. In fact, many of the emotions we experience begin in the body.

According to professor of psychiatry Dan Siegel, "The flow of energy and information from the body up into the cortex changes our bodily states, our emotional states, and our thoughts" (2011, p. 59).

It's commonly accepted that children perceive many feelings about the world through their bodies; what may not be so clear is that changing the body position can markedly change a child's feelings about the world. Siegel recommends, "The next time your children need help calming down or regaining control, look for ways to get them moving" (p. 59).

Yoga postures remove undue stress from the body's systems; "organs are supplied with fresh blood, and are gently massaged, relaxed and toned into a state of optimal health" (Iyengar, 2001, p. 43). Different positions affect the nervous system in different ways. Forward bends and supported inversions are calming (Cole, 2008). Backbends activate the sympathetic nervous system; spinal rotations make the spine more supple, increasing energy levels (Iyengar, 2001).

Despite these rules of thumb, students do not always react predictably or consistently to poses. You must observe your clients carefully to determine whether the postures you have selected have the desired effect (Kraftsaw, 1999).

For example, you would expect calming postures to soothe excited children. Many children, however, require moving through a series of energetic postures first before they can begin the quieting process. While heart-opening backbends typically elevate the body's energy, these poses may intensify anxiety among individuals experiencing depression. A restorative forward bend might better ease a depressed child into yoga therapy.

GETTING STARTED

Consider a child who sits in his chair with his head hanging, chest sunken, and shoulders slumped. This posture reveals a lot about how that child feels. With his lungs and heart literally depressed, it's nearly impossible for him to take a deep breath.

How do you change that child's experience? Start by moving his body in the least invasive manner. To begin unlocking his upper body, introduce gentle shoulder rotations from his seat. Help him reach toward the back of his chair one arm at a time, slowly stretching the front of the shoulders. As he grows more familiar with the movements, he may be comfortable stretching both arms behind his chair in a simple chest stretch. With very little change to his position, he begins to experience more openness in his rib cage and deeper respiration.

Sometimes a child needs to turn inward to reduce the anxiety he feels from the world around him. Teach him to use his body to release in a standing or seated forward fold. Talk to him about the quiet inner place he is visiting in this position. As he grows receptive, ease him into movement— reaching up first, then hanging down. Have him move with the breath, inhaling up, exhaling down. The child feels safe, continually returning to the comfort of the forward bend. Whether or not he understands the concept of turning inward and opening outward, he will experience these sensations through the changes in his body and respiration.

STRETCHING FOR STRESS RELIEF

Have you ever noticed stiffness in your back or legs after a lengthy car ride? That's because the body adapts to positions sustained for long periods of time. When you attempt to stretch your limbs, the resistance you feel is your body's mechanism to protect the joints from becoming unstable and the muscles from injury.

The muscle spindle fibers that attach to the tendons send a warning during forced stretching, explains Mel Robin. If the movement is gentle, however, "the Golgi tendon organs sense the stretch, . . . relax it . . . and reset the muscle spindle tension" (2009, pp. 449–450). If you move too quickly, bounce, or force through the stretch, the muscles will contract rather than stretch (Robin, 2009).

Teaching children to move slowly can be challenging; finding comfort in each phase of a motion helps them to control their pace. Slow repetitions while moving in and out of poses are often more relaxing than holding a lengthy stretch. Using props to support the child in postures mitigates tension as well. Playfully rocking back and forth combines fun and gentle stretching in motion.

Emotional upsets trigger the nervous system to activate motor neurons, increasing muscle tension, a habitual pattern for many children with special needs. Even at rest, muscles maintain varying degrees of tonus. But "gentle, prolonged stretching [is] thought to desensitize the stretch reflex" (Cole, 2008, p. 88). The longer the hold, the greater the release; stretching helps a child feel less "uptight" (Robin, 2009).

FLEXING THE CERVICAL SPINE

An animal in the wild bares its throat only out of fear or as an act of surrender. Exposing the throat or belly in spinal extensions may arouse feelings of vulnerability for humans as well. Conversely, tucking the chin into the throat contributes to feelings of safety.

Consider the child sitting in the slumped posture. He is exhibiting the "flexional tonic reflex," the body's tendency to fold inward for self-protection. Forming a fetal shape in response to fear, sadness, or stress activates parasympathetic dominance of the nervous system—promoting calm (Robin, 2009).

Some children have such a strong flexion reflex that the effort to lie flat on their back is stress-making. In these cases, help children into a more flexed variation for supine poses by bending their knees and placing their hands on their belly (Robin, 2009). Elevate the child's head on a pillow or folded blanket to create cervical flexion. If there are no props available, invite the student to rest his head on your knee or to lie on his side with his knees tucked in.

Pressing the chin into the throat notch increases pressure to the baroreceptors, lowering heart rate and blood pressure (Robin, 2009) and activating the solitary tract nucleus. This inhibits sympathetic dominance of the nervous system and slows the heart rate by stimulating vagal motor neurons (Cole, 2005).

It is important to note that there are some children for whom intense neck flexion is potentially damaging. Instability between the first and second cervical vertebrae (atlanto-axial) is found in approximately 10%–20% of children with Down syndrome, according to Sonia Sumar in *Yoga for the Special Child* (1998), contraindicating deep neck flexion, extension. or rotation.

INVERSIONS

Inversions induce relaxation by shifting blood pressure toward the upper body. The increased pressure "stimulates vagal motor neurons, slowing the heart" (Cole, 2005, p. 346). Inversions are contraindicated for children with a history of seizure or heart disorders. (See Chapter 15.)

Some inversions from supine positions, such as Bridge pose, involve a slow elevation of the hips and chest above the head, while increasing cervical flexion. A favorite among many students on the autism spectrum, the pose combines pressure at the throat notch with movement in the pelvis. This enhances relaxation because "sacral movements stimulate the PNS and increase vagal activity," explains Stephen Porges (personal communication, 2012; Cottingham, Porges, & Lyon, 1988).

Inverted poses with the legs elevated are especially calming. Resting the legs on a wall with the back supported and the chin slightly tucked is restorative. This posture, another favorite among my students, creates an atmosphere of tranquility and trust. Lying alongside a child with your legs up the wall, you may rest quietly or engage him in a discussion about his day— a new challenge in class or on the bus. In this safe, comfortable pose, children often share concerns that can be addressed with yoga breathing or posture.

As beneficial as inversions are, I do not recommend teaching headstand to children. It is my belief that many young necks are not yet strong enough to support the full weight of their body. Adults understand the use of the arms, shoulders, core, and legs in this inversion, but children often lack the proprioceptive skills to put all of these pieces together, especially while upside down.

In Chapter 15 you will learn many safe and simple inversion positions, including alternative postures for children who crave pressure on their heads.

OCULAR PRESSURE

Gentle pressure around the orbit of the eyes or on the forehead triggers the parasympathetic vagal heart-slowing reflex (Robin, 2009). When an exhausted child rubs her fists into her eyes, she is stimulating the vagus nerve, slowing the heart rate and preparing her tired body for sleep (Cole 2005; Robin, 2009). Stimulating this reflex through yoga postures has a similar effect.

You can help children create light pressure on the bones that surround the eyes by using a small eye pillow or by resting their forearms on their brows during supine relaxation posture. This blocks the light, promoting relaxation, and puts weight around the orbit of the eyes, triggering the parasympathetic nervous system (Cole, 2008).

Many children are calmed in poses that combine cervical flexion with ocular/frontal pressure. In postures with the forehead touching the ground, the pressure on the forehead is soothing, and the contact with the earth is grounding.

QUALITIES OF CALM

Roger Cole describes "eight relaxation-inducing conditions: physical comfort, muscle release, warmth, a reclined or inverted posture, darkness, pressure on the bones around the eyes, giving oneself permission to relax, and holding the pose for a sufficient amount of time" (2008, p. 88). Cole suggests combining as many of these elements as possible in yoga postures to deepen relaxation. (See Appendix 4, "Conditions for Calm.") Even children who lack the disposition to remain in a pose for long will benefit.

As discussed in Chapter 6, a child with a deficient vagal system lacks the tools to self-calm. Porges suggests that repetitive behaviors common to children with ASD, such as "rocking and swinging, in which the position of the head is changed relative to the heart, . . . stimulate the peripheral baroreceptors that regulate blood pressure . . . [and] may reflect a naturally occurring behavioral strategy to stimulate and regulate a vagal system that is not efficiently functioning" (2005, p. 73).

In addition to the inverted postures already discussed, yoga therapy includes many soothing rocking postures that can be performed slowly or quickly (see "Postures for Vagal Stimulation" in Chapter 18).

Another application of this information in yoga therapy is through variety and pace of posture. For a child whose vagal system may be compromised, varying the speed of movement is especially important. By choosing a combination of postures that are faster paced (triggering sympathetic dominance) and slower (parasympathetic dominance), you may increase their body's capacity to switch between these functions of the nervous system.

High levels of cortisol perpetuate a nervous system in stress mode. Many children with special needs lack the ability to consciously slow their breathing and quiet their minds. By choosing postures that trigger the child's vagus nerve and slow his heart rate, his breathing will slow down; he may experience a reprieve from the continual anxiety associated with high levels of stress.

"Since there is now documentation that children with autism have lower levels of vagal tone and do not efficiently regulate it (i.e., control of the vagal brake), yoga could be an efficient portal to improve this system" (Porges, personal communication, July 20, 2012).

RELAXATION THROUGH TOUCH

Learning to use and receive touch for calming is an important component of yoga therapy. As discussed in Chapter 4, it is steady, firm pressure that interrupts the otherwise constant stimulation from the nervous system (Coulter, 2001). When performing prone backbending or intense flexion postures, the child creates the pressure with his or her own body.

Touch is also a tool that may be used directly by the therapist, as long as she recognizes when to touch, how to touch, and when not to touch a child. According to occupational therapist A. J. Ayres (1995), light touch activates the nervous system, whereas deep pressure is relaxing.

For children with sensory challenges, often seen among those on the autism spectrum, touch can be extremely unpleasant. Temple Grandin, an expert on animal handling, is on the autism spectrum. She describes the evolution of her relationship with touch in her book *Thinking in Pictures*. "The application of physical pressure has similar effects on people and animals. Pressure reduces touch sensitivity . . . Slow application of pressure is the most calming" (2006, p. 85).

Grandin describes her own discomfort at being touched until she invented her squeeze machine, an apparatus that applied steady firm pressure to her entire body—under her control. After learning to experience comfort in touch, she was finally able to pet her family cat, who had previously run from her rough handling. She also learned to tolerate touch from others. "It was difficult for me to understand the idea of kindness until I had been soothed myself . . . I believe that the brain needs to receive comforting sensory input. Gentle touch teaches kindness" (pp. 84–85).

In fact, most children find comfort in touch. It makes them feel safe and cared for. Stroking the skin releases endorphins and reduces stress, according to Dacher Keltner (2009): "Touching instills trust and spreads goodwill . . . through the release of opioids and oxytocin. They trigger the activation of the vagus nerve, the nerve bundle in the body devoted to trust and social connection, . . . and shift the . . . HPA axis activity—to more peaceful settings" (pp. 197–198).

Because the responses to touch are so varied, it's important to secure permission before touching a child. For touch to retain its soothing properties, it must be something that a child chooses and feels the right to reject.

Baby posture is the most calming posture in your catalog listing. Curling up into a fetal position (see p. 168), is the favorite of most of my students, including those on the autism spectrum. When doing Baby pose, I offer children a back massage as long as they are quiet and in the posture. This is highly motivating.

As a licensed massage therapist, I have the authority and experience to touch. When training other professionals in yoga therapy, I suggest securing parental permission before doing massage. Using a touch that is firm and steady or resting your relaxed, weighted hands on the child's back is generally soothing. To be certain, vigilantly observe the effects of your touch in posture.

One question always precedes the touch: "May I rub your back? If you don't want to be touched, it's always okay to say no." Many children, including those with ASD, grow tolerant of touch in therapeutic yoga postures. In addition to the calming posture itself, a significant factor is having a choice. If they prefer not to receive massage in the posture, they are still experiencing the soothing effects of deep pressure on their foreheads and on their folded joints.

While working with children with emotional behavioral disorders at a state hospital, I was often surprised at their receptivity to touch in Baby pose. These students, some of whom had been abused by or abusive to others, often attended classes armored in padded parkas and down vests, even on the warmest South Florida days. They peeled off their layers when it was time for Baby pose, just long enough to receive a steady, comforting hand on their backs. As soon as it was over, they piled their heavy clothing back on (Goldberg, 2004a).

Even when you are fairly certain of the answer, continue to ask before touching a child. There are days that someone may not want to be touched. And perhaps a child who has said no for days, weeks, or months may one day say yes. I worked weekly with a nonverbal high school girl with schizophrenia who was extremely resistant to touch. Each week I extended the invitation and was consistently refused. No one was more surprised than I when one day she said yes! She permitted me to rest my hand on her back. The next week she moved my hand to show me that she wanted her back scratched. From then on, even during the lessons where she seemed disinterested in the other postures, she always participated in Baby pose. We had found an experience of touch that was soothing for her and a special form of communication between us.

Teaching children about touch—how to receive it, how to refuse it, and how to share it—is especially important for those with special needs. Children with language limitations are often handled by adults when words fall short of the desired responses. Receiving touch in a safe environment while they are comfortable, and learning how to refuse or invite it, is both empowering and calming.

MUDRA: THERAPEUTIC HAND POSITIONS IN POSTURE

Mudra is the ancient yoga technique of using hand gestures and body positions to close or seal an energetic circuit (Saraswati, 1999). When working with children with special needs, the position of a child's hand can make a difference in his behavior and how he feels. There are hand positions that help individuals turn their focus inward and increase their sense of connection to the earth beneath them. Others increase their attention to the world outside (see Weintraub, 2012).

Having a sense of where they are in space (proprioception) and how to bring their bodies under control is challenging for many with special needs. Often children just don't know where their hands are. Some children on the autism spectrum experience involuntary or repetitive hand movements, especially when they are anxious or unfocused. Children with ADHD are often fidgety and impulsive, with hands flying at their schoolmates. By teaching children specific positions for their hands, we can help them curb some of these involuntary or thoughtless movements.

Keeping the hands in contact with the body during postures helps keep the child's attention on his movements. LifeForce yoga therapist Joy Bennett recommends a simple mudra with the thumbs tucked inside the palms, fingers curled around them. "This may offer some sense of security, grounding, and calming. Placing the hands over the heart is also soothing to the nervous system" (personal communication, October 10, 2012).

Most children can imitate simple hand positions. This provides a means for those with developmental disorders or limited mobility to participate in and benefit from this calming aspect of yoga therapy. (See "Therapeutic Hand Positions in Posture" in Chapter 15.)

Relaxation Through Breathing

The breath speaks the language of body and mind. When you create a slow steady rhythm with the breath, you signal the body that all is well.

While teaching therapeutic yoga in a middle school class for varying exceptionalities, I observed an unexpected form of participation. Samuel, age 12, a heavy mouth breather with ASD, frequently panted with mounting frustration throughout the day. He rarely joined his classmates when we brought out the yoga mats and frequently paced around the room during class. The final relaxation was especially challenging.

One day, while guiding the class through slow belly breathing during relaxation, the room grew quiet. The labor of Samuel's breathing—a background sound to which I had grown accustomed—had subsided. For those few moments, Samuel's breathing had deepened and slowed. In his own way, he was participating in the relaxation process (Goldberg, 2004a).

STRESS AND BREATH

The influences of the nervous system on respiration are clear to anyone who has ever watched a scary movie. You suck in your breath when you see the villain approach. You hold until your breath explodes in a shriek when the villain strikes. When the hero prevails, you release a great sigh of relief.

Similarly, the rate and quality of respiration can significantly change the nervous systems. "Abnormal breathing patterns can stimulate autonomic reactions associated with panic attacks," explains David Coulter (2001, p. 90). In fact, how a child breathes contributes to his levels of stress. While "poor breathing habits . . . produce anxiety and chronic overstimulation of the SNS," calm respiration slows down the heart and lowers blood pressure, stabilizing the system. "Our ability to control respiration consciously gives us access to autonomic functions that no other system of the body can boast" (pp. 90–91).

Think of the child slumped at his desk: His breathing is likely shallow and superficial. Consider a child on the autism spectrum whose elevated cortisol levels may result in accelerated rates of respiration. How might their emotional states change if they deepened or slowed down their breathing? According to research by Philippot, Chapelle, and Blairy (2002), breathing patterns account for 40% of the changes in a person's feelings related to anger, fear, sadness and joy. In a 2011 analysis of yoga therapy in the treatment of psychiatric disorders, Cabral, Meyer, and Ames found yoga breathing an outstanding therapy in treating anxiety and post-traumatic stress disorder.

Changes in respiration alter emotional responses. Breathing at a rate of five to six breaths per minute, "coherent breathing, is a safe and easily accessible method to reduce anxiety, insomnia, depression, fatigue, anger, aggression, impulsivity, inattention, and symptoms of PTSD, . . . [It] has no adverse effects, and can be used in children" (Brown, Gerbarg, & Muskin, 2009, p. 81).

TEACHING BREATHING

Belly breathing is an excellent tool for relaxation. To teach it to your students, it's important to feel it in your own body. Place your hand on your abdomen. Notice whether it moves when you breathe. Explore what happens when you deepen your breath. Can you allow your belly to expand with your next inhalation? Exhaling, feel your abdomen gently contract. Continue to breathe in and out through the nostrils, feeling your abdomen expand with the inhalation and contract with the exhalation.

To help a child relax, teach her to become aware of her breathing. Involve all of her senses. While she rests on her back, place her hand on her belly so she can feel the motion within her own body. Resting a hand on her belly during quiet breathing also gives the child a focus for a wandering mind. You may also lie on your back next to her. Your presence will help her sense the slower rhythm of your respiration, calming her, too. Lying prone is also an effective position for children to feel the motion of their respiration. Their belly presses into the floor

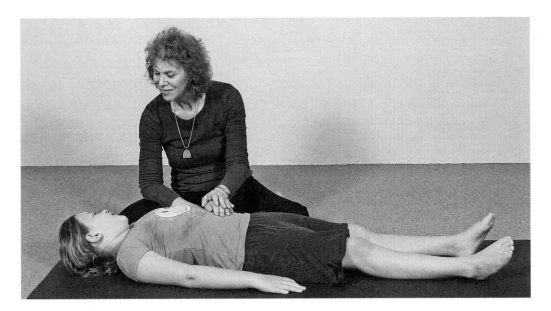

9-1 Belly Breathing

as they breathe in, lifting them slightly away from the ground; with the exhalation, they sink back down.

The most important tools to promote belly breathing are repetition and practice in a soothing, safe environment. Coulter (2001) explains that if we try to force a slowing down of respiration to an unnatural rate, the practice itself can become stressful, resulting in an increased heart rate rather than the desired decrease. Don't try to teach a child to slow down his breathing in the midst of a tantrum. Even doubling the length of the exhalation in relationship to the inhalation, the usual trigger to the parasympathetic nervous system, will not alter a child's nervous system if he is in full blown stress mode. Instead, practice frequently during quiet times to help children prevent or reduce meltdowns. June Groden recommends establishing a verbal cue for exhaling slowly at the first sign of anxiety (personal communication, October 10, 2012).

When working with kids on the autism spectrum or with other visual learners, LifeForce Yoga therapist and holistic nurse Laurie Schaeffer, of Kenai, Alaska, found inspiration in the book *Yoga Education for Children*. Adapting the lesson called "Breathing with a Staircase" (Saraswati, 1990), she uses a whiteboard to draw an upward slanting line, then a downward slanting line. She asks the children to inhale as she draws the upward line and to exhale as she draws the downward line. Initially she keeps the lines of equal length, but as the children get accustomed to the rhythm, she extends the downward line, the exhalation, a little longer. "With the drawings, they are able to see and follow the movement of the breath," Laurie explains. She has fashioned visuals with balloons to clarify the emptying of the lungs, making space for new fresh air. This practice can be expanded into an anatomy lesson about the respiratory system (personal communication, September 24, 2012).

Creative Relaxation practitioner Linda Citron, RYT, uses a small Hoberman Sphere, a miniature geodesic dome that expands to several times its size. Holding the "breathing ball" at waist level, she demonstrates the expansion and contraction of the abdomen. "It's mesmerizing," she says, "and helps most any child visualize the action of respiration" (personal communication, June 2, 2012).

For auditory learners, use the rhythm of your voice to create a pace. "Inhale through the nose, tummy gets bigger; exhale through the nose, tummy gets smaller." Measuring breaths with handclaps or music helps create a steady rhythm for respiration. You might try coordinating breathing with a drumbeat, lengthening exhalations with increased beats. A gentle gong or bell serves as well.

Don't let the child struggle or get out of breath. Some children hold their breath when they are agitated—a pattern you do not want to reinforce. It is for this reason that I do not recommend retaining the breath as in classical yoga breathing practices (pranayama). It's important that children with special needs learn first to breathe rhythmically and deeply, without gaps or retentions.

Some children habitually breathe by pulling the belly in. Work with them on relaxing the belly area first before trying to lengthen their respiration. Take care not to make children overly self-conscious. Sometimes they try so hard to follow your instructions that they force the belly out with the in-breath and hold it, followed by a small explosion of breath with the exhalation. Children on the autism spectrum, often very literal, are especially prone to this kind of forced breathing.

Sometimes it's tempting to demonstrate or exaggerate instructions by breathing in and out through the mouth, but this is not the optimal relaxation breath. Teach children to perform all exercises with respiration through the nostrils unless specifically directed otherwise. If poses with instructions to breathe through the mouth create confusion for a child, skip them until you've reinforced nostril breathing.

Not all children can breathe through their nostrils, because of allergies or chronic congestion. In fact, many children habitually mouth breathe. Let the child breathe in whatever way he can!

For many children, it's a lot easier to lengthen the exhalation through the mouth than through the nostrils. Blowing bubbles, straw breathing, or keeping crepe paper in motion with the exhalation can be lots of fun for children. These activities are useful for helping children develop muscle tone around the mouth (see p. 255), the diaphragm, and the abdominals, as well as controlling and extending the duration of the exhalation. In addition, these exercises are valuable for enhancing social interaction. Follow these playful practices with a few moments of gentle belly breathing to trigger the quieting reflexes in the brain.

Another technique for slowing the breathing has long been used to combat respiratory problems and their associated anxiety. Cooling breath, slowly exhaling through pursed lips, "lengthens exhalations, slows the heart rate, decreases the amount of air remaining in the lungs after exhalation, and reduces fear and anxiety" (Coulter, 2001, p. 91). A similar effect occurs by engaging the abdominal muscles to slow the rate of exhalation through the nostrils.

Slow, steady release of sound is an effective tool for slowing exhalation. One such technique is called Buzzing Bee Breath. The inhalation and exhalation are through the nostrils, but the breath is moved down into the throat, creating a rumbling or humming sound with the exhalation. Depending on the cognitive levels of the child, this can be a means to play with breathing while lengthening exhalation.

This technique is not recommended for all children. I generally avoid postures with crazy faces or odd sounds when working with children susceptible to imitating this kind of behavior in socially inappropriate ways. It is for this reason that I do not recommend the lion pose, which releases the breath in a ferocious roar, the tongue stretched toward the chin. This is great fun for many children but should be used selectively. Another excellent tool for slowing the breath through sound is chant and singing, detailed in Chapter 20.

If children have limited abdominal proprioception, it's often more effective to alter their respiration through movement rather than instruction. Select postures that speed them up and then slow them down (see "Creating a Pace," Chapter 18). When they slow down, remind them to breathe, creating a seamless rhythm with your words and voice.

You may use your own body as a guide. Sit back to back with the child and breathe with him. You must be in a calm state for this to be effective. By sharing

9-2   Back-to-Back Relaxation

the slow steady rhythm of your own breathing, you have a sort of conversation with the child. As he rests against you, he observes the expansion in the back of your body with each breath in, the release with each breath out.

You might ask the child to rest his head on your back, and then take a turn resting yours on his. This lets him know how you feel, that you trust him and he can trust you. This practice deepens your bond with a child, without the need for words.

Relaxation Through the Mind

My teacher, Swami Vishnudevananda, used to say, "You can't wash one side of a cloth; you can't separate the body from the mind." Whether or not a child has the facility to regulate his thoughts, you can help him change how he feels and thinks by changing his posture and his breathing.

In their thorough investigation of alternative therapies in mental health, Brown, Gerbarg, and Muskin concluded, "Mind-body practices such as yoga postures, yoga breathing, and relaxation have the potential to calm the mind and improve mental focus" (2009, p. 208).

TEACHING FOCUS

My friend and long-time yoga teacher JoAnn Evans believes that relaxation is "an activity of the mind. It's not something that happens to you. It's something that you do. It requires the complete focus of the mind. The scattered agitated mind, skipping all around, can never relax."

In *The Brain That Changes Itself* (Doidge, 2007), scientist and researcher Michael Merzenich makes a compelling case for training the mind in what yogis call one-pointedness. According to author Norman Doidge, Merzenich made an important discovery: "Paying close attention is essential to long-term plastic change" (2007, p. 68). The brains of animals he studied did not make lasting changes when they "performed tasks automatically . . . they changed their brain maps, but the changes did not last." More important, Merzenich observed that multitasking, a skill so prized in our society, actually interfered with an individual's ability to learn and retain information.

Relaxation is a skill, like reading or basketball, taught through repetition and practice, with simple, achievable steps. Yoga therapy teaches children how to focus the mind. It provides instruction in directing the thoughts to one point; the effectiveness of this method is observable.

Balance poses are an excellent example. It's nearly impossible to support the body on one foot without fixing the mind on a single spot. Try it yourself: Stand on your right foot while looking around the room, talking on the phone, or with your eyes closed. It's very difficult! Now, stand on both feet and locate a spot on the floor approximately your height in front of you. Keep your eyes fixed on this point, breathing deeply and steadily for about a minute. Shift the weight slowly to your right foot. Without moving your eyes or disturbing your breathing, lift your left foot an inch off the ground.

How did you do? Much better the second time, right? More important, how did you feel after the second attempt?

The effectiveness of focus is rewarded with improvement. Although there may be physical impediments to balance within the vestibular system, most children are able to improve these skills with instruction and repetition. Whatever the outcome, even the practice helps steady a scattered mind and reduce distraction from the world of sensation.

The focus of the eyes, the concentration, and the steadiness of the breath are comparable to meditation.

MEDITATION FOR CHILDREN WITH AUTISM

Many children with special needs are victimized by their own minds. Thoughts, feelings, sensations bombard them continually, increasing their levels of stress and forcing them into fight or flight. Improving focus in posture is a preparatory step toward meditation. Regulating the breathing, practicing quiet relaxation and turning inward for mindfulness practices are additional ways to introduce children with special needs to the process of stilling the mind.

"Meditation is a conscious process of self-regulation that tempers the flow of thoughts, emotions, and automatic behaviors in the body and mind" (Sequeira & Ahmed, 2012, p. 4). This tool for developing one-pointed mental focus has been the subject of scrutiny in recent years, in the search for more economical and less invasive alternatives to treating chronic disease, according to these researchers.

Children with autism are believed to lack "theory of mind" (Baron-Cohen, Leslie, & Frith, 1985). That is, they may not understand that other people experience different thoughts and perceptions from their own. This concept has been used to explain lack of empathy and awkwardness in social interactions.

Theoretically, an individual who does not recognize that others perceive life differently from him may not recognize that he has a "self" that is independent from others. Sequeira and Ahmed (2012) suggest that by first experiencing an increased sense of self through meditation, children may also increase their awareness of others as different from them. *The Bhagavad Gita* describes the awareness that comes through stilling the mind: "In the depth of meditation, the Self reveals itself" (Easwaran, 2007, p. 142).

The researchers suggest a variety of meditative techniques when working with children on the spectrum, including the use of rhythm, mudra, chant, movement, and imitation. "Successful programs do not require that children remain sitting still for very long but encourage social bonding, joy, and confidence" (Sequeira & Ahmed, 2012, p. 6).

Imitation, which triggers the firing of mirror neurons—an area that appears deficient among children with ASD (Iacoboni, 2008)—is an effective form of meditation. The use of playful rhythmic movements has been shown to increase the attentiveness of children with autism and to foster imitation (Shannahoff-Khalsa, 2010).

Butterfly meditation is a simple calming practice that combines imitation and rhythmic motion. After fluttering her hands all about, the child sits palms up, hands on her thighs. She turns her gaze to the "butterfly" in her right hand. Then she looks to her left. With practice, the child turns her gaze to the butterfly in the palm of her right hand, floats it up off her knee a few inches, and then floats it back down. She shifts her eyes to the left palm and repeats (see p. 147).

Sitting in front of the students, model this sequence. As the children imitate you, they potentially activate mirror neurons, creating new experiences and feelings based upon these actions (Iacoboni, 2008). Looking up at the children, it's heartening to see the serene faces gazing at their palms in this simple meditation. Even those who are not watching their hands are moving in rhythm. Others, just sitting, seem calmed by the quiet that surrounds them. This sequence creates an atmosphere for inward focus.

Rhythmic rocking combined with chanting or singing is also soothing. Repeating calming vowel tones improves focus for many children (see Chapter

20). Using unfamiliar sounds removes emotional triggers from the words (Paul, 2004). Many children are calmed by Sanskrit chants or lullabies in other languages. When sung slowly, these meditative songs are effective in redirecting anxious children to rhythmic breathing.

CREATING CUES FOR RELAXATION

In yoga therapy, continually remind children what it means to be relaxed: "Safe, comfortable, quiet—this is relaxation. So, the next time someone tells you to relax, remember how it feels: safe, comfortable, quiet" (Goldberg, 2004b). Helping children associate this word with a particular feeling or experience also serves as a cue, enabling them to recall it as needed.

Notice where children hold their tension, and teach them to notice it, too. Some will start to hunch up their shoulders as anxiety builds. Watch for clenched jaws or wrinkled foreheads. Some may squeeze their knuckles or fists. Develop a simple cue to use whenever you observe this pattern of elevating tension, such as "Let go" or "Release." For example, when you observe a child's shoulders starting to hunch, you say "Let go," as you gently but firmly rest your hands on his shoulders. When he relaxes, you say, "Nice letting go" (see Photo 15-3). Practice this during periods of calm.

On page 236, you will learn postures for children to use as transitional tools during schedule changes or after challenging events. By using cues to help children release habitual holding throughout the day, you may defuse escalating levels of physical tension.

PROGRESSIVE MUSCLE RELAXATION

Progressive relaxation is a technique long used in yoga. Its effectiveness was researched by Edmund Jacobson in 1929. In his groundbreaking book *You Must Relax*, published in 1934, Jacobson espoused the principle that movement is not required to relax; it can be achieved through awareness and redirection of the mind. This notion was popularized by Herbert Benson in *The Relaxation Response* in 1975. June Groden of the Groden Center uses an adaptation of Jacobson's approach specifically for children and adults with special needs when working with individuals with severe emotional or physical challenges (personal communication, October 10, 2012).

TEACHING "TENSE AND RELAX"

Just as it sounds, Tense and Relax is a process of increasing and decreasing tension in specific muscles and areas of the body. Yoga anatomist David Coulter encourages extremes in this exercise: "The more vigorously they hold tension, the more the Golgi tendon receptors will stimulate relaxation in the affected muscles" (2001, p. 549). Most children look forward to this practice because it feels good to release tension, and they are in control of the process.

To help children learn this technique, make the practice fun. Exaggerate the tense portion. Hold one arm out to the side, repeating "Tense, tense, tense, tense, tense." Finally, announce "Relax," letting your arm drop with a sigh of relief. Do both sides. You may work with the face and other limbs, as well. As children imitate you in this sequence, they experience release through the letting go and laughter.

There are many opportunities to learn about the process of relaxation through this sequence. Discuss the differences in the muscles when they are tense—firm, strong—and relaxed—soft, squishy. When they tense, ask "Would you want to hold this all day?" Compare to a relaxed arm. "Which one feels better?"

Some children may have difficulty tensing their muscles. Let them squeeze a soft plastic ball, observing how it changes when they squeeze—flatter, smaller—and how it changes when released. Experiment until you find a meaningful way to demonstrate this distinction.

Children on the autism spectrum often imitate this activity without requiring a lot of talk or explanation. By demonstrating the meaning of the words—*tense* = tight fist; *relax* = arm dropped to side—you help the child associate these terms with a physical experience. Because tensing and releasing alters the level of contraction in the musculature, the practice helps their bodies become more relaxed. When you change the body, you change the mind, giving this simple practice great value.

Years ago when teaching yoga to college freshmen, I was approached by a young woman nearly in tears. Because she had severe asthma, she explained, people had been *telling* her to relax since she was a child. "Try to relax when you can't breathe," she laughed. "And the more I panicked because I couldn't calm down, the more breathless I became. In my 19 years of struggling with this condition, it wasn't until now, through yoga, that anyone ever taught me *how* to relax" (Goldberg, 2004a, p. 71).

FINAL RELAXATION

Sivananda yoga classes typically conclude with a deep relaxation (*savasana*) of about 15 minutes. This includes progressively scanning the body, tensing and releasing muscles from the tips of the toes to the crown of the head. Using auto-suggestion, the student sends the thought to each of the organs to relax and release unwanted tension, followed by a period of quiet (Vishnudevananda, 1988).

The final relaxation for children with special needs, called "Floating on a Cloud," may range from 1 to 10 minutes. Sometimes it's useful to gently hold a child's ankles when beginning this posture to help direct her awareness to her lower body. This is a grounding posture. Rather than exaggerating progressive muscle relaxation in this posture, keep it brief so they don't get distracted. If the children are responsive, continue to guide them in progressively tensing and relaxing their fingers and arms, their shoulders and face.

End your relaxation session with a mindfulness practice. You may suggest that children curl up on their sides like a tiny seed to plant in their healing garden. "Plant a seed of friendship, love, kindness. Sitting up slowly, feel your roots spread down into the ground, and your branches reach up high toward the sun." (See scripts for "Floating on a Cloud" and "Mindfulness Practice" in Chapter 18.)

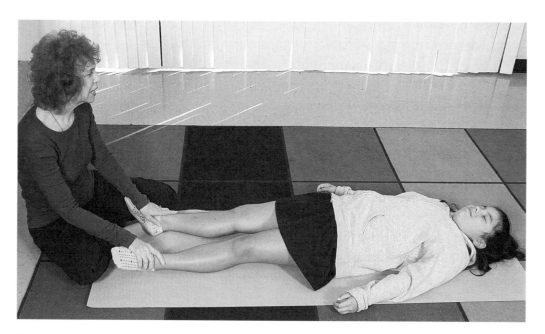

9-3   Grounding for Final Relaxation

PART II

PROCESS: PRINCIPLES OF CREATIVE RELAXATION

Creative Relaxation is the program I developed for training therapists, educators, yoga teachers, and parents in yoga therapy for children with autism and special needs. It adapts yoga exercises for use in public school education and varied therapeutic settings. While Creative Relaxation may be used with all children, it is specifically designed for those with autism spectrum disorder, Asperger's disorder, emotional behavioral disorder, attention deficit hyperactivity disorder, sensory processing disorders, physical and learning disabilities, and children with anxiety.

The principles of Creative Relaxation are to create a sacred space, engage the child, provide tools for success, and develop opportunities for independence (Goldberg, 2011).

CHAPTER 10

CREATE A SACRED SPACE

"MORE AND MORE experimental evidence indicates that environment can affect the wiring of the brain." Perhaps homes, offices, and schools will one day be designed to "provide an enriched environment for enhancing brain function" (Gage, 2003, p. 53).

Sacred Space for Children: Feeling Safe

Learning requires trying something new or in a different way, experimenting with the unfamiliar. The child who puts himself in your hands must feel certain that he is protected, secure, and safe. Not feeling safe triggers the amygdala, generating anxiety (Cole, 2008).

Creating a sacred space requires being present for a child. That means attuning yourself to his wants, needs, and potential sources of discomfort and adjusting your environment and expectations to them.

I discovered the importance of creating a sacred space when I was a reading specialist over 30 years ago, working with middle school students, some of whom were reading at first- and second-grade levels. With fragile egos and erratic hormones, these kids were at risk of dropping out or getting into trouble—anything to avoid revealing their difficulties with reading.

A child who has been unsuccessful in school for so many years is especially mistrustful of trying again. He feels like a failure as soon as he walks into the classroom. Rather than repeat things that had not worked before, I tried to make the children comfortable. We talked and listened to one another. I filled my classroom with magazines and books based on their interests. I gave each child my full attention and praised even the slightest effort. They began to feel comfortable enough to start taking risks.

Students dared to sound out the one letter or syllable that they recognized in a magazine with appealing photos. They began to ask when they got stuck, because they wanted to know. They made a guess about what something might mean, based on whatever they recognized. They began to learn because they felt safe enough to try.

CREATING A MOOD

You can create an inviting atmosphere in even the most unlikely environments. Make one corner of your classroom into a sacred space by using a dim lamp and playing soft, relaxing music. Display photographs of sleeping animals or a beautiful sunset. Plants, a tree bough, or a small fountain will contribute to the healing mood of your space. Identify this as the yoga space with mats for postures or beanbags for relaxation.

If you have to move the yoga materials, put them back in the same place each time so that children identify this area as their sacred space.

An attitude of ahimsa (do no harm) on your part creates a mood within your classroom or office. Acknowledge any effort by the child. Praise quiet in the room, and include those who appear not to be participating when they are quiet, too. As long as a child is not hurting himself or another, find no fault.

EXPRESSION, VOICE, AND BREATHING

Be mindful of your facial expressions. Strain in your face or a tense stance may be perceived as a judgment by a very sensitive child. Take care to keep a relaxed expression and presence. You can achieve this through vigilance of your breathing, which serves as a mirror for your own emotional state.

Use the tone, volume, and speed of your voice to create a mood. By slowing your own breathing, you may lower the pitch of your voice. A deeper pitch, softer volume, and slower pace of speaking create an atmosphere of acceptance.

When you breathe rhythmically and deeply, you appear open. In fact, relaxed breathing makes you a better listener, explains acupuncture physician Steven Templin: "Your rate of respiration creates a mood, building rapport, an atmosphere of respect and safety" (personal communication, June 5, 2012). Your physical state is communicated to the child, and has an impact on him. When your heartbeat is balanced, or coherent, you "can entrain another person's heartbeat into the same coherence" (Soosalu & Oka, 2012, p. 139).

LIGHTING

For most children, it's a great relief to have the lights in a classroom or office switched off. "Any light that reaches your eyes sets off nerve impulses that directly inhibit your anterior hypothalamus, weakening the calming signals it sends to your brain" (Cole, 2008, p. 89). For some children, the continual humming of fluorescent lighting can be distracting. When they are lying face up on the floor, the glare is intense. If you have access to a window and can substitute natural lighting, that's ideal. Alternately, turn off as many lights as you can or use a lamp with a dim or softly colored bulb.

Some children, however, are uncomfortable with darkness, which is a challenge when working with groups. One therapist who works with small groups compromises by letting each child make a choice about the lighting. For example, she might conduct the first half of class with the lights on and the second with the lights off.

I have worked with a child who likes yoga therapy but screams when lights are turned off. Placing her near the window and alerting her just before switching off the lights mitigates most of her discomfort, but there have been days when she is inconsolable. If she appears fearful, she and an adult partner take a walk until she is calm. After the first weeks of each new session, the child generally adapts to the darkened room and is full of smiles.

It's important to distinguish between a child's will and her needs, so that taking a walk is not a reward for screaming. If the child's response becomes a battle of wills, you probably need to endure the screaming. In most cases, once the child realizes that she cannot bring about the desired change, she adjusts. Otherwise, the inappropriate behavior is rewarded and repeated.

In a private setting, you can accommodate individual needs more easily than in a group class. Don't let it become a war of wills. Experiment with lower light gradually, as her tolerance increases. If the child is truly frightened, keep the lights on and use an alternate method to signal the beginning of the session, such as music on and shoes off. When she is relaxed and comfortable, you may begin to address the sources of her fear or means to mitigate it.

TEMPERATURE

An ideal setting for yoga therapy would allow open windows and fresh air. Keeping the room a comfortable temperature can be a challenge in schools and offices where windows are sealed and thermostats are not accessible. Being too warm makes children sleepy and lethargic; cold triggers the sympathetic nervous system (Cole, 2008). If you are in a cold space, as schools and offices often are, use an energetic sequence that accelerates the child's rate of respiration. Keep blankets or sweatshirts available for the child, particularly during the final relaxation. If your space is warm, prevent overheating by using a slow, calming routine.

SCHEDULING TIME

Choose the best time of day for yoga therapy. You want your students to be alert, but not hyper. Use active routines early in the day. Calming postures work well as down time. It's best to practice on an empty stomach, so schedule your lesson an hour or more before lunch. If you do have to practice after lunch, avoid inversions and postures with abdominal pressure, because they could cause children discomfort. (See Chapter 16, "Yoga Therapy After Lunch.")

If a child tends to fall apart at 3:00 on most days, try an experiment. Practice yoga therapy at 2:30 to see whether this interrupts the negative pattern of behavior.

MUSIC

Music creates a mood for yoga therapy. "Music resonates through the limbic system, where memories are stored, and in the amygdala, which governs emotions . . . Just as two pendulums will ultimately swing together, our heart rate and movements will speed up or down to keep time with a beat" (Keedle, 2012).

The sound of music is useful to signal the beginning of a yoga therapy session. I prefer music that does not follow a specific rhythm or pattern, rather like a meandering brook, so my students do not anticipate what is coming or get involved in the tune. Using the same CD at each lesson helps children associate the soothing sounds with the relaxation process. As soon as they hear the opening crescendo, they begin to settle down for class (Foss, 2002).

Joy Bennett of Joyful Breath Yoga Therapy also recommends instrumental music, but "nothing too loud or too stimulating. Tibetan bells or 'singing bowls' have great resonance; children are soothed by their rich sounds and tones." Joy stays away from "children's music. Autistic children often find it too loud, and it aggravates them" (personal communication, October 9, 2012).

10-1 Tibetan Bowls

On occasion, a child may find your choice of music distracting or unpleasant. You may wish to experiment with the effects of different music and rhythms. Yoga therapist Molly Lannon Kenny of Samarya Yoga Center in Seattle sings Sanskrit chants to her students. One little girl asks her to sing the Gayatri Mantra during relaxation at the end of every class. This ancient chant, invoking the healing power of the universe (Paul, 2004), comforts the child (personal communication, August 9, 2012).

Because of sensory processing issues, Oklahoma speech and language pathologist Angela Moorad explains, "Some kids can't tolerate music at all and some need the beat of the music to help keep them alert. That's why it's so important to know the needs of the kids in the group" (personal communication, October 12, 2012).

Even the beautiful sounds of bowls or gongs can be like fingernails on a chalkboard for some children. Upon entering the studio where I teach, the parent of a child on the autism spectrum looked in horror at the Tibetan bowl sitting on the table. Vehemently shaking her head, she warned me that this sound would send her daughter into an anxious fit. For this reason, I recommend experimenting with instruments and unusual sounds in private sessions, where you can assess a child's response first. In small classes, where I know each child, I typically end a session by playing the Tibetan bowl. When working with large or new groups of children with varying sensitivities, however, I avoid sounds that may agitate or startle a child.

In private practice, you can involve the child in the choice of music or eliminate it altogether. Create an alternative signal for the beginning of the yoga session by adjusting the lighting (turning off overhead lights) or by covering the computer desk with an Indian blanket. Signaling that it's time for yoga therapy is helpful in creating a mood.

Rules for Yoga Therapy

Providing clear guidelines will help children stay within acceptable limits of behavior. When you introduce and enforce a set of basic rules, without judgment, you maintain discipline without criticism and without losing your own calm. For example:

RULES FOR CLASS

1. Remove your shoes
2. Stay on your own mat
3. Keep your hands and feet to yourself
4. This is a QUIET zone
5. Listen and follow directions

Adjust these rules to suit your client and the setting. For instance, some children may respond better to more literal instruction such as "Keep your hands and feet on your mat." Establish a hand gesture to signal quiet. Others may need more specific instruction such as "Raise your hand first before you speak."

Use praise and encouragement to reinforce the rules. With some children, you may select one rule and work with that before moving on to the next. For example, if you are working with a child who finds it difficult to stay on his mat, make this the focus of your lesson. Every time he sets a foot on his mat, praise that behavior: "Nice job getting on your mat." If he sits on the mat for a second, immediately say, "I like the way you are sitting on your mat." Determine if there is a minimum amount of time the child must stay on his mat before moving on to another task. "If you stay on your mat while I count to three, we'll take a run around the room (or have a nice rest)." Then come back to the mat for another count of three.

Remember, you must mean what you say (the child will hear that in your voice), and only praise that which is consistent with your rules and directions.

The advantage of these rules is that they offer a tool for correcting behaviors without making anything personal. When Joel pokes Mark, remind Joel of the rule about keeping his hands and feet to himself. If Julie attempts to take Brian's spot by pushing his mat away, remind Julie, "Stay on your own mat." Rather than criticizing behaviors or finding fault, you are enforcing the rules of your program.

INDIVIDUAL SPACE

In yoga therapy, you have the opportunity to create a physical space for each child that is his or hers alone. Use a yoga mat or towel, carpet samples (donated by retail outlets), or masking tape to identify personal space. By delineating each child's space, you help him stay within predetermined boundaries, maintaining control. This is also helpful for children who lack proprioception. In addition, you offer a sense of security for those who are fearful of or uncomfortable with close contact with others.

A word of caution here: Sometimes children will become preoccupied with the arrangement of this space. One child spent her entire session smoothing out and adjusting her new yoga mat. Each time she began a pose, she became distracted by some slight but compelling irregularity in the position of her mat. This was especially disappointing because she practiced regularly with me at school (where she did not bring her own mat). It was only when she came to the studio where I was teaching that this occurred. For some children, the less equipment, the better!

When using yoga mats, position them on the floor before the children take their seats. This minimizes their preoccupation with placement of the mat. Initially you may permit the children to choose their own spaces. If the class is unruly, assign a place to each child before they sit down. At schools with multi-colored carpets, you may delineate space by colors. Shalya will sit on the blue square and Sophia on the red. Carpets with a map of the United States work well: Jake sits on Alabama and Derek on Florida.

Sometimes during class it becomes apparent that certain children should not sit together or that one needs to be closer to you for more assistance. When you make changes in arrangement, it's best to do so before the next session begins. If you do need to separate children during a class, explain: "Let's try Alex sitting here and Ethan over there." Avoid any critical tone in your voice or manner. Find an opportunity to praise the children who have been moved as soon as you observe them following instructions. Remember, the purpose of the reassignment is to assist the child in knowing where his space is and to create an optimal environment for instruction.

It's important that all children can see you. Stagger the mats so that no child obscures another's view. When working with visual learners, I use a cue card easel with all the postures that I'll be teaching. If it is set on a chair or table higher than where I am sitting, it is visible to all students.

When working with groups, the rule "Keep your hands and feet to yourself" serves to protect each child and is a guide for class conduct. In private sessions, this rule also helps protect you. Practicing without shoes improves balance in standing poses, increases safety with groups in small spaces, and enhances relaxation. Flying feet are a challenge even without shoes in small spaces.

Most children are delighted to remove their shoes, although in school teachers often prefer that children keep their socks on. If possible, keep extra washed socks on hand to deal with occasional smelly feet. In a clean studio or office space, both shoes and socks off works best.

Occasionally a child is resistant to removing shoes. Remind him of the rule and offer him a choice: He may sit out, watching from his desk, or he can sit just outside the designated space where the rest of the class is and participate from there, for safety. Be sure to make yoga especially fun so the left-out child will be tempted to engage. If the child decides to remove his shoes (and he probably will), he may join the circle.

Some children become anxious when asked to remove their shoes or to sit on the floor. To avoid contributing to their discomfort, you may conduct yoga therapy in your office or classroom seated in chairs, with or without shoes. You will find lessons in Chapters 16–20 for seated postures. When you teach children relaxation techniques they can use at their desks, the classroom becomes a more peaceful space.

CONSISTENCY

Being consistent is one of the most difficult jobs for a teacher or therapist. Children are acutely attuned to deviations from what they perceive "should" be. Add the challenge of making sense of an already confusing world, and you can see the importance of staying within set rules.

Still, no two children or situations are exactly alike. For this reason, it is important to have a set of standards that you can adapt for each child. Consider the rule to listen and follow directions. Your response to exceptions to this rule depends on the child, the outcome of the action, and your goals for the session. For example, you may be working privately with a child who is fixated on a toy. If you try to force the object away from the child and he has a meltdown, you will lose his attention completely. If you ignore the behavior, you are being inconsistent. Instead, amend the rule by permitting the child to hold the toy while he does specific postures. However, when two hands are required, he will be expected to put that object aside while doing that pose. The reward for following directions will be praise and permission to once again hold his toy. By adapting the rules so the child can experience success, you will likely increase his attention to your instructions and willingness to participate.

DISTRACTIONS

Choose a space that is simple and clear of clutter. "Every child benefits from a safe, calm, and distraction-free environment" (Kranowitz, 2005, p. 251). Keeping the practice area spare is especially helpful for those on the autism spectrum. Temple Grandin clarifies this in her book *Animals in Translation:* "Animals and autistic people don't have to be paying attention to something in order to see it. Things . . . pop out at us; they grab our attention whether we want them to or not" (2005, p. 51). Once individuals with ASD get focused on one thing, she explains, it's really difficult for them to escape the object of their focus.

Grandin explains that neurotypical individuals focus more on "the big picture" rather than "all the tiny little details that go into that picture" (p. 57). The ability "to filter out distractions is a good thing," Grandin continues. People with ADHD are prone to "sensory overload" because "every little sensory detail in their environment keeps hijacking their attention" (p. 67).

Examine your space from the perspective of one who sees all the details and is easily distracted from the "big picture." In a yoga studio, move props, pillows, bells, and drums out of sight before beginning class. Resisting the impulse to touch or play with instruments during class adds an unnecessary distraction for many children. When teaching in a classroom, move the desks to one area to create an open space. Remove books and games; cover or hide computers from view. After lunch or snack time, clean the area before seating children on the floor. Remember, one stray potato chip can become the source of preoccupation for some individuals.

Avoiding the distraction of the teacher's body is something that can be easily accomplished. When dressing for children's classes or private sessions, avoid clothing that is tight fitting or revealing. Wearing loose trousers and a plainly colored shirt that covers the entire torso eliminates that concern.

Children with special needs, especially those on the autism spectrum, often have a keen sense of smell. For this reason, avoid perfumed hair products, deodorant, or skin creams. Do not use candles or incense, which may be irritating to sensitive eyes and noses.

A Sacred Space for the Therapist: Maintaining Control

The application of yoga as therapy as discussed in this book is not exclusively for yoga teachers. These techniques have been distilled for use by educators, therapists, parents, and clinicians. For this reason, it is imperative that you offer only those aspects of yoga that you feel comfortable teaching (See Golden Rule 5 in Chapter 5). It's better to start simply and gradually increase the demands of your lessons, using the same principles for yourself as you will for your students.

CHOICE OF ROUTINE

Your selection of routines and poses can help you maintain control. For example, you might begin with seated postures only. It is common for children, especially those on the autism spectrum, to become distracted while transitioning from one position to another. Sometimes, when a child stands, he runs. By selecting postures where children remain seated on the floor, you may feel more confident in controlling your client or group.

DURATION OF CLASS

The length of a session has an impact on the child's ability to attend and stay focused. Expecting a child to sit or follow directions for a period beyond his capacity often leads to outbursts or meltdowns. I usually recommend 30-minute classes, but that can and should be adjusted for comfort and control. Divide a large or unruly group in half so that each half-group has a 15-minute session. Adjusting the duration of sessions to the child's capacity prevents upsets and helps maintain a safe and comfortable space.

CLASS SIZE

Creating a sacred space applies to the size of the class that you can safely manage. When conducting a pilot program (Appendix 3) in an autism cluster, I had only three students per class and was assisted by another professional. I routinely teach camp groups of 15 or more children with varying disabilities. This decision must be determined by your ability to keep each child safe and to address their needs.

TEACHER/CHILD RATIO

When teaching large groups, it is advisable to have one or more assistants. That way one of you can carry on the instruction while the other addresses individual issues. Having assistance is especially important when working with children with severe challenges. It's ideal to have a partner for each child or to see the child privately.

SAFETY FOR ALL

For your safety and the security of the child, reserve the right to request the continual presence of a parent while working with his or her child, either in a waiting area or with you in the room. It's important to have an emergency number where someone can be reached immediately when parents are not present and to keep a fully charged phone in the office or classroom at all times.

CHAPTER 11

ENGAGE THE CHILD

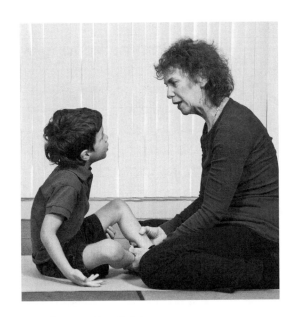

11-1 Engage the Child

CONNECTING WITH A child is the first step in creating a therapeutic relationship. We've talked about creating a sense of safety and acceptance. Those are things that you do *for* the child. Engaging the child, however, involves interaction, communication, a give-and-take in which the child participates.

Meet the Child Where He Is

Children want to be acknowledged; it is a requisite for classroom success. "Every child needs to know that someone is paying attention to his strengths and weaknesses, likes and dislikes, ups and downs" (Kranowitz, 2005, p. 251).

In *The Heart of Yoga,* T. K. V. Desikachar describes the work of his father, Krishnamacharya, who helped sculpt the tradition of yoga therapy as it is known today. Instruction must address the uniqueness of each individual. "The starting point is never the teacher's needs, but those of the student" and these may change from day to day (1995, p. xviii).

Swami Vishnudevananda taught many facets of yoga: posture, breathing, relaxation, diet, positive thinking, philosophy and meditation. The teacher's task was to welcome the student through whichever doorway he entered yoga, to meet the student wherever he was. The paths are many; the way is one.

This principle is interdisciplinary. "One of the tenets of social work is to start where the client is," explains Rich Foss, LCSW. To do this in his office in a Florida high school, he invites kids to put their feet up on his desk, hang them over the back of their chairs, or sit on the floor. "Anything to put the child at ease" (personal communication, September 5, 2012).

Communicating with Children

There are many ways to connect with children with diverse needs. You communicate with your tone of voice, your body position relative to the child, your gestures and posture, and your breathing.

TONE OF VOICE

You already know that your voice creates a mood. With highly sensitive children, however, your manner of speaking can disrupt or deepen your connection with a child. In *Overcoming Autism*, co-author Claire LaZebnik describes her son with ASD: "Tone of voice is huge with Andrew, who will often cry if he feels that an adult is angry at him or disappointed in him." A "cheerful" tone, on the other hand, helps him avert frustration and keeps him engaged when faced with a challenge (Koegel & LaZebnik, 2004, p. 111).

Suit your tone to the child. If he seems excitable, tone yourself down a notch. If he appears flat, generate modest enthusiasm without overwhelming him. Keep your gestures fluid to avoid startling children, and maintain smooth, rhythmic breathing. These behaviors invite interaction and express support.

Pause in your instruction if children start to get loud, and wait for them to quiet down to be heard. Without raising your voice, you can engage them if they are looking forward to or are curious about what's coming. Your own enthusiasm and tone maintain interest as well as control.

SAY WHAT YOU MEAN

Adults often bewilder children by saying something other than what they mean. For example, if you are angry but you say that you are "fine," you confuse the child about what it means to be "fine." You may be able to fool adults with what you say, but children are attuned to nonverbal cues. They will respond more to your tone of voice and posture than to your words. Children with language deficits may be even more sensitive to the mood, the tone, the manner in which you present yourself and your instruction. Match your words with your feelings to maintain satya, truthfulness, and clarity for children.

COMMUNICATE ON THE CHILD'S LEVEL, LITERALLY AND FIGURATIVELY

In yoga therapy, adults and children are literally eye-to-eye. Placing yourself on the level of the child rather than hovering above can mitigate anxiety and increase receptivity.

Temple Grandin discusses the importance of staying "down low to the ground" which is "a lot less scary" (2005, p. 45) for animals when working in any novel situation. Unthreatened, the animals were more likely to approach her. She has found their response comparable to that of individuals with autism.

SPEAK THE CHILD'S LANGUAGE: MODALITIES IN LEARNING

When you interact with a child, it is your responsibility to make yourself understood. This requires an understanding of the child's communication style.

Have you noticed that people learn in different ways? My husband likes to read directions thoroughly before beginning a project. He's a visual learner. My son can listen to directions and then perform the task perfectly. He's an auditory learner. It's preferable for me to have someone walk me through the steps. I can't just watch them do it; I have to perform each task myself while I am getting the instructions. I'm a kinesthetic/tactile learner.

In schools, most information is presented orally. Children with autism, however, tend to be visual learners. Those with learning disabilities and attention deficits are often kinesthetic/tactile learners. Some children learn by hearing alone without associating the visual aspects of the material.

In yoga therapy, you give instructions (auditory), demonstrate (visual), assist students as they move in and out of the poses (kinesthetic), and touch or tap them gently in posture to direct their awareness to muscles that need to be activated or released (tactile). In this way, you engage all of the senses of your students and communicate via multiple modalities. Some students will need more of one type of instruction than others. Observe which teaching techniques are most effective for each child. By adapting your teaching style to the child's learning style, you learn to speak the child's language (Goldberg, 2011).

Here's an example of combining modalities when teaching Folded Leaf, a seated forward bend. Sit alongside or in front of the child so you are completely within her field of vision and hearing. First guide the student in sweeping the arms (both or one at a time) up and down in the pose. You may model, tap the child's hands or move her arms to cue the motion. Be attentive to sensitivities to touch when tapping and cueing in this manner. Chant "Hands go up, hands go down," in rhythm with the motion and breath. Following your visual instructions and the sound of your voice, the child experiences the movement in her body and the feeling of her breath; she is learning with multiple senses.

Don't hesitate to lie down right next to children to engage their attention or model a pose. Use your voice, tactile cues such as tapping the muscle required to move a limb, and illustrations of the postures to determine which techniques are most effective for children. Combine modalities when working with diverse groups.

Make Yoga Therapy Fun

Adapt, adjust, and find the most comfortable, enjoyable, rewarding way for children to practice, and they will reward you with their enthusiasm!

11-2 Communicating on Child's Level

Lina Maria Moyano, LCSW, combines yoga with Floortime, a "relationship-based therapy" with children on the autism spectrum. "When you play with a child, you need to slow down so you can let the child explore and become a leader in the interaction. We connect from the heart, relax and have fun" (personal communication, December 7, 2011).

Creating a connection through music, posture, and play engages children in yoga therapy. Whether they lead or follow or make up their own dialogues, music gives them the freedom to express themselves while having fun.

Speech-language pathologist Molly Lannon Kenny of The Samarya Center uses musical instruments during yoga for a variety of activities, including "musical conversations" (personal communication, October 12, 2012). Nancy Williams, author of *Yoga Therapy for Every Special Child,* uses "drumming to facilitate imitation of sequenced patterns." She explains, "I alter rhythm, count, volume and patterns to cue auditory and visual processing. This stimulates prosody for speech" (personal communication, October 15, 2012).

Having fun and laughing together is unifying and bonding. Steven Gutstein (2005) describes shared laughter as a motivating factor in early childhood development and says that children with autism can learn this skill through "experience sharing."

It is possible to teach children to smile at appropriate times, even if it is not something that they infer. In fact, changing facial expressions can alter the body's biochemistry (Weintraub, 2012). Take a moment right now to smile; notice how different you feel!

Here's a method to create smiles (see more in Chapter 19) in yoga therapy, using Cat pose. Coach the child to look up and say, "Meow." His mouth forms a smile. This is "Happy Cat." When the child demonstrates his Happy Cat, it's natural for you to smile, too. Show him your Happy Cat smile, and coach him to smile back. The child may begin to associate the arrangement of his face and the sensations around his mouth with the words "smile" and "happy." He is learning another form of communication.

Make Yoga Therapy Self-Rewarding

Some children need to see the benefits of yoga therapy before trying it. I met much resistance when working with students in a center for emotional behavioral disorders. A number of the high school boys didn't want to get down on the floor; yoga was for nerds. My colleague and I brought in a young man, a body builder, to help us lead the group. Suddenly yoga therapy was very cool!

You may engage some students by photographing them (with parental permission) in two or three postures at the beginning of a series and then six to eight weeks later. Some children enjoy making a friendly wager: How long will it take until they are half an inch closer to the ground in standing forward bend? To reach their goal, they may be willing to try other poses that you recommend. As students attain increased comfort in a pose, the postures become self-rewarding.

FINDING COMFORT

Earning a child's trust is important if he's to feel safe with you. By presenting postures that are neither stressful nor beyond the child's capacity, you enhance his capacity to release anxiety.

Help children to find comfortable variations of postures. When modeling, offer various options within poses. In this way you teach children to listen to their own bodies, rather than forcing their bodies to adapt to someone else's way.

Supported postures, using props, may create a more comfortable experi-

11-3   Comfortable Variations in Folded Leaf

ence for some children. Kianga Jinaka, RYT and Creative Relaxation practitioner, worked with a teenaged boy with schizophrenia. Because he was so tense, she created a nest with bolsters and blankets, choosing a restorative posture. Feeling comforted, he settled in and began to relax. In time, he began to express his feelings and request more poses.

Engaging Through Contracts

Contracts engage children, without overwhelming them with excessive choices. By involving them in selecting what they will practice, you provide a sense of control. Contracts offer many opportunities to practice the art of compromise. Here's a formula for creating contracts for yoga therapy:

1. *Rules.* Take time to clarify, discuss, and secure agreement on the rules that you have selected; see if the child has any to add. Some children will need reminding of these each time you meet, and they may be renegotiated periodically.

2. *Content and structure.* After initially assessing the child, determine the duration and objective of the lesson. From Part III of this book, make a list of the postures that are appropriate for this lesson, using written names or visual cue cards. You and the child will choose postures from your list through discussion or with visuals. As the child progresses, you may give him greater freedom in posture selection. Be sure to include appropriate counterposes (see Chapter 15).

Here is a sample contract:

1. **Duration:** 15 minutes

2. **Objective:** Strengthening postural muscles of the upper back

3. **Starting positions:** Seated, standing, prone

4. **Child's choice:** 3 poses

5. **Therapist's choice:** 3 complementary or counterposes

6. **Sequence:** Determined by therapist for flow and balance of postures

7. **Conclusion:** Floating on a Cloud

You can imagine how much communication and negotiation goes on through this process, even if the child is nonverbal.

You may let the child select the music from two or three suitable options. He may also choose between a sequence seated in chairs or on the floor. Remember not to overwhelm him with too much choice.

3. *Assessment.* Upon completion of the sequence, you and the student will determine if this contract should be adjusted. Was it too hard, too easy, just right? Would you use it again? You may use previous contracts as starting places for new ones and to help the child keep track of his progress.

Engaging the Child by Using What's Familiar

One of the most challenging aspects when initiating yoga therapy is its "newness." When I first began teaching yoga at a camp for children with autism and varying disabilities, almost everything about my program was unfamiliar. The first sessions were challenging for the children and exhausting for me.

As the weeks progressed, the campers became more accustomed to what I was asking them to do. I could see the possibilities for the program. The following summer was very different. Many of the returning campers remembered portions or all of what they had learned. They followed with greater ease and modeled for their peers.

Each summer, there are more children who are familiar with the program. They smile when I begin their favorite postures. The boys groan when I suggest giving their foot a hug in the hip rocking pose. The girls whisper "Yes" when I lead them into a posture where back rubbing is involved. Some grow animated when we try something new: "We haven't done this one!" Many still resist new challenges, but it's not so disturbing as it once was, because they have successfully tried new postures before.

There is no way to avoid the newness of an unfamiliar program. But there are techniques you can use to ease children into yoga therapy.

USE FAMILIAR PHRASES

To begin your class seated on the floor, you need a term for this position. Choose a phrase that the children will recognize: cross-legged, crisscross applesauce, seated pose. Once children respond to this phrase, use it consistently. The same is true for all of the starting positions and posture names.

USE FAMILIAR IMAGERY

Children on the autism spectrum tend to be visual learners. Yoga therapy is easily adapted to this modality, because it draws on images from everyday life—a table, a butterfly, a dog. Select names of animals or trees that children recognize. Children in Massachusetts will be oak trees; Floridians will be palms. For relaxation, choose familiar images: floating on a cloud, reclining at the beach, resting near a stream.

MAKE THE UNFAMILIAR KNOWN

One therapist brought a bellows to her office because this object, the name of a breathing posture, was not one her clients recognized. Once they could see and feel the action of air moving through a bellows, the posture became real to the children. Bring in photos of frogs or a real rocking chair to make these posture names meaningful.

Engaging Children Through Imitation

We know that the learning process begins when children copy or repeat our behaviors, expression, and language. It has long been hypothesized that individuals with autism find imitation difficult because it requires identifying with others, having a theory of mind (Baron-Cohen, Leslie, & Frith, 1985). In fact, lack of imitative play is one of the criteria for a diagnosis of autism according to DSM-IV.

Marco Iacoboni's fascinating book *Mirroring People* (2008) discusses the process of learning and developing socially through imitation. Iacoboni conducted fMRIs to confirm his theory that when observing faces, the mirror neurons, the insula, and the limbic system, particularly the amygdala, reveal increased activity in the brain. With typical individuals, this brain activity increases whether imitating *or* observing the expressions of another person. The neurons fire just as if the person were making those expressions. Iacoboni theorizes that this begins the process of empathy.

This, however, was not the case in the brains of many individuals with autism.

According to Iacoboni, individuals with autism demonstrated impairment in "social mirroring, which is supported by the neural interactions between mirror neurons and the limbic system" (p. 172). Iacoboni reported findings by Dapretto and colleagues (2006) that severe impairment in children with autism corresponded with lower activity in mirror neuron areas of their brains. Functional MRIs by the researchers showed that children with autism did not follow pointing gestures or the eyes of individuals they observed. More highly functioning individuals with autism watched the mouths of speakers, rather than the eyes.

Without observing facial expression, there is little opportunity to fire mirror neurons. The process of empathy requires an identification with others that seems more challenging for individuals with autism because of neurological differences (Iacoboni, 2008).

An encouraging study has been conducted using an integrated approach to yoga therapy for children with autism by Shantha Radhakrishna (2010). Six children and their mothers met for instruction five times a week over ten months. Researchers reported improvements in the participants' imitation skills, particularly in "body, postural and oral facial movements. Parents reported changes in the play pattern of these children with toys, peers and objects at home . . . In addition, children exhibited increased skills in eye contact, sitting tolerance, nonverbal communication and receptive skills to verbal commands related to spatial relationship" (p. 26). Shannahoff-Khalsa (2010) found that rhythmic movements, simple chants, and breathing techniques invited focused attention and imitation among children with autism.

If a child lacks the tools to imitate an adult, you can initiate the process to create connections in natural ways. When teaching yoga therapy to preschoolers, I worked with a three-and-a-half-year-old girl who spent a good deal of her day hopping up and down. She laughed and seemed to be enjoying herself so much that I couldn't resist joining her. While hopping, I would say, "Shake it out, shake it out," giving a name to the position she was in. After a few moments of jumping about (I didn't have the endurance to maintain this pose for long), I said, "And stop!" After a pause (a chance for me to catch my breath), I would rejoin her in hopping, repeating "Shake it out."

After a while, the child began to imitate my stops. Whenever she came to a stop, even for just a moment, I would praise her lavishly for such "good stopping." As soon as she began to jump, I would rejoin her and we would start the whole process again. It was the first time that I had been able to coax her from her hopping and create an activity that we shared. And it was the beginning of her responding to the words "And stop," which was reinforced and became very useful to her classroom teacher.

A study conducted in 2001 by Field, Sanders, and Nadel compared the response of twenty children with autism to adults who either played with or imitated them. Children who had been imitated "spent a greater proportion of time looking; vocalizing; smiling; and engaging in reciprocal play." They found that by the third session, "the children in the imitation group spent a greater proportion of time . . . being close to the adult . . . and touching the adult" than those who had not been imitated (p. 317).

This gives credence to an experience that I had many years ago when working with a group of children with ASD. None of these children were verbal; many had significant cognitive impairments. At first I tried to teach by demonstrating postures and talking about their breathing. It soon became clear that this was having no effect. The boys ambled around the room and had to be continually urged back into the yoga space.

Not knowing what else to do, I began interacting with the children in a different way. Instead of trying to direct their activities, I participated in them. One student continually stared at a spot above his head, as if he could see through the ceiling. I thought, perhaps he has a direct line to an angel above us who is so beautiful, so compelling, that there really is nowhere else worth looking at in this room. So, I sat alongside the child and shared his view, imagining something beautiful above us. Another boy ambled around the yoga area on all fours; I did the same. One boy lay on the floor. For safety's sake I did not lie down, but I sat close by, quiet.

After a few weeks, I began to notice changes in the children. They recognized me and became more animated when I arrived to sit in their circle. The boy who stared at a spot above his head elected to sit right beside me. The students (and these were big boys) came close, leaned against me, almost sitting in my lap. They surrounded me in a way that acknowledged my presence. The boy who lay on the floor began to permit me to support his head with my hands while he rested on the floor. This seemed to me an act of trust. The children had permitted me into their dialogue. We were interacting, engaged, sharing a moment.

CHAPTER 12

PROVIDE TOOLS FOR SUCCESS

To HELP CHILDREN feel accomplished, provide opportunities for their success by adapting instruction to their learning strengths. Many children with special needs respond well to a highly structured environment, simplified instruction, and the use of visual supports.

Consistent routines and carefully planned transitional activities are useful for children with sensory processing disorders (Kranowitz, 2005); familiar settings mitigate motor-planning challenges (Miller, 2006). Children with autism are often distracted and overwhelmed by sensory stimulation. "Organization and structure reduce anxiety," explains Janet Janzen, who recommends a "balance of activities that are . . . familiar and new" (1996, p. 363).

Structure in Instruction

Children with special needs are often fearful of change or interruptions to their routines. When a child knows what is expected of him, what is going to happen next, and that it is possible to achieve what he has been asked to do, he is less likely to resist or feel overwhelmed. Children on the autism spectrum are responsive to structure (UNC, 2012).

SCHEDULES

I recently visited an autism cluster where yoga therapy is included in the curriculum, using S.T.O.P. and Relax. Transitioning children from a classroom activity to yoga and back to their seats could be disruptive in any classroom setting. Yet the teachers managed to keep their programs running smoothly. I wanted to know how.

Every teacher agreed that scheduling yoga therapy into their day was essential to its success. According to the University of North Carolina's Project TEACCH, "Many [autistic] students have problems with sequential memory and organization of time . . . a schedule can help a student organize and predict daily and weekly events. This lessens anxiety about not knowing what will happen next" (UNC, 2012).

Behavior therapist and yoga teacher Crystal Wissinger, of Imagine Wellness LLC, uses a visual schedule while teaching yoga to children with autism and other exceptionalities. "I use visuals from Baron Baptiste's book *My Daddy Is a Pretzel* (2004) with cards, color coded by starting positions. I number them and place them on a board in a vertical row, large enough to be seen by the entire group so they know what's coming" (personal communication, July 31, 2012).

Wisconsin school media specialist Kelly Hagen shared that afternoons had been a difficult time of day for children with ASD. To address this, teachers implemented a scheduled period of yoga therapy using the *Creative Relaxation*: *Yoga for Children* DVD (Goldberg, 2004b). "The boys are able to focus better in the afternoon after the calming effect of your DVD" (personal communication, December 4, 2008).

SOCIAL STORIES

Stories personalize abstract concepts for children. Carol Gray of the Gray Center in Michigan devised "social stories" to prepare children for something unfamiliar. Autism educators have found this sort of rehearsal especially helpful for preparing a child for something new, to discuss what will likely occur and to address concerns of the child (Janzen, 1996).

You may use this principle to personalize a story before beginning yoga therapy by adding photos of the child and the yoga area, his name, and the schedule. In the S.T.O.P. and Relax curriculum, the storybook *It's Time to Relax* includes simple illustrations to clarify written instruction. "On Wednesday at 10:00, I will go to relaxation class. There will be mats on the floor and music playing. I will take off my shoes and sit on a mat" (Goldberg, Miller, Collins, Morales, 2010).

Substitute Patterns

Repetitive or stereotypical behaviors are believed to calm or soothe individuals with autism, but they are often socially excluding. Autism coach and Creative

12-1   Story Book S.T.O.P. and Relax

Relaxation practitioner Barb Hennessey of Florida finds that yoga-based relaxation strategies can change a child's demeanor quickly, especially if he practices them regularly. "If a child is hand flapping, a calming intervention takes his mind off the repetitive action and redirects him to the replacement behavior" (personal communication, October 3, 2012).

Substitute a yoga activity that is comparable to the sensory experience the child is seeking. Instead of humming incessantly, suggest he chant "OM" or "HUM." For spinning, try a fast variation of a rotational pose like Twister. For hand biting, experiment with sitting on the hands in seated postures. Substitute Butterfly Hands for hand flapping, with long rests between flutters.

Identify a cue to interrupt the repetitive activity, such as a hand clap or a word. When the child responds to the cue, praise him. Establish a specific duration for the alternative activity, such as to the count of ten. Follow with a calming posture or sequence.

Simplifying Instruction

When I began teaching children on the spectrum, I often gave long lists of directions at one time. Seeing the confusion that ensued, I began dividing instructions into single steps. Simplify your language by choosing the smallest number of words needed to express yourself.

LANGUAGE FOR LITERAL LEARNERS

Individuals with autism often interpret language literally; they may be confused by subtle imagery or metaphor. If you tell a child to "give it a rest," he may lie down on his mat. Avoid nuance and say precisely what you mean: "Please sit quietly."

Avoid complex sentences. If you say, "Feel free to move your mat if you are feeling crowded," every child may begin moving his mat or pushing others away. Instead, say, "Mark, please move your mat here, and Peter, over here."

Avoid excessive detail and choices. Let the child choose between two options, once you've determined her ability to respond. Lengthy explanations can be confusing or distracting. Watch the child. If she strays off task, you may be speaking too slowly or too long. If she is following your instructions, you know you are being effective. Use what works.

GIVE THEM TIME TO RESPOND

It's a common pitfall for parents or adults who work with children with special needs to ask too many questions or assist a child before it's necessary (Gutstein, 2005). I recently had a delightful child with Down syndrome in a group yoga therapy class. As agreed, her mother observed silently. After the 30-minute class, the mom was astounded by the extent of her daughter's participation. The mother confessed how difficult it had been not to prompt her daughter or "check in" during class. To her credit, what she discovered by being a silent observer was how much more independent her daughter was capable of being than she had known.

Continually observe the child to see if she is engaged. As long as she is following your words, give her time to process instructions and follow them at her own pace (see Appendix 5). You can always prompt her or repeat the instructions, as needed.

Simplifying Postures

Providing students with tools for success often requires simplifying the poses so a child loses neither enthusiasm nor self-esteem while learning new skills. Eliminate aspects of a posture that lead to frustration or are beyond a child's capability. Children with motor-planning challenges may benefit from mastering each phase of a pose separately before trying to put it all together.

For example, if a child has difficulty standing independently, she can practice Tree pose from her seat. Raising her arms like branches, she can sway them in the breeze. Perhaps she can follow the motions of her arms with her eyes. With this sequence, she experiences success in the pose. You can also include children of varied skill levels in the same class, each performing the posture in her own way.

Systematic repetition within evolving frameworks that can be expanded also helps children succeed (Gutstein, 2000). Yoga therapy establishes a starting point that is familiar and returns to it frequently during instruction. Beginning and ending sequences with foundational postures, you gradually increase challenge.

For some children, it's best to begin therapy with just one starting position. If a child is low toned or lethargic, she might prefer lying on her back, hugging her knees. There are a number of supine poses to playfully release tension and get her feet and arms in motion. Work from this position for as long as needed to help the child experience success. When she is ready to practice seated poses, continue to start and end her program with supine knee hugs.

Avoid Frustration

Usually you can tell when a child is ready for an additional challenge and when he is at the edge of his tolerance. If he is red in the face, his hands are clenched, or his breathing is shallow, he is likely experiencing frustration.

Ending an activity when a child feels successful makes him more willing to try a pose again next time. There is a physiological reward for meeting a moderate challenge: increased levels of dopamine, which feels good. Frustration, on the other hand, elevates the levels of stress hormones and curbs dopamine production (Sapolsky, 2003). This feels bad.

Yoga philosophy acknowledges all effort, without attachment to the end result. Part of your ability to help a child feel successful is to reassure him that each variation is a "correct" form of a posture. With a structured, sequential approach, you help the child become proficient with each phase of a pose while minimizing frustration.

Visual Instruction

Just as we acknowledge a child's challenges, it's important to use his strengths to enhance success. Most people on the autism spectrum process visual information more effectively than auditory, according to Mesibov, Shea, and Schopler (2004). The TEACCH approach to autism education uses visual supports to "promote feelings of security, competence, and independence" (p. 41).

Yoga is ideal for visual learners because the teacher positions herself directly at the student's eye level, using her body as a visual tool and making instruction easier to follow. There are many opportunities to exaggerate movements and use gestures to catch the child's attention.

MODELING, CUEING, AND PROMPTING

Modeling is an excellent visual tool for teaching movements and behaviors. The importance of imitation has already been discussed. I generally model every posture that I teach. If I tell the children to sit down and then stand up to help a child, the other children stand up, too. Kids do what you do, not what you say.

When modeling for a child, stand or sit in front of him and act as a mirror. Move your left foot when you tell him to move his right, and your left arm when you tell him to lift his right. If modeling in this way creates confusion for you or the child, stand or sit alongside him instead.

A cue is an action or object that is used to trigger a desired response, and a prompt calls attention to a missed cue to "ensure a correct response" (Janzen, 2009, p. 197). The previous chapter described multimodal cues such as tapping or helping a child move a limb while you give oral instructions. Illustrations of each posture serve as visual cues. Showing the child an illustration while giving instructions combines visual and auditory information. Visuals showing a child where to place his feet or hands or where to look are prompts.

S.T.O.P. AND RELAX VISUAL CURRICULUM

In 2000 I had the opportunity to collaborate with a group of autism specialists and a school psychologist at a public school in South Florida. Our early focus was to prepare elementary school children with ASD for the transition to middle school. In Appendix 3 you will find a summary of the efficacy of the yoga-based program developed from 2000 to 2004 for children with autism spectrum disorders. The need for a visual curriculum was the inspiration for S.T.O.P. and Relax, the yoga-based program developed by Sally Miller, Debra Collins, Daniela Morales, and myself (2006/2010).

When I first began working with visuals, it was like having two assistants. Children who had required a great deal of guidance or who had not been able to follow the routines came into postures when they saw the illustrations. While they followed the visual, I could assist others. Some held the pose for just a moment, but their response was evident.

In addition to children on the autism spectrum and those with motor-planning challenges, visuals provide a specific focal point for children with ADHD, whose attention easily strays. Cues that are illustrated without a lot of detail or background activity minimize distraction. Visuals are helpful for therapists or educators who may be less adept at demonstrating and helping children into postures.

Lee Day of Pensacola has been a special educator and consultant for 25 years. Now a yoga teacher, she has been using the S.T.O.P. and Relax visual curriculum for the past two years with elementary aged children with varying needs at a private school for autism. She has observed "noticeable improvement in the ability of the students to remain on their mats, focus, and follow instructions. They remain calm and engaged. Children especially enjoy the breathing exercises and the music."

Lee uses the PowerPoint variation of the curriculum. "Increasing the size of the visual prompt clarifies instruction. These students receive daily academic instruction via computer assisted technology; it may be that the familiar, 'projected' format is preferred in learning yoga, too.

"Viewing the cue card images rather than having to focus on a human instructor may be less confrontational for these special students," Lee explains. "The cleanly drawn images, in shades of gray, lacking specific facial features, are

rock the baby

12-2   Visual Cue S.T.O.P. and Relax

preferable to photographs for similar reasons" (personal communication, September 25, 2012).

Yoga teacher and Creative Relaxation practitioner Natali Robert of Miami finds that "visuals provide a lot of structure." Beginning a new program with a large group of children of varying ages and challenges, she set up the S.T.O.P. and Relax easel with the seated posture displayed as students arrived. "Even with all the noise and confusion on the first day, as soon as children saw the visual cue, they knew what to do. They came in, sat on their mats, and were ready to begin" (personal communication, October 14, 2012).

Creating a Ritual

It's especially important when working with anxious children to keep to a routine. Whereas adults often thrive on change, children, particularly those with special needs, are comforted by predictability. By beginning your session in the same way each time, you will help facilitate the child's transition into the relaxed, attentive state required for yoga therapy. Creating a consistent conclusion to the session will also ease his return from deep relaxation to the next event in his day. You may choose any routine you like. But to get you started, here's a sample:

When children enter, have quiet music playing. Establish a location where they will leave their shoes (and their outside voices) at the door. Have the mats and room organized. Begin in a seated position, with legs crossed. If possible, dim or shut off overhead lights. For the first lesson or as needed, use Rules for Class (Chapter 10).

Start each session by taking three soft Huh breaths: inhale elevate the shoulders; exhale drop the shoulders with the sound "Huh." Then do three seated circles in each direction. You may include a song such as "Namaste" (see Chapter 20) or chant a vowel sound such as "AH" or "OH" after a deep breath. Repeat the sound three times.

Continue from the seated position with postures that establish rhythmic breathing. Practice seated postures long enough to create a mood for relaxation, but not so long that children lose interest.

From this point, you will continue with your routine (see Chapters 15–20). Keep in mind that your lesson may need to be adapted to accommodate what you see when the child or group walks into your space. Plan to be surprised!

For the conclusion of the session, dim the remaining lights and invite the children to lie on their backs and "float on a cloud." Lower your voice and slow it down. Talk about softly breathing, in and out through the nose (see the script in Chapter 18).

Watch the children carefully during deep relaxation. Conclude while they are comfortable to ensure a positive experience.

Ask the children to roll onto their sides and curl up in a ball for a moment, and then to come to a seated position. This is the opportunity for sharing kind thoughts, such as "Peace to all." Complete the sequence with three Huh breaths, just as you began.

You can change the final message of the class and any of the postures in between, but keep the format consistent so that your students have a sense of ritual and sameness.

FAMILIAR SEQUENCE

In addition to using rituals to begin and end classes, many children find comfort in familiar sequencing of postures. Working within familiar frameworks (Gutstein, 2000) also creates a safe environment to interject change.

Joseph, a nine-year-old with ASD, was new to my weekly camp program. Reluctant to participate in yoga therapy, he was initially disruptive and had to sit out. After a few weeks, he moved into the circle, but with his back to me. Although he declined my invitation, I continued to include him in the class by inviting him to participate in partner poses, offering to light his "candle" and praising him for sitting on his mat.

One day before class I dropped my visual display of cue cards. Several cards fell out, and I quickly put them back into the binder before beginning class. As I was teaching the seated postures, Joseph interrupted me. "You skipped Pretzel," he called out. I had not even noticed that I had altered the sequence, switching Pretzel pose with the posture that had previously come after it. But Joseph knew exactly what sequence I had been using and just where Pretzel was "supposed" to appear! I thanked him for the information and acknowledged how carefully he was paying attention.

The following summer, when we resumed yoga therapy, he began to lift one foot off the ground for Candle pose. He was always ready for that posture, knowing that it followed Rocking Chair, and he smiled enthusiastically when I "lit" his candle. He was closely following the class sequence and, in fact, participating in his own way. In recent months, Joseph has begun participating in nearly all the postures.

One teacher in an autism cluster with fourth- and fifth-graders follows the same sequence faithfully each day. She uses the S.T.O.P. and Relax curriculum, because most of her students respond well to the visual cues. She had been including yoga therapy three days a week, but she (and the parents) noticed that the children were calmer and more productive on the days she did yoga, so she increased the frequency.

When I observed her class, I suggested adding a few new postures to her routine. She had, in fact, considered making changes but had good reasons to keep things as they were. Having set aside a 30-minute slot in her busy schedule, adding new poses would require eliminating others. She explained that each child had a different favorite, and she couldn't leave out a posture without someone getting upset. To prevent disappointment and the chaos it might cause, she had decided to keep the routine the same.

Nonetheless, she developed an innovative strategy for bringing variety into her program. The children had become so accustomed to the routine that they needed very little guidance. In fact, many of the children could repeat the entire lesson, along with her usual suggestions for each posture. So, each day she selected a different child to lead the group, flipping the cue cards she had laminated for student use on the easel stand. This has become an excellent practice in communication skills and hand-eye coordination and is a confidence builder for the "teacher for the day."

As these examples demonstrate, many children with ASD have an incredible capacity to memorize whole chunks of information (Janzen, 1996, Grandin, 2005) and repeat it verbatim. They can also become so attached to a particular sequence of events or way of doing things that they find changes disturbing.

I worked with an older student, age 19, with ASD for a number of years. In addition to taking group classes with me, her parents used my DVD at home. Sometimes in class she would quote me to myself. In fact, Siri was more familiar with the way I taught on the video that I was myself. It was a huge struggle to help her understand that we would be doing things a little differently each time we were together, unlike the video, which was always the same.

It was because of this challenge that I began to save time at the end of each session for requests or variations in postures. This provided a set time for Siri to share the "right" way on days we tried variations of familiar poses.

It also underscores the importance of changing something in every lesson—adding at least one posture or substituting a variation of a pose. Interweaving new and familiar poses, as Janzen recommends, helps children feel comfortable because so much of what is shared is familiar.

This attachment to sameness is another reason to use rituals for the beginning and ending of yoga therapy. The end of the session was a difficult time for Siri. She never wanted to leave. In fact, transitional periods are often the most challenging times for children with autism and other special needs. Establishing a ritualistic conclusion helps prepare them for the inevitable end of an activity.

Transitions

One of the most difficult times in the day of a child with special needs is when something changes. As discussed in Chapter 6, unexpected changes are especially upsetting for children who feel little control over themselves or their environment. Yet, a child's day is full of change: moving from one classroom to another, going to lunch, switching from computer time to math lessons.

A transitional cue is an object that reminds the child of his "targeted destination" (Janzen, 1996, p. 444). Visuals, sounds, words, phrases, and yoga postures can all serve as transitional cues to help children prepare for what is coming next or to ease the conclusion of one activity and the movement to another.

STRUCTURED TRANSITIONS WITHIN YOGA CLASSES

Janzen (1996) suggests using a consistent cue a few minutes before the specified ending time for a favorite event. For example, you can let a child know with a signal such as flashing lights or a hand clap that class will end in five minutes. Tell the child: "You may [or I will] choose one more posture and then it's time to float on a cloud."

If a child seems fatigued or attempts to run off during the session, take control before he reaches the meltdown phase (Janzen, 1996). Say, "It looks like you are almost ready to finish yoga. Let's float on a cloud for a moment, and then we'll end class for today." In this way you maintain structure by reinforcing the consistent transitional cue that signals the end of each session, even as you accommodate the needs of the child. And you conclude the activity in a positive way.

YOGA POSTURES AS TRANSITIONAL PROMPTS

Yoga postures are effective tools for helping a child transition from activity to activity within the day. You can use visual cues to signal the pose. After doing the posture, show the child another visual to indicate the next event on his schedule.

Postures can be used when moving from seated at the desk to standing up for another activity, while waiting in line, or to help a child cope with unexpected schedule changes (see Chapter 18, "Postures for Transitions"). Once you are familiar with the posture catalog, you may select any pose to use as a transitional tool.

Rewards and Reinforcement

According to Project TEACCH, "All students should receive praise and social reinforcers . . . Some students may need constant and frequent reinforcement, while others can handle more intermittent reinforcement. The type of reinforcer must be appropriate and natural to the activity the student is doing and to the level of student understanding" (UNC, 2012).

FINDING THE POSITIVE

For many children, positive reinforcement is an effective tool for modifying behavior. To keep students on task, you may need to acknowledge each positive step they take. In each phase of a posture, praise effort. This form of simple, frequent reinforcement is extremely effective. It's a lot of work, requiring your full attention and meticulous consistency.

CATCH THEM BEING GOOD

Use the child's name while praising him. Find an opportunity for every child to "shine." If a child has been struggling with a difficult position, be sure to acknowledge his effort—"Good try, Michael!" If a child has been talking, compliment him when he is being quiet. Any opportunity for praise will do!

To bring a distracted child back to her mat, praise everyone in the group who is performing the task. "Sophie, good job sitting on your mat!" As soon as the roaming child takes her place, add, "I like the way Shayla is on her mat." Each time she returns to her mat for a moment, note this accomplishment.

If a child is not doing the pose but remains sitting quietly, praise his quiet. Acknowledge appropriate behavior and any form of participation, even if it's just *not* causing a disruption. This requires tremendous effort for many children.

CAUTIONS WHEN USING PRAISE

Praise will strengthen both appropriate and inappropriate behavior (Janzen, 1996). If you comfort a rebellious, screaming child with a hug, you reinforce that behavior. It is far more effective to ignore the attention-seeking scream and then hug the child later when he or she is following your instructions. As difficult as it can be to ignore such behaviors, be vigilant in rewarding only what you want the child to do again.

David Walsh (2011) warns about the perils of creating "praise addicts" who may avoid challenges for fear of not earning praise. If you sense that a child's dependence on praise is holding him back, consciously lessen the frequency of your praise and work on helping him develop more independence.

Handling Difficult Behaviors

There may be times when you need to remove a child from a group session because his behavior is unacceptable. If you know that the child has the capacity to control the behavior, ask him to sit out for a specific time period. Try to choose a posture that is really fun for the other children while the child is sitting out, so he can't wait to return. As soon as you invite him back, forget all about the previous problem. At your first opportunity, find something positive to say about the child's behavior or effort.

AVERTING MELTDOWNS

When a child starts to fall apart, it's useful to have a plan to redirect him or her back to a calm place. Although there is no foolproof method, there are techniques that have been effective.

What Can You Change?

The first step is to change what the child is doing and whatever conditions you can. Something is upsetting him, and although you may not know what that is, you can see that continuing the current activity will lead to a higher level of agitation. Consider the things that you can change quickly: what you are asking him to do, the position the child is in, the manner of his breathing, the lighting or smells in the room, the music or sounds you are making, his proximity to you or others. Begin to systematically change as many of these as you can with the least disturbance to the child.

Consider the Obvious

Does the child need to use the bathroom or have a drink of water? Is what you are asking him to do too difficult? Perhaps he is tired and needs a rest. If you intuit any of these things or past experience suggests these patterns, attempt to provide what he needs.

Change the Breathing

If a child is on the verge of a meltdown, you can be fairly certain his breathing is growing fast and shallow. If children have learned and practiced techniques that involve deepening their breath, they will often respond to a familiar cue. Saying, "Take five deep breaths" or displaying a visual cue card showing "Huh Breath" has brought many children back from the brink. Select a pose that opens the chest. Some will respond better to a moving breathing flow such as Bellows Breath. If the child has not yet learned to respond to these signals, this will be something you will want to work on as soon as he is receptive. But not now.

Change Location

Sometimes relocating a child away from others will help calm him. But if the child is resistant to touch, don't move him. Instead, move the other children in his area. Move yourself slightly away. If these actions help, you know it was part of the problem. If not, try moving closer to the child to see if that is effective. Be quick and discreet without a big fuss about any of these moves.

Change Posture

If the child is lying down, ask him to sit up and hug his knees. If he's sitting on the floor, have him curl up on his side or elevate his hips. Flexing the spine and tucking the chin into the throat notch generally trigger a calming effect. If he is seated in a chair, ask him to open his chest or hang down in a forward bend. If he is standing, invite him to "Shake It Out" or hang down like a Rag Doll. These postures may redirect the child's focus, averting explosive behaviors.

If the child has a favorite posture, use it. I recently worked with a group of children on the autism spectrum, one of whom was on the verge of a melt-down throughout most of the session. Knowing that he loved the singing and rocking motion of Seesaw posture, I interjected this pose frequently throughout the class. Each time he started to become physically aggressive, we rocked. He would smile and appear engaged. Inversions calmed him briefly, as long as I returned to Seesaw in between.

Change the Environment

Stop singing or talking for a moment to see if you can effect a change in the child. Make your voice very quiet. If the lights are on, turn them off. If the windows or doors are open, close them. There might be a smell or sound that's imperceptible to you, but irritating to the child.

Angela Moorad, a speech and language pathologist who incorporates yoga in her work, said that during the rare instances when a child starts to fall apart during a session, she immediately stops all sensory stimulation: "For some kids this means turning off the music; for others it means taking a break and resting in a comfortable position on their mat. Many love child's pose; others like lying on their stomach or side" (personal communication, July 27, 2012).

Easing demand on the child in whatever ways you can often averts melt-downs. By observing the child throughout every phase of the program, you can more effectively redirect him or her at the first sign of upset.

One of the best behavior management tools is structure. Simplifying instruc-tions, providing transitions, using schedules, and providing visual tools make success possible for most children. With careful observation, you can help chil-dren avoid frustration and avert meltdowns. Remember that with children, less is often more. Don't overexplain or analyze. Simply tell them what you want them to do, help them do it, and praise their effort. These tools for success lead to increased capacity for independence.

CHAPTER 13

DEVELOP OPPORTUNITIES FOR INDEPENDENCE

You learn to speak by speaking, to study by studying, to run by running,
to work by working; and just so you learn to love . . . by loving.
—SAINT FRANCIS DE SALES

Bᴇ COMBINING TECHNIQUES from all of the principles of
yoga therapy, you create opportunities for children with special needs to become
more independent. It is a highly individualized process. That's why it's so important to know as much as possible about the children you are working with and to
continually reassess your strategies.

Personal Log of Progress

Establishing a personal log of progress motivates children to practice postures independently.

Often children with special needs lack a clear sense of where their bodies
are in space. This makes observing their own progress in yoga therapy more
difficult. Although excessive emphasis on measuring success is not desirable,
demonstrating the changes that come with consistent practice can be motivating and empowering. This can start by measuring the distance of fingertips from

the floor in a standing forward bend, over a period of two months (see Chapter 11), and recording them in their own journal of progress. Some children may add personal comments, such as "Rag Doll felt good today."

Children may also create simple logs for school or home that note the times and duration of their practice. During her homework session, Brenda completed five Huh breaths. After the spelling test, Karen did Twister and Butterfly Hands from her seat.

The purpose of keeping a log is to support and encourage—not to add burdensome recordkeeping. A detailed handwritten log may be perfect for Mark; an illustrated schedule with checkmarks better for Joel; and a monthly calendar with inches marked just right for Peter.

Independence Through Body Awareness

Children gain independence by increasing their body awareness. As they learn how it feels to relax, they are better able to observe when their tension levels are elevating.

Many children with special needs take medications to help control their behaviors and stabilize their nervous systems. There are also children who experiment with illegal drugs to help alleviate symptoms. These situations are far beyond my scope of practice, so I never make recommendations about medications. Nonetheless, I have had children respond to yoga therapy in the same terms they use to describe their experiences with drugs.

High school students in a program for emotional behavioral disorders would sometimes come up from standing forward bend and announce, "I feel high." After deep relaxation, some compared the feeling to being "stoned." This presents the therapist with an extraordinary opportunity to discuss alternative means of feeling relaxed and loose. If it's appropriate, you may share that many people use yoga postures and breathing as alternatives to drugs or alcohol. Yoga is free, legal, and something children can do independently throughout their day.

Many years ago I taught yoga therapy to a group of fourth-graders with emotional handicaps. Midway through the ten-week program, a child with ADHD and obsessive-compulsive disorder shared a remarkable observation: "I can tell when I need my meds." The deepened body awareness that he experienced through yoga therapy helped him to notice subtle changes within his own metabolism. Although he needed a parent or school nurse to administer his medications, this experience elevated his sense of awareness and self-control.

Adaptations

Adapting postures to meet the needs and capabilities of the child is the heart of yoga therapy. As Lauren Allen explains, "It's all about making kids feel successful." She combines her knowledge as a yoga teacher with physical therapy for children with profound challenges. "If I've got a child with severe brain damage who cannot stand, I'll have him do Tree lying on his back. He goes home saying, 'I did yoga. I can do Tree pose!' He feels good about himself."

Lauren explains that standing postures are powerful tools for strengthening and stabilizing the pelvis. Kids with cerebral palsy (CP) often have one side stronger than the other. "When they stand on one foot, their pelvis drops. Tree pose helps build pelvic stability, essential for walking, running, and stair climbing." Starting by placing the heel of one foot on the other, with the toes remaining on the floor, children gradually progress to lifting the full foot off the floor.

It's a challenge to maintain a child's interest and enthusiasm. Lauren continues, "Many kids with CP have been in therapy all their lives. It gets old. Doing something that typically developing children do is huge for them." It can be tough to motivate adolescents, especially when they are in pain. "I send them home with yoga postures. Then it doesn't seem like therapy and they stick with it."

Lauren uses yoga breathing and repetition of mantra to help patients anchor their minds during therapy. She devised a simple mantra—"Let go"—to combine with the breath: "Breathing in *let*, breathing out *go*." She finds this technique especially useful for children ages eight and up, who understand that there is a purpose to the discomfort they must endure. Breathing and mantra are tools they can use independently to help "get them through the pain" (personal communication, July 22, 2012).

Connect with Community

Teaching family classes is a marvelous form of yoga therapy. Including siblings provides models for the special-needs child and offers a bonding opportunity for the family. Parents of kids with exceptional challenges frequently keep full schedules with little time for relaxation. Sharing even one quiet moment with their child can be a rare gift. Yoga, the great equalizer, seats everyone on the ground. Poses may be challenging, but everyone can succeed in some way. Imagine how it feels for a child to partner comfortably with his sibling in class, or to discover that he can do a posture as well as or even better than his mom. Doing yoga with a group in a natural setting gives children with special needs an opportunity to feel part of a typical community.

Teaching Self-Control

Many skills taught in yoga therapy can be generalized into aspects of self-control. To help children with autism gain control Janice Janzen suggests, a "balance of activities that are . . . active and quiet" (1996, p. 363).

CONTROLLING VOLUME

Most children love to make noise. But noisy children can easily get out of control. To maintain order, teachers may avoid this risk by keeping children quiet throughout most of their day.

You can teach children when to be noisy and when to be quiet. This shift is made routinely in yoga therapy. Children bark in Stretching Dog pose and then rest silently in Baby; loud meows precede quiet purrs in Cat pose; yoga singing varies from chanting with full volume to a whisper. These contrasts provide practice in learning to modulate the level of their voices. This in an important life skill, yet there are few opportunities to practice it. Many children realize that they are too loud only after they have been penalized for the behavior.

To practice the shift from barking Dog to quiet Baby, start and end with quiet Baby. Hold this longer than the barking Dog pose. Remind children that Baby is a quiet time—"Don't make a sound." Repeat the sequence several times. If children abuse the noisy time or can't be quiet in Baby, quickly move on to another pose. But try again at the next session. As dreadful as it can be for those few seconds, I have found this to work with many children on the autism spectrum, with ADHD, and other special needs. After steady practice, kids learn that if they want to bark, they have to be quiet, too.

For yoga singing or chanting, use your hands to guide children as they alter

13-1 Tree Hands to Signal Quiet

their volume. First explain how it will work, and be certain that each child can see you. Beginning with the "OH" sound, for example, start with your palms together, the signal for quiet. Then gradually open your hands wider, inviting an increasing volume. As you begin to move your hands back together, the children gradually quiet their voices until they end with their mouths closed in a silent M, their palms together. Most of the children love to do this. If they get out of control—and they will test the limits of your tolerance—give them one more chance or simply end the practice until next time. Since this is so much fun, children quickly learn to comply with the rules in order to do it again and again.

One caveat: You've got to let children get really loud in order to make this enjoyable and to teach the distinction between the extremes. So save this for days when you can handle a lot of noise!

TEACHING CHILDREN TO WAIT

To keep yoga therapy a quiet time, ask the child to hold questions and comments until a designated time in the session. But don't wait too long; let him speak with permission before losing control. You might start with just a moment's delay, by saying, "Let's finish this posture before questions." By providing time at specific intervals, you minimize interruptions during the session as well as rewarding a child for waiting.

Carefully observing the child, you can extend the periods between talk at a pace that he finds tolerable. With practice, many children are able to complete an entire session without interruption. It's a good idea to save time at the end of each session for children who want to ask questions or make special requests. This keeps the child on task, encourages self-control, and rewards patience.

CUEING FOR SELF-CALMING

Debra Collins, a school psychologist who works with children on the autism spectrum, includes yoga breathing and postures in her therapeutic approach. In the hallway one morning, she encountered a particularly anxious child, close to tears. "I knew she was familiar with the S.T.O.P. procedure for self-calming, so I cued her and she immediately began to self-regulate." Then the child was able to discuss the problem. "She had been panicking about the difficult spelling words her teacher had assigned that day." Together, they established a simple plan including self-calming and study. "Success!" Collins beamed (personal communication, June 12, 2012).

Choices

During yoga therapy, I frequently compliment children on making "a good choice." In a group class, moving a mat away from another child is a good choice to avoid a potential clash. Deciding to try a difficult posture, quieting down when asked—these are choices that a child makes in every session. Sometimes you can see children considering their options, especially when they are tempted to mimic another child's inappropriate behavior or to engage in a minor skirmish over territory. When you successfully redirect a child to participate with the group or to follow your instructions, remind her that she has made this choice.

If you have the flexibility in school, you may give the child a choice about when to do yoga therapy, such as after spelling or before lunch. At school or home, you may agree on one hour per week, but the child may decide if she wants two half-hour sessions or four 15-minute sessions. As discussed, she may help choose the content of the lesson, the sequence of the postures, music, and lighting. The more the child participates in these choices, the more independent she will become in her practice of yoga therapy.

Awareness of Stress

Catherine Faherty (2000) credits a behavioral strategy called "Mind the Gap" to Jack Wall of the Charlotte, NC, TEACCH Center. He described the gap as the moment between an event that elevates anxiety and the child's response to it. Faherty explains that many children with ASD seem as surprised by their own outbursts or aggressive behaviors as the people around them. They are not aware of the warning signs that indicate they are close to a behavioral precipice. The gap is "the time a choice can be made as to what actions to take" (p. 262). Faherty suggests using visuals and social stories to educate children to identify signs of anxiety and their triggers.

Yoga therapy offers children tools to make choices rather than be victims of their own stress response. Having learned to recognize the difference between tension and relaxation in their bodies, they can more easily learn to identify the warning signs that precede potentially explosive behaviors and better regulate their own behaviors.

SENSE OF CONTROL

Acting out or aggressiveness may be a form of communication—a way to express frustration or discomfort by individuals with cognitive or language impairments. By providing an alternative mode for this expression, students begin the process of taking control of their behavior; they have the opportunity to be better understood.

June Groden of Providence, Rhode Island, explains the importance of recognizing the antecedent to a maladaptive behavior: "Once the triggers are identified, you can cue the student to start using the relaxation procedures he has learned. The cue can be a word like 'relax'; the student learns that this means *not* throwing, *not* hitting." He can begin the self-management process as soon as his teacher brings his awareness to the trigger. He later learns to identify the trigger himself and uses relaxation as a self-control procedure (personal communication, October 10, 2012).

In 1988 Groden and Prince reported an increase in self-control among clients with special needs by substituting a "relaxation response in place of the typical maladaptive behaviors" exhibited during high stress. With practice, "44% of the clients are able to relax when given a verbal cue by their teacher, and another

31% were able to use the procedure independently" (Groden, Cautela, Prince, & Berryman, 1994, p. 186).

Scheduling Yoga Breaks

As discussed in the previous chapter, staying on task, following a series of instructions, and completing tasks at the designated time can be difficult for children with special needs. "A schedule can aid students in transitioning independently between activities," according to the Project TEACCH website (UNC, 2012).

A child whose schedule includes yoga and movement breaks has a built-in tool to defuse the escalating levels of tension that may arise throughout his day. To enhance self-control, Janzen suggests giving children with autism "frequent opportunities to move about and engage in strenuous exercise" (1996, p. 363). Bobbi Jarvis, of Exercise Breaks in the Classroom, teaches energetic sequences to "get the wiggles out." Once students learn the routines, they take turns leading their classmates. Parents report seeing their kids take breaks independently during homework sessions (personal communication, July 23, 2012). In her Action Based Learning program, Jean Blaydes Madigan (2009) promotes the use of movement, including standing, stretching, and balancing exercises, throughout the school day to help children manage their own behavior.

Yoga breaks offer opportunities for a child to let off steam, release tension before it escalates, and self-regulate. Scheduling yoga therapy into a child's day creates a predictable pattern of practice that he can learn to use independently.

"MY" TIME

Help each child to select a personal posture—something that releases tension or is especially calming, his MY (My Yoga) Time. A child may have several MY Time poses: one for independent use, one for out-

13-2   Yoga Breaks for Tension Relief

side, and one for inside. Be certain to reinforce the most calming one to be used at your signal to avert upsets.

If the child is struggling during school or therapy, signal him to use this pose. As he develops more independence, he can tell you when he needs a yoga break. By implementing self-calming techniques, he learns to self-regulate without interrupting his classmates or family. Discuss changes in MY Time postures as needed. Be certain that the child chooses postures he can do safely on his own.

IDENTIFYING FEELINGS

Yoga breaks may help prevent extreme reactions to events that will inevitably occur throughout the day. Help the child identify how he feels after doing specific poses. Explore methods for changing his feelings by using these poses. Appendix 6 provides a MY Time worksheet to help children process feelings by personalizing yoga postures.

Help the child to use MY Time during quiet moments of the day—before reading or movie time, after rest—so he associates it with a reprieve. Prompt the child to use his MY Time whenever he appears slightly agitated. Share it with parents or others who work with the child.

Independence Through Touch Pressure

As discussed in previous chapters, firm, steady pressure can be calming to individuals with extreme tactile sensitivity. Children who seek stimulation or relief by hitting or pressing their heads into a wall may benefit from postures that increase pressure against the crown or forehead. Yoga therapy offers an alternative behavior that is appropriate, noninjurious, and within their control.

The fetal pose (Baby), which combines deep flexion with ocular pressure, is an easy pose for most children. To intensify the pressure, the child may roll onto the crown of his head by slightly elevating his hips, with his palms below his shoulders for support (see Crown pose, p. 173). You may kneel alongside him to secure his balance. If the child has good balance and seeks more pressure, he can straighten his knees, pressing his feet and palms into the floor. Others may come down to this pose from Stretching Dog, by bending their elbows and placing the forearms on the ground. Stay close in order to steady children in these challenging balance postures.

If a child finds one of these postures calming, cue him to take the pose when he becomes agitated or begins to seek head pressure. You can teach the technique to the child's parents and teachers so they can cue or assist him as well.

Prone poses, especially when combined with backbending, increase pressure to the abdominal organs. Although helpful for many children, these postures are not recommended for children with extremely high tone, according to Lauren Allen, PT. "High tone kids often have problems with bowel movements," she notes, but you don't want to stress their systems further. Soothing postures like Knee Hugs and Baby bring "firm, steady pressure to this area and can help relax the intestines and sphincters" (personal communication, July 22, 2012).

Many children can learn to perform these self-massaging postures independently.

REFUSING TOUCH

There are individuals on the autism spectrum or with extreme tactile sensitivities for whom touch, even by loved ones, can be painful or frightening. In *Thinking in Pictures*, Temple Grandin describes her resistance to being hugged: "I wanted to experience the good feeling of being hugged, but it was just too overwhelming. It was like a great, all-engulfing tidal wave of stimulation . . . it flipped my circuit breaker" (2006, p. 58).

Teaching children that they are in charge of their bodies is an extremely important life skill, especially for those with language or developmental disorders. Knowing that they have a choice about whether or not to be touched is empowering.

To help children learn how to refuse touch appropriately, let them practice in a posture. With their permission while they are in Baby pose, begin a back massage. When they say, "Stop please," or use a hand signal, you immediately stop the massage. If they want you to resume, they signal or say, "More please," and you oblige. Practice this frequently so they become comfortable saying, "Stop" or "More."

A nonverbal child may push your hand away as you approach. This is a form of communication. Acknowledge that you understand he does not want to be touched today, and, if appropriate, thank him for the information.

LEARNING TO TOUCH

You can also provide opportunities to learn about touch. With family classes, invite partners to exchange massages in Baby pose. Typically, the child gets a back rub from her parent, and then she gives one. Another way to participate in this activity without direct contact is for the child to give herself a massage while her parent does the same. This form of parallel partnering works very well with those who resist touch.

Some children may not want to be touched themselves but are willing to touch another person. However, they may not know how to do so appropriately. Grandin (2006) described the challenges she had learning to pet an animal properly because she didn't know how touch was supposed to feel.

While a child sits near her parent in Baby pose, you can teach her simple ways to offer comforting touch. You might rest your palm on her mother's back. Invite the child to try if she chooses. You may show a child how to place her hands close to her father without touching at all, while sending caring thoughts. Teach this technique to the parent, as well.

Children who observe this process often become less anxious about receiving touch. Many people with autism, according to Grandin, "crave pressure stimulation even though they cannot tolerate being touched. It is much easier for a person with autism to tolerate touch if he or she initiates it" (p. 58).

There will be children who are just too uncomfortable to receive touch, and it's important to accept and understand that. But they may be willing to allow their parent's hands close while they convey loving thoughts. This is empowering to the child because his needs are honored. It is also an experience of grace for a parent whose touch has been rejected by her tactile-intolerant child.

Putting It All Together

Morahina Rodriguez of New York City is the mother of a 19-year-old daughter on the autism spectrum. She had been searching for a therapy to help her daughter connect with her body, "to become grounded." Her daughter has many sensory challenges and is "very jumpy." She has obsessive-compulsive disorder and her anxiety sometimes leads to involuntary movements. Morahina's research led her to the parents' guide *Yoga for Children with Autism Spectrum Disorders* by Dion and Stacey Betts (2006). To prepare her daughter for the practice, she wrote a "social story" and established a schedule—"structure and pictures help her a lot." Three days a week, at the same time of day, Morahina would bring out the yoga mats to signal the beginning of their class. Since yoga was new to them, they followed my DVD.

"Everyone has such a busy life," her mother explained. "But we set this time aside. We bonded as we lay on the floor together. It was good for both of us."

Her daughter needed a lot of prompting and assistance. "At first it was hard to do the postures. But she was prepared and she knew the schedule, so she tried." When she became distracted, her mother would model the postures. Balance postures were the most challenging for her daughter, so Morahina made adaptations to help her feel successful.

From the beginning, her daughter loved Seesaw pose. She liked holding hands with her mother and swinging back and forth; she would laugh when the singing began. She was fully engaged.

Walking Crab and Drawbridge helped increase her body awareness. She grew calmer during Baby pose, one of her favorites. Morahina taught her to use her breathing when she was anxious, to relax her face and shoulders. "When she relaxes, she has less involuntary movement."

With regular practice, her yoga improved. "I think she has more feeling in her body now. She likes Stretching Dog and Fruit Picking. And she loves Rocking Chair—she thinks it's hilarious!" Over time her daughter was able to do all of the postures; even the balance poses improved. She appeared less anxious, more comfortable in her body. She grew so accustomed to the routine that on the days that her mother forgot, she would remind her that it was yoga time.

The daughter's fear of dogs had made it difficult to go outside. Morahina coached her to breathe and relax. "Now she makes the connection. After so many repetitions, she does it automatically, whenever she feels fearful." When she sees a dog, "she is able to self-regulate by taking a deep breath" and consciously relax her body.

I had the good fortune of meeting Morahina when she attended my Creative Relaxation training in May 2012. She plans to become a yoga teacher so she can share yoga therapy with other special children. Her message is to be "persistent and consistent. Stay with a routine, even if your child gets only one pose correctly. Believe in your child—and give him or her a chance to learn. Never give up" (personal communication, July 20, 2012).

PART III

APPLICATION:
POSTURES, LESSONS,
AND ACTIVITIES

CHAPTER 14

GUIDELINES FOR INSTRUCTION

THIS CHAPTER PRESENTS an overview of the posture catalog in Chapter 15. It serves as a key to the elements included for each of the 60 postures described in the next chapter. In addition, you will find guidelines for implementing instruction of the poses.

FOUNDATIONAL POSTURES

Foundational postures are the starting positions for all postures: seated, hands and knees, prone, supine, and standing. Some foundational categories also include postures listed by their direction of movement—forward or back bending, twists, and inversions.

STARTING POSITIONS

The foundational posture indicates the primary starting position for each pose. Alternative starting positions are described here.

BENEFITS OF POSTURES

General benefits provided in the foundational listings apply to all postures in that category, and are not repeated in posture descriptions. Additional benefits are listed for each pose.

The needs, strengths, and challenges of each child supersede any information provided here.

INSTRUCTIONS FOR THE CHILD

Each listing provides child-friendly language for teaching. It's essential to use language that the child can understand; assess its effectiveness by the child's response.

For some children, fewer words are better: "Please sit. Hold foot. Rock the baby." Others may need visual or gestural cues to support your words. For children who enjoy imagery and detail, weave a story around the animal or object named in the posture, or explain its anatomical benefits.

POINTS TO REMEMBER

Following are expanded guidelines to accompany those in the catalog.

Assisting Versus Correcting

Make few corrections, but offer lots of assistance. There's an important distinction. Assisting a child provides relief from discomfort and an experience of support in posture. Corrections about form, however, are not generally beneficial. A child who struggles in many areas hardly needs another source of criticism. Strive to elevate the child's self-esteem as well as his self-awareness.

Breathing

You may include breathing instruction in every posture. For example, begin each exertion with an inhalation and release the effort with an exhalation. You may guide children to inhale when they reach up and exhale when they reach down; inhale while lengthening the body, exhale while twisting; inhale into chest openers and backbends, exhale into forward bends.

Unless otherwise specified, remind children to breathe through the nose. Take care that the child is neither holding his breath nor exerting excessive effort in the breathing process. If breathing instruction is distracting to the child, omit it.

Creating a Pace

Use your voice—volume, tempo, pitch, projection—as well as the speed with which you move from posture to posture and your choice of postures to create a pace. To energize children, increase the volume and power behind your voice. Soften your voice and slow it down for calming postures. Elevate your pitch when instructing children to inhale; lower it for the exhalation. Elevate it when guiding children to look up; lower it for downward motions.

Most children find it easier to do several repetitions of a posture rather than to engage in lengthy holds. Maintain a steady rhythm of postures without long pauses to keep distracted children on task. You may start slowly and then accelerate into more energizing poses, or start quickly and end slowly. Adjust your pace according to the presentation and response of the child.

You will find songs in Chapter 20 to accompany many postures and create a pace.

Using Both Sides of the Body

Model poses by sitting in front of or alongside the child. When the instructions guide you to do a posture on one side (i.e., the right leg), repeat the pose on the other side.

VARIATIONS

These are suggestions for making a posture more or less challenging or to appeal to the child in another way. If a posture is contraindicated for a child, there may be a suitable variation presented.

PRECAUTIONS: READ THESE BEFORE ATTEMPTING POSTURES

Yoga is an extremely benign form of therapy. Still, there are postures that are not suitable for some individuals. Inversions, for example, are contraindicated for many conditions (see Chapter 15, p. 170). This is something you need to know before beginning your program.

Choose only those postures that you are absolutely confident will benefit the child. Consult the child's family and medical team as well as an experienced yoga therapist. If you are uncertain, omit the pose.

COUNTERPOSES

A counterpose stretches or releases the very muscles that were contracted in the previous pose. For example, a counterpose to Drawbridge, supine hip elevation, is Folded Leaf, seated forward bend.

A restorative counterpose is one that requires less effort than the posture that precedes it. Shake It Out is a playful counterpose for releasing tension after most any posture. There are counterposes that are calming, such as Baby, and focusing, such as Tree Hands. Some children will benefit from a restful counterpose after each exertion. Others may do a long series of postures before needing or wanting a rest. The counterpose to all postures is Floating on a Cloud.

When you sequence your postures, be certain to include counterposes that are balancing for the child's musculature and degree of exertion.

SEQUENCING

This section suggests which postures will work well with, before, or after the pose. Those that work well *with* one another are complementary. They may be similar in their starting position or benefits, or they may fit together in a natural flow of movement. Poses that work well *before* help prepare a child for the subsequent posture. For example, Rocking Chair is an excellent preparation for Candle pose. Similarly, some postures work well *after* others, such as Butterfly Meditation after Butterfly Hands.

When You Begin

- Keep a respectful distance.
- Keep it safe.
- Keep it simple.
- Keep it positive.

CHAPTER 15

CATALOG OF POSTURES

THIS CHAPTER DESCRIBES six hand positions (mudras) and 60 yoga postures selected specifically for children with special needs. The postures are suitable for most, but not all children. Review contraindications and variations with care.

Therapeutic Hand Positions in Posture

Mudras are hand positions to help children contain and direct their energy. By making children aware of the placement of their hands, you give them an additional point of focus in posture and a tool to control errant hand movements.

1. **Tree Hands:** Palms and extended fingers pressed together, thumbs at the center of the chest. Holding the hands in this position turns a child's attention inward. Use this posture to signal quiet or to help a child refocus.

2. **Interlaced fingers:** Interlacing fingers directs the child's attention to the point of contact. When a child interlaces his fingers and hugs his thighs into his chest in Seated Egg or Knee Hugs, he creates a closed circuit with his body.

In an active posture such as Rocking Chair, interlacing fingers behind the knees assists with balance and helps the child maintain inward focus while in motion. For children whose hands stray during class, use interlaced fingers beneath their heads in supine resting postures.

3. **Grounding hands:** The experience of connection to the earth is elusive for many children with sensory challenges. Pressing the palms into the floor is grounding, as in Warrior Lunge, Stretching Dog, and Balance Beam. Pressing the palms firmly down in supine inversions such as Drawbridge and Crab increases stability when elevating the hips. If a child appears anxious, a posture with palms pressing firmly into the ground will likely help him recenter.

4. **Hands on body:** Keeping the hands in contact with the body is the simplest hand position of all. Holding the legs or feet while in Folded Leaf, for example, gives the child a point of focus, enhancing her capacity for stillness. Between standing poses or after Shake It Out, have children bring their palms to their sides. In supine resting postures, some children are better able to turn their awareness inward with their hands on their bellies. During school or therapy, have children rest their hands on their knees to refocus.

5. **Open hands:** Palms relaxed and upward facing. Much more difficult than it might seem, this is a posture of surrender. Seated with the palms turned upward on the knees is a posture of receptivity. Reclining on the back with the palms up, back of the hands on the ground, is the classic relaxation posture. Open hands send a signal that the child feels safe. Invite children to assume the open hand position, but consider other options if a child appears disconnected from his body or the ground beneath him.

6. **Personal mudras:** Some children may learn to use hand positions

15-1 Open Hands Floating on a Cloud

independently as self-regulating tools. Observe a child's hand placement while he is calm; this may be his personal mudra. Remind him to use this when he needs redirecting.

Teach the hand positions in the postures, in combination with relaxed breathing, and at intervals throughout the day to create a yoga therapy practice for every child.

Foundational Posture 1: Seated

The seated position on the floor is with ankles crossed and hands on knees, creating a stable base. Sitting on a cushion or with the back against a wall helps some children stay upright. In most instances, you may substitute the child's preferred seated position, such as sitting on his feet or with legs straight. Most of these postures can also be performed in a chair, and many can be done standing.

Seated postures increase hip flexibility. With the chest and back upright, respiration is improved. Children can stretch and move their limbs and spine while seated. These poses are useful as warm-ups for beginning your session or as yoga breaks during the school day, during transitions or other therapies. Children with limited mobility may do an entire yoga therapy session from their seats.

1. **HUH BREATH**
   Starting Position: Seated; any foundational posture
   Benefits: Deepens breathing, extends exhalation; tension release; signals class beginning and ending
   Instructions for the Child: When we are tense or upset, sometimes our shoulders get really tight. We may even forget to breathe! As you breathe in, raise your shoulders up high. Breathe out and drop them down with a "Huh!" (Do three times.)
   Points to Remember: Facing the children, prompt them by pointing to your shoulders as you speak. If the child is comfortable with touch, sit behind him with your hands cupping his shoulders. Elevate and lower his shoulders with his breathing.
   Variations: Try one shoulder at a time. Placing the child's right hand on his

15-2 Huh Breath

right shoulder, gently elevate his elbow to help him feel the upward and downward movement. Repeat on left.

Precautions: Adjust your instructions to the rhythm of the child's breathing. Watch for breathlessness among children who are exhaling too long or who are breathing too slowly or too rapidly.

Sequencing: Works well to signal beginning and ending of each session, as yoga break, or as transition.

2. SEATED CIRCLES

Starting Position: Floor or in chair

Benefits: Calming, activating the vagal nerve; directionality, sensory awareness

Instructions for child: Hold onto your knees and make slow circles with your whole body. Stop and go the other way.

Points to Remember: To create a soothing rhythm, chant "Circles, circles, circles" with the movement. Some children will move their heads only or rock side to side. Sit behind the child, holding his shoulders, upper arms, or elbows to assist.

Variations: Start with small circles, then bigger. Reversing in this posture is difficult for some children; they may need assistance. With children in close proximity, keep the circles small and hands on knees.

Precautions: Watch for signs of dizziness or self-stimulation, especially with head circles.

Counterpose: Seated Egg

Sequencing: Works well with Huh Breath and Pretzel

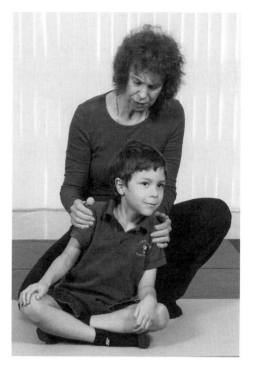

15-3 Seated circles

3. ELBOW CIRCLES

Starting Position: Floor or chair; standing

Benefits: Flexibility in the shoulder girdle, back strength; stress relief; bilateral coordination

Instructions for child: Hold onto your right shoulder with your right hand. Move your elbow around in a big circle. Now go the other way. [Repeat left.] With one hand on each shoulder, make elbow circles in one direction. Reverse.

Points to Remember: Using the elbows, which the child can see, helps him create the motion. Hold the child's shoulders or elbows to help him find fluidity and to reverse directions.

Variations: Touch the elbows in front, crossing the midline; reach the elbows back. Practice without the hand hold, circling each shoulder separately and reversing; then circle them together.

Precautions: Avoid with neck or shoulder injuries. Prevent the overzealous child from forcing the shoulder beyond its natural range of motion.

Counterpose: Butterfly Hands

Sequencing: Works well with Seated Circles, Bellows Breath

15-4 Elbow circles

15-5   Tense and relax

4. TENSE AND RELAX

Starting Position: Any foundational posture

Benefits: Intense contraction enhances relaxation; observe habitual patterns of tension; self-regulation

Instructions for the Child: Stretch out your arm and make a tight fist. Hold it. Tense, tense, tense. And . . . relax. Now, shake it out, and relax!

Points to Remember: Students enjoy the dramatic and extended chanting of "Tense, tense, tense . . . aaaaaand relax." Start briefly; hold longer with practice. Completely release before tensing another area of the body. When working with large groups or in small spaces, stretching the arm in front prevents invading another's space.

Variations: June Groden (Autism Society of America conference, 2008) recommends stretching the arm out to the sides as a less-aggressive position. If the posture promotes aggressive behavior, tense hands and face only, with arms down at the sides. Children may progressively tense and relax body parts seated or while lying supine in Floating on a Cloud.

Precautions: Some conditions are accompanied by extreme tonus. In such cases, substitute calming poses, massage, or gentle stretching to release tension.

Counterpose: Butterfly Hands

Sequencing: Works well with Elbow Circles

5. BUTTERFLY HANDS

Starting Position: Seated, standing, supine

Benefits: Stress relief, self-regulation; creative play, language skills; proprioception, directionality

Instructions for the Child: Your hands are butterflies! Fly your butterflies high and low. Fly them in front; fly them in back, and out to the sides. Now fly your butterflies all around. Slowly bring your butterflies to rest in your lap.

Points to Remember: Coordinating the movement with prepositions such as up and down reinforces the meaning of these directional terms. Useful for yoga breaks.

Variations: Sing the Butterfly Song (see Chapter 20). Ask the child to describe his butterfly—its color, size, shape. Combine with a lesson on butterflies or color. Use to redirect repetitive hand flapping.

Precautions: If children get excited or overstimulated with this pose, keep the flight brief with long resting pauses.

Sequencing: Works well after Bellows Breath or Tense and Relax

15-6   Butterfly Hands

6. BUTTERFLY MEDITATION

Starting Position: Floor or chair

Benefits: Mindfulness, self-calming; language skills; motor planning, sensory awareness

Instructions for the Child: Bring your butterflies to rest on your knees, palms up. Look at the butterfly in your right hand. Let your butterfly float up, and let your butterfly float down. Turn to look at your other butterfly. Butterfly floats up; butterfly floats down. Let both butterflies rest.

Points to Remember: It's essential to model the pose to convey its meditative properties. When first starting, gaze once on each side. Increase repetitions as appropriate.

Variations: This is very challenging for children who have difficulty controlling the motions of their hands or following verbal instructions. Try letting the butterflies rest briefly on the body: "Butterflies float up and rest on your head. Butterflies float down and land on your knee."

15-7   Butterfly Meditation

Precautions: This is an advanced posture, requiring the ability to sit still. Use selectively.

Counterpose: Shake It Out

Sequencing: Works well after Butterfly Hands and as a yoga break in classrooms or therapy sessions

7. BELLOWS BREATH

Starting Position: Seated, standing, or supine

Benefits: Deepens breathing, enhances neck flexibility, opens chest and shoulders, strengthens mid-back muscles; visual focus; directionality

Instructions for the Child: Interlace your fingers and place your hands behind your head. Breathing in, open your elbows wide and look up toward the sky. Breathing out, elbows and head come back down, look down low. Inhale, look up; exhale look down. Your arms pump the breath in and out like a bellows.

Points to Remember: When assisting, gently guide the motion without pressure or force. Once the child gets the feeling, encourage him to continue on his own.

Variations: If the hand position is difficult, let the child touch his crown or hold his ears. Practice the eye motion only. If combining the breathing and motion are difficult, practice the arm movement first. Then teach the breathing before putting it all together.

Precautions: Avoid with neck or spinal injuries or atlanto-axial instability.

Counterpose: Because of the neck flexion and extension in this pose, it does not require a counterpose.

Sequencing: Works well with Butterfly Hands, Tense and Relax, Elbow Circles

15-8   Bellows Breath

8. FINGER STRETCH

Starting Position: Floor, chair, standing, or supine

Benefits: Extension stretches elbows, wrists, and fingers; bilateral coordination, motor planning; stress relief

Instructions for the Child: Do your fingers get stiff from holding your pencil for a long time? Let's stretch them out. Thread your fingers together. Then turn your hands inside out by pressing your palms away from you.

Points to Remember: Helpful before and after test taking. First interlace the fingers and open and close the palms. Then stretch the palms apart, without the arms. After practice, put it all together.

Variations: Stretch each finger with the other hand to prepare for the pose. Switch the finger position by putting the opposite forefinger on top. Stretch the arms over head and to each side for a lateral stretch.

Precautions: Avoid with finger, wrist, elbow, or shoulder injury. Avoid hyperextending the elbows or overstretching the shoulders.

Counterpose: Butterfly Hands

Sequencing: Works well with Bellows Breath

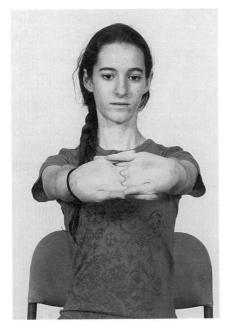

15-9 Finger Stretch

9. BUTTERFLY KNEES

Starting Position: Seated with soles of feet together, knees out to sides; supine

Benefits: Stretches inner thighs, external hip rotation; creative, interactive play; language skills

Instructions for the Child: Bring the bottoms of your feet together. Holding your feet, lift your knees up and down, up and down. Go fast, like a butterfly fluttering its wings. Now slow it down.

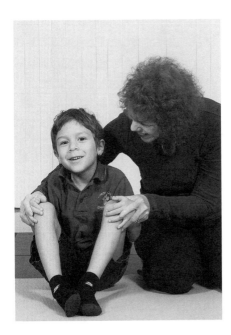

15-10 Butterfly Knees

Hold onto the outside of your knees. Breathe in, knees come up; breathe out, knees come down.

Points to Remember: Demonstrate how to get into the posture by grasping one foot at a time, placing the soles together. To assist, sit beside or in front of the child and hold his knees gently. To make this posture playful, emphasize speed. To turn the focus inward, move the knees slowly in rhythm with the breath.

Variations: Ask the child about his butterfly—what color is it? What kind of flowers does it like best? Practice the slow motion of the knees alone before adding the breathing. Discuss the difference between moving slowly and moving quickly. How does each feel?

Precautions: Some children may become overzealous. Slow them down or move one knee at a time. If the child is uncomfortable, place pillows beneath the knees for support. Avoid with hip, knee, or low-back injuries.

Counterpose: Drawbridge

Sequencing: Works well before Sandwich

SEATED FORWARD BENDS

Forward bends stretch muscles in the back of the body and strengthen those in front. Keeping the chest open strengthens the mid-back. Forward bends massage the abdominal organs, improving digestion and elimination, and increase hip flexibility.

These poses calm and soothe the nervous system, helping children identify and release tension in their bodies. Coordinating movements with breathing— inhale up, exhale fold—is an important tool for relaxation.

10. SANDWICH

Starting Position: Seated with soles of feet together

Benefits: Same as Butterfly Knees; spinal flexion; mindfulness; balance

Instructions for the Child: Let's make a jam sandwich. Do you like strawberry or grape? Spread the jam on one slice of bread (sole of foot), and then on the other (sole of foot). Press your two slices of bread together. Reach down and take a big bite. Or lift your sandwich up to your mouth. Delicious!

Points to Remember: The instructions make this an energizing, playful pose.

15-11   Sandwich

15-12   Sandwich Balance

Combine with Fruit Picking (Posture 56). To balance, the child may elevate one foot at a time to start. This requires abdominal strength and focus.

Variations: To make this a calming pose, instruct children to reach their nose down toward their toes. Rest and breathe in the posture. Encourage children not to force, but to find a comfortable variation in the posture.

Precautions: Same as butterfly knees. Children for whom inversions are contraindicated (see p. 170) or with injuries or limitations to the spine or neck should not lower their heads.

Counterpose: Drawbridge, Crab, Seated Egg

Sequencing: Works well with Butterfly Knees (already in position) or after Fruit Picking

11. SEATED EGG

Starting Position: Seated with knees bent, soles of the feet on the floor

Benefits: Spinal flexion; mindfulness: grounding; balance

Instructions for the Child: Give your knees a big hug by wrapping your arms under or

15-13   Seated Egg

around your thighs. Clasp your hands together, and rest your chin or fore-head on your knees. Imagine what it feels like to be a baby chick, snug inside your egg. It's peaceful and quiet in there. Breathe in and out.

Points to Remember: Use this pose to regain quiet if a child becomes excited or a class grows unruly. Good for yoga breaks.

Variations: Make this into a balance pose with toes touching the ground. Lift one foot and then the other, sitting up on the sit bones (ischial protuber-ances), not the coccyx.

Precautions: Avoid if child is extremely withdrawn or has knee, lower-back, or shoulder injuries.

Counterpose: Drawbridge, Airplane

Sequencing: Works well after Rocking Chair or Seesaw to regain calm and inner focus

12. FOLDED LEAF

Starting Position: Floor with legs extended; chair

Benefits: Deep back stretch, heels to crown; mindfulness, deepens breathing

Instructions for child: Sit up straight and tall with your legs stretched out. Take a deep breath in and reach your arms way up high. Breathe out and stretch your arms down low. [Repeat] Imagine the wind on your back, folding your leaf down. Rest your hands wherever they touch.

15-14   Folded Leaf

Points to Remember: For tight hamstrings, bend the knees or place a rolled towel beneath them. Practice touching knees, thighs, or ankles, easing rather than forcing into the pose. For Half Folded Leaf, bend one knee as in Butterfly Knees with the other leg straight. To exercise the eyes, follow the fingers up and down.

Variations: In the chair variation shown, the child opens her chest before hinging forward. If preferred, the arms may hang down. The children sit sideways at desks with attached chairs.

Precautions: In the floor variation, don't hang the head down; this increases tension in the neck and lower back. Never push a child into the pose. Avoid with low-back pain, neck instability, or hernia. When head hangs down past the knees in a chair, the same precautions as for inversions apply.

Counterpose: Drawbridge, Crab, or Half Fish

Sequencing: Works well after Rock the Baby, Pretzel

15-15   Folded Leaf in Chair

SEATED TWISTS

Most twists can be performed seated, standing, or supine. Twists involve bilateral motions and crossing the midline of the body, and they improve motor planning. Rotations massage and tone the abdominal organs, enhance digestion, and stretch and strengthen trunk and back muscles, shoulders and arms. Increased flexibility in the pelvic girdle facilitates sitting, walking, and running. Gentle compression of the spinal disks through twisting improves circulation to the spinal nerves and disks.

These precautions apply to all twists: Injuries to the nerves, disks, or abdominal organs contraindicate seated twists, as do neck, shoulder, back, or spinal instability. Do not twist on a full stomach.

13. PRETZEL

Starting Position: Seated on the feet and shins; cross-legged, chair, or standing

Benefits of the posture: Neck and spinal rotation, stretches quadriceps; directionality, proprioception; creative play, language skills

Instructions for the Child: Sit on your feet. To warm up, turn your head right, then left. Facing forward, stretch both arms in front toward me. Wrap both arms around you to the right, turn your head, too. You're all twisted up like a pretzel. [Repeat left] Shake your arms to shake the salt off your pretzel!

Points to Remember: Use Pretzel to reinforce right and left. Use a visual cue or landmark in the room to identify directions. To simplify, omit directional terms, do neck rotations only, or sit cross-legged.

Variations: In a chair, the child turns his upper body right, draping his right arm over the chair back, holding his left thigh or the chair seat with his left

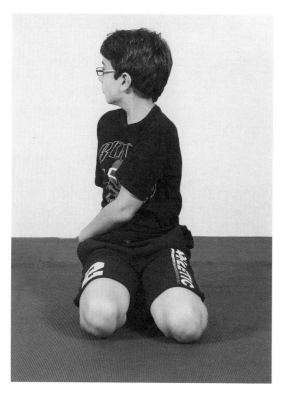

15-16   Pretzel

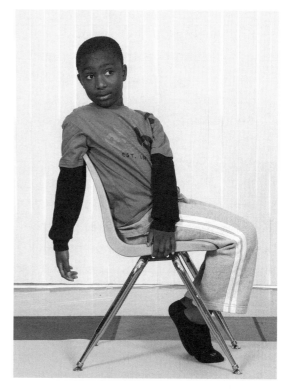

15-17   Pretzel Chair

hand. Generate discussion about the kind of pretzel they are (salted or sweet), and where they might go to eat a pretzel (ballgame, movies).

Precautions: See description above; use alternative starting position with hip, knee, ankle, or foot injury.

Counterpose: Folded Leaf, Drawbridge

Sequencing: Works well with Twister

14. TWISTER

Starting Position: Cross-legged, standing

Benefits: Stress relief; creative play; language skills

Instructions for the Child: Sit crisscross. Let's twist from side to side. Feel the power of the twister growing, speeding up. Let your arms fly out and around you, side to side. Start to slow it down, coming to a stop.

Points to Remember: Use the phrase "side to side" or a swishing sound as a chant to keep the child focused in the posture. Speed it up or slow it down, creating a pace that suits the child at the moment. Use this stress reliever as a yoga break.

15-18   Twister

Variations: This is a faster version of Pretzel and can also be done standing. Compare this motion to a spinning washing machine or helicopter blades. Use this posture to teach about weather conditions such as tornadoes or hurricanes.

Precautions: See description above.

Counterpose: Seated Egg

Sequencing: Works well after Pretzel

15. ROCK THE BABY

Starting Position: Floor with legs extended; cross-legged or chair

Benefits: Calming; creative play, language skills; compassionate touch, mindfulness

Instructions for the Child: Hug your right foot close, as if you were holding

15-19   Rock the Baby

a baby. If your arms are long enough, wrap them around your knee. Otherwise, hold onto your foot. Be gentle—you don't want to wake up the sleeping baby in your arms. Let's sing or hum while rocking the baby side to side. Give your baby a hug and then tuck it in, safely back to the ground.

Points to Remember: Sitting cross-legged may be easier for balance. Demonstrate the foot hold if it's more comfortable than hugging the knee. Make this a meditative pose by humming quietly, or a playful posture, with children singing. (See songs in Chapter 20.) Talk about the care required when holding a baby. With older children, discuss babysitting.

Variations: To assist a child, support her foot and shin from below with your palms or forearms while you rock her leg. Avoid pushing; allow her body to surrender to the rocking motion. Conclude by tucking the baby into its "crib" on the floor and giving it a gentle massage, teaching appropriate touch.

Precautions: See description above.

Counterpose: Seated Egg

Sequencing: Works well with Twister

SEATED PARTNER POSES: FORWARD AND BACK BENDING

These postures promote social interaction, communication, and creative play. They provide an opportunity for you to bond with the child and build trust among family members or classmates.

Supervise the partner postures with great care. In groups, be sure there is sufficient space behind and between children to avert collisions. Avoid these poses rather than chance an injury or rejection of one child by another. If children are not comfortable with touch or are not able to restrain aggressive impulses, skip these postures for now. You can work side by side with the child or mirror him without touching. Use walls or cushions for support if the child prefers to work without a partner.

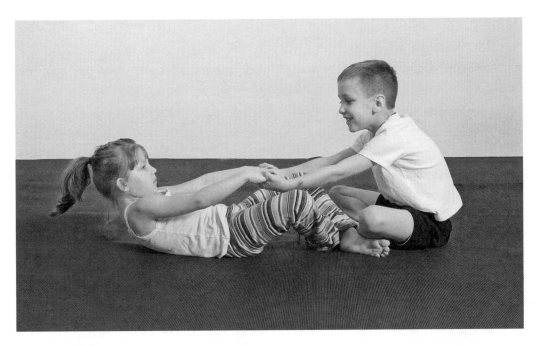

15-20   Seesaw

16. SEESAW

Starting Position: Cross-legged, close to and facing partner

Benefits: Balance, flexibility; vestibular stimulation, proprioception

Instructions for the Child: Sit crisscross and face your partner. Hold hands gently. Check behind to make sure you have space to lean back. Let's sing and rock! Now stop and thank your partner.

Points to Remember: See Seesaw song, Chapter 20. You may partner with a child to demonstrate slow, gentle rocking. Sit behind a child to help him rock while he partners with another child or adult. Sometimes there are skirmishes over partners. Do not reward inappropriate behaviors by giving in to unreasonable demands.

Variations: If touch is a challenge, sit beside the child, rocking independently. For auditory sensitivities, eliminate the singing.

Precautions: Most children enjoy this pose, but this is not for all children. Do not tolerate unnecessary roughness.

Counterpose: Forward and back motion provide a counterpose

Sequencing: Works well with Lawn Chair

17. FLYING BATS

Starting Position: Seated with soles of feet on floor, facing partner

Benefits: Having fun, cooperation; abdominal and back strength; balance, flexibility; proprioception, motor planning, bilateral coordination

Instructions for the Child: Find a partner your height. Sit close and hold hands inside your knees. Touch the bottom of one foot to your partner's. Lift your foot up and lower it down. [Other side] If you are ready, lift both feet. Hold on! Come down carefully. Let go and thank your partner.

15-21   Flying Bats One Foot

15-22   Flying Bats

Points to Remember: Children must sit close enough to maintain hand hold. When partnering with a smaller child, use the tops of your feet or shins to support his heels. To lift *both* feet (see photo), hands must be inside the knees. Stand or kneel alongside children to support their hands or feet. Lower feet before releasing hands.

Variations: Children may lie on their backs with knees bent, feet facing their partner. Straighten one leg at a time to touch feet. To work without a partner, rest the feet on a wall. In a space with soft carpets, partners count to three, let go, and enjoy a half backward roll.

Precautions: Match children by strength and capacity. Not suitable for children who are extremely low or high toned. Avoid with neck, shoulder, back, or spinal injuries or instability.

Counterpose: Crab

Sequencing: Works well with Seesaw

18. BACK-TO-BACK BREATHING

Starting Position: Cross-legged back-to back with partner

Benefits: Calming, breath awareness, mindfulness

Instructions for the Child: Let's rest our backs for a minute. I'll support your back and you can support mine.

Points to Remember: Asking the child to help you rest engages him in this posture. Choose a quiet time for this posture, and adjust the duration to suit the child. Start by mirroring the child's rhythm of breathing, and gradually slow your breathing. Do not ask the child to adjust his respiratory rate. Invite this process nonverbally through shared relaxation.

Variations: If the child is uncomfortable with your being so close, leave a small space between. Or sit side by side. Use any comfortable seated position for the child. You may sit back to back in chairs or standing with children of similar height.

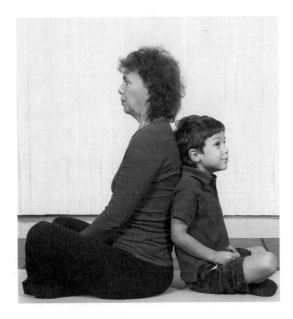

15-23   Back-to-Back Breathing

Precautions: Avoid with children who head butt. Sitting still is very challenging for some.

Counterpose: Drawbridge, Bug on Its Back

Sequencing: Works well with Lawn Chair

19. LAWN CHAIR

Starting Position: Seated back to back with partner, legs straight

Benefits: Cooperation; flexibility, strength; vestibular sense, proprioception, motor planning

Instructions for the Child: Sit back to back. Finley, start to lean forward in Folded Leaf; Marion will rest her head on your back. Pretend you are sitting in a comfortable lounge chair at the beach. Slowly reverse.

Points to Remember: This posture combines forward and backward bending. Partner with the child or match children by height and size. Carefully monitor this pose, assuring that neither child is being pushed beyond a comfortable limit.

Variations: Children with very tight hamstrings or hip inflexibility, may sit cross-legged. Children may partner side by side. The forward motion (Folded Leaf) can be done independently; use a bolster or cushions for the backrest.

15-24   Lawn Chair

Precautions: Avoid with children with hip, neck, or back injury or instability, abdominal complaints, headache, or dizziness. Do not partner children who may head butt or be aggressive.

Counterpose: Includes forward and back bending, so no counterpose required

Sequencing: Works well with Back Rest Breathing or after Seesaw

Foundational Posture 2: Hands and Knees

Standing on hands and knees increases strength in the back, shoulders, wrists, and knees and flexibility in the shoulders and ankles. Avoid if a child has an injury in any of these areas. These postures improve balance and bilateral coordination.

This position is a useful transition when moving from seated to prone or from seated to standing posture. Fully grounding through the palms, knees, lower legs, and feet promotes gravitational security and sensory awareness.

If a child lacks abdominal tone, use prone or seated variations to prevent low back injury. Children with neck instability should do the seated variations for the following poses. If highly flexible children hyperextend their elbows or destabilize their wrists in this position, have them turn their fingers slightly inward or keep their forearms on the ground.

20. TABLE

Starting Position: Hands and knees with back level

Benefits: Motor planning, proprioception

Instructions for the Child: Come onto your hands and knees. Make your back flat as a table. I might eat my lunch on your table!

Points to Remember: Line up the hands with the shoulders and the knees with the hips. Children with motor-planning challenges often need help getting into this posture. Sit in front of the cross-legged child. Asking for his hands, gently guide them forward toward the floor in front of him. His hips will follow. Don't be concerned with the position of his feet for now. This may take several lessons. Or, place visual cues on the floor in front of him so he will know where to place each hand. Sit beside him and model the motion.

15-25   Table Preparation

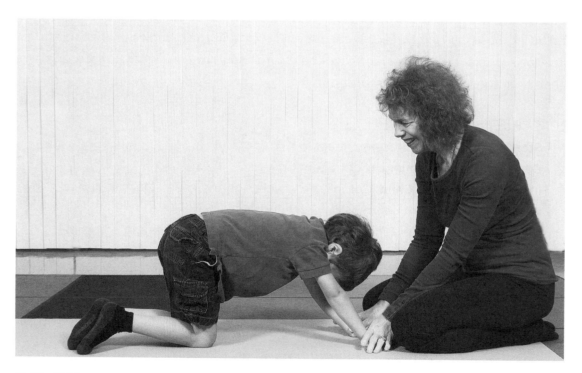

15-26   Table

Variations: The child may sit cross-legged and place his hands on the ground in front of him for Half Table. In a chair, he'll place his hands on his knees.

Precautions: See description above.

Counterpose: Crab, Drawbridge

Sequencing: Works well as a starting position for Cat, Stretching Dog, and crawling poses

21. HAPPY CAT

Starting Position: Table; seated on floor or chair

Benefits: Creative play, language skills; visual-motor coordination, cross patterning; deepens breathing; spinal extension; stretches chest, abdomen

Instructions for the Child: It's time for Cat! Starting in Table, look up high and stretch your chest. Take a deep breath and say, "Meow." Smile like a happy cat! Let's crawl in a big circle around the room. Follow me. Remember to smile with each "meow"!

Points to Remember: This is a playful pose. Practice the smile after the pose to reinforce the facial expression. With noisy children, purr in the posture to quiet things down.

15-27   Happy Cat

Variations: Children with severe scoliosis may benefit from doing this posture seated or standing with their hands on the wall so as not to sink into their weaker side. For language development, use this posture to work on the sounds of M-E-OW. Talk about cats—color, size, names.

Precautions: Same as for Table. Take care that the child does not sink into the shoulders or overly arch the lower back or neck.

Counterpose: Angry Cat, Baby

Sequencing: Works well with Angry Cat, Stretching Dog

22. ANGRY CAT

Starting Position: Table; seated on floor or chair

Benefits: Creative play, language skills; visual-motor coordination; deepens breathing; spinal flexion; combined with Happy Cat, increases blood flow to organs of chest and abdomen, strengthens spine

Instructions for the Child: From happy cat, now we'll be an angry cat. Press into your hands and take a deep breath. Breathe out as you round up your upper back like an angry cat. Look down, and don't say a word. Now become

15-28   Angry Cat

a happy cat. Breathe in, look up, and say, "Meow." Smile! With your next breath out, round up your back and don't say a word.

Points to Remember: For language development, switch between noisy cat "meow" and silent cat.

Variations: Same as Happy Cat. With noisy children, remain in Angry Cat.

Precautions: Same as Table. Take care that the child does not sink into her shoulders or wrists.

Counterpose: Happy Cat, Baby

Sequencing: Works well with Happy Cat, Stretching Dog

23. BALANCE BEAM

Starting Position: Table

Benefits: Improves vestibular sense, proprioception; mindfulness, focus

Instructions for the Child: Wiggle your right toes. Straighten your right leg and lift if off the ground. And lower. Wiggle your left fingers. Straighten your left arm and stretch it in front. And down. Now we'll put it all together. Look at your spot on the floor. Wiggle your right toes and raise your right leg. Wiggle your left fingers and raise your left arm. You are straight as a balance beam!

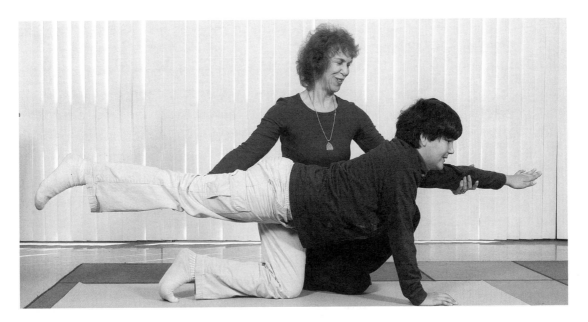

15-29   Balance Beam

Points to Remember: Use a prop to provide a focal point for the child's eyes. This pose takes a great deal of body awareness and coordination. Work with one limb at a time. To support the child, place your palms beneath his elbow and his knee. For a child who prefers not to be touched, support him with a chair or cushion to familiarize his body with the positions.

Variations: See "Motor Planning and Bilateral Coordination: Small Steps," Chapter 18.

Precautions: Same as Table. Visual and sensory limitations inhibit balance.

Counterpose: Baby, Folded Leaf

Sequencing: Works well after Cat

24. FROG

Starting Position: Table

Benefits: Stretches calves, ankles; deep flexion hips, knees; hip, lower back flexibility; motor planning; inner calm; creative interactive play, language skills

Instructions for the Child: From Table, squat down toward your heels. Can you croak like a frog by the pond? Now hop from lily pad to lily pad.

Points to Remember: Squatting requires tremendous flexibility in the back of the ankles. Some children will be more comfortable on their toes. They may keep their hands or fingertips on the floor to maintain balance. Stretch the legs first in Stretching Dog and Folded Leaf.

Variations: Some children will be more comfortable hopping like a kangaroo, without the low squat. Frogs may "chase flies" by moving their heads in all directions, searching for prey. They can stretch their mouths open to catch the flies and "swallow" them down. A child who cannot squat can sit cross-legged and croak or catch flies.

Precautions: Avoid with ankle, knee, hip, or low-back injuries. Not recommended for children who are extremely tight in the calves or Achilles tendon.

Counterpose: Bug on Its Back, Drawbridge, Balance Beam

15-30   Frog

Sequencing: Works well after Stretching Dog

25. VOLCANO

Starting Position: Frog

Benefits: Creative play, language skills; relieves stress; strength; flexibility; proprioception; energizing

Instructions for the Child: Sit like a rock, all tucked in with your feet on the ground. You've been here like this for a long time. Start to feel a rumble inside yourself. Rumble, rumble, rumble. Begin a slight sway from side to side with your hips and arms. Your insides are getting hot. You feel them bubbling up, and up, and up until they burst out in an explosion of lava! Leap up high.

Points to Remember: Children in Frog will stretch out their limbs as they grow into an exploding volcano. This is a sophisticated concept. You may want to include some information or illustrations first about volcanoes before teaching this posture.

The extreme leap requires tremendous strength, balance, and coordination. For children with limited motor control, use only the rocking motion and the rumble, but not the leap.

Variations: This can be done from a seat by stretching the arms and reaching high. In a standing position, a child can hug his arms into his body to start and then reach and jump.

Precautions: Same as for Frog. Avoid the leap if child is unsteady on her feet, is extremely low toned, or has injuries to the spine, hips, or other joints.

Counterpose: Bug on Its Back, Baby

Sequencing: Works well with Frog

15-31   Volcano

HANDS AND KNEES COUNTERPOSES

15-32   Baby

26. BABY

Starting Position: Table

Benefits: Back flexion relaxes back after extensions; calming, introspective; soothing pressure of folded limbs trigger PNS; proprioception, motor planning

Instructions for the Child: From Table pose, sit on your feet. Bring your head down to the ground or onto your hands. Curl up into a little ball, just like a tiny baby. You are safe and quiet in this pose. You are peaceful. Breathe and relax.

Points to Remember: Some children have difficulty getting into this posture. Help the child into Table. Then guide his hips toward his feet. Do not force his head down, but suggest he rest it on the ground, on a cushion, or in his palms

15-33   Baby with Massage

with his elbows on the floor. You may use additional imagery in this posture: curled up like a tiny seed planted in the ground; tucked in like a mouse in its hole. This posture may be useful for a child whose mother is pregnant.

Variations: Massage the child's back in the posture. Teach healing touch by letting the child share massage with you, parents, or classmates. Supervise partner massage. Long Arm Baby is the same pose with the arms stretched overhead on the ground. Seated, a child may rest his head on his desk.

Precautions: If children have difficulty breathing in this position, have them lie sideways with an arm or pillow beneath the head. Avoid with knee, ankle, hip, or low-back injury or headache. This is a very slight inversion, although the chest and head are fully supported.

Counterpose: This is a counterpose for all back bends; use as a resting pose after energizing postures

Sequencing: Works well with Cat, Balance Beam, Stretching Dog, Hi, World

27. HI, WORLD

Starting Position: Baby

Benefits: Creative play, language skills; transitions; energizing; back, shoulder, arm flexibility

Instructions for the Child: It's time to wake up from Baby. Sit up. Stretch your arms way up high. Say, "Hi, World!"

Points to Remember: Baby is a very calming, introspective posture. Children sometimes have difficulty reengaging or proceeding to the next posture. This playful transition signals that it's time to wake up and reconnect with the outside world. Vary the volume—a shout or a whisper.

Variations: This posture can be used to transition between other events in the child's day—when waking up in the morning, after quiet time, or at the end of a yoga session.

Precautions: Same as for Baby.

Sequencing: Works well after Baby

15-34 Hi, World

CONTRAINDICATIONS FOR INVERSIONS

Inversions are any position in which the head is below the level of the heart, whether by lowering the head, elevating the chest, or elevating the chest and legs (Rosen, 2002). High blood pressure, elevated intracranial pressure, stroke, glaucoma, detached retina, carotid artery stenosis, congestive heart failure, and hiatal hernia all contraindicate inversions (Cole, cited in Rosen, 2002). Avoid inversions if the child has a history of seizures, heart disease, spinal, back or neck injury or instability, headache, or after eating or drinking.

INVERSIONS FROM HANDS AND KNEES

Hands and knees inversions build strength and flexibility. Most children find these forward bending inversions calming. The pressure against the hands and feet helps children feel grounded, increasing proprioception and gravitational security.

28. STRETCHING DOG

Starting Position: Table
Benefits: Stretches hips and back of the body; strengthens legs, shoulders,

15-35   Stretching Dog—Grounding Feet

arms, and wrists; motor planning, balance; creative play, communication skills; slows respiration, mindfulness, focus

Instructions for the Child: My dog stretches his spine every morning. From Table, push the bottoms of your toes into the floor. Press your hands down and raise your hips up high, just like a stretching dog. It feels so good; wag your tail!

Points to Remember: To ground the child, press the balls of his feet down before he begins. Starting with the tops of the toes on the floor won't work. Being upside down often confuses a child about direction of motion. Using both hands, hold onto his trousers near the outer hip, holding his clothing only. Instruct him to lift as you provide an upward pull to create the lifting experience for him. Hold briefly and repeat.

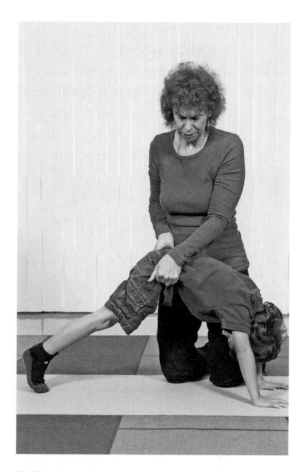

15-36   Stretching Dog

Variations: Rest the child's head on cushions or blocks to increase stability in the posture. Use visual and verbal cues only if a physical assist is not appropriate. What kind of dog are they? Let them bark or howl. Combine with Snake three or four times for an energizing sequence.

Precautions: See contraindications for inversions. Avoid for children with foot, leg, or spinal injuries. Do not lift a child with gravitational insecurity or anxiety.

Counterpose: Baby, Snake, Airplane

Sequencing: Works well with Snake

29. WALKING DOG

Starting Position: Stretching Dog

Benefits: Same as Stretching Dog; bilateral movements, cross patterning

Instructions for the Child: Let's take your dog for a walk! Start by moving your right arm forward. Add your left leg. Next move your left arm and right leg forward. Put all this together for Walking Dog.

Points to Remember: Walking Dog requires coordination and sensory organization. Tap the hand and opposite foot, to assure cross patterning in the pose. Walk in posture alongside the child to cue or model the motion.

Variations: Practice crawling on hands and knees for Walking Dog. Gradually introduce the motion with limbs straight.

Precautions: See precautions for inversions. Same as for Stretching Dog.

Counterpose: Baby, Crab

Sequencing: Works well with Stretching Dog, Snake

15-37   Walking Dog

30. CROWN POSE

Starting Position: Baby

Benefits: Balance, mindfulness; core body strength, stretches back of body; touch pressure and inversion without excessive stress on neck; alternative to headstand

Instructions for the Child: The crown is the top of your head. From Baby, press your palms down under your shoulders. Slowly roll the top of your head onto the floor, lifting your hips slowly. Use your hands for support. Feel the gentle pressure on your crown. Roll down; rest in Baby.

Points to Remember: For children who crave pressure on the head, this pose may deter self-stimulating or injurious behaviors. This is an advanced posture. Proceed only if you are able to support the child. Sit or stand alongside her to assure stability. Keep the palms down beneath the shoulders for support. Be certain she remains on the crown so weight is distributed evenly on the flattest part. Avoid rolling sideways or overflexing the neck.

Variations: Teach children who seek pressure on the crown to do this posture at your cue, hands beneath their shoulders. Children may need an assist coming up. The girl in the photo shows an advanced variation, holding her ankles.

15-38   Crown pose

Precautions: This is an inversion: see precautions. Avoid with gravitational insecurity, shoulder or neck instability or injuries, or vestibular challenges.

Counterpose: Knee Hugs and Neck Rolls, Airplane

Sequencing: Works well with Stretching Dog pose; always follow with Baby

Foundational Posture 3: Prone

Lying on the belly increases pressure on the abdominal organs, stimulating digestion and elimination. Deep touch pressure in prone poses can reduce sensory overstimulation. Learning to lengthen and elevate the spine against gravity improves back strength, proprioception, motor planning, and vestibular systems.

Children who self-stimulate the genitals while prone should do these poses on hands and knees or seated. Reintroduce the posture periodically to see if their attention can be redirected.

PRONE BACKBENDS

Backbends are energizing, activating the sympathetic nervous system and increasing alertness. They open the chest and stretch the front of the body. Strengthening the muscles in the back of the body improves the ability to sit and stand upright.

Backbending requires a gentle approach and is not recommended for children with spinal, neck, or back injuries or hiatal hernia. Protect the neck by keeping it aligned with the spine in these postures.

31. SNAKE

Starting Position: Belly

Benefits: Strengthens shoulder, wrists; creative play, language skills; breathing

Instructions for the Child: Press your hands into the ground, and come up on your elbows. If this feels good, stay there or stretch your arms to come up higher. Look up. HISSSSSSSSSSSS! Can you slither on your tummy like a snake?

Points to Remember: Make this pose playful. If the chest sinks and shoulders are hiked up, the elbows should be kept bent and forearms down. Help the child stabilize the pelvis and legs before attempting the full variation. Avoid com-

15-39   Snake Elbows Bent

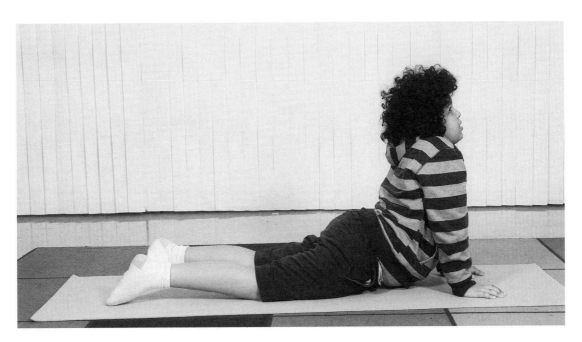

15-40   Snake

pressing the lower back. To make this an energizing sequence, switch between Stretching Dog and Snake as slowly or quickly as is comfortable for the child.

Variations: From the Bent Elbow variation, make this a moving sequence. Come up with the inhalation; float down with the exhalation. If the belly pose is not comfortable, the child can hiss in Table or seated.

Precautions: Avoid with spinal injuries, low-back pain, or neck instability. Hiked shoulders can cause strain in upper back. Avoid lumbar compression by grounding the pelvis.

Counterpose: Baby, Stretching Dog

Sequencing: Works well with Stretching Dog or in combination with Superman for an energizing sequence

32. AIRPLANE

Starting Position: Belly

Benefits: Strengthens back and legs; deepens breathing; creative play, language skills

Instructions for the Child: Where would you go if you could fly through the sky? Stretch your arms out to your sides like airplane wings, palms down. Wiggling your fingers, lift your arms up and down. Wiggle all your toes; raise each leg up and down. Let's warm up the engine with a deep breath and lift everything up! Fly like an airplane—whoosh!

15-41 Airplane

Points to Remember: Make this a strengthening pose, or focus on the playful aspects. Let children call out where they want to fly. After the pose, talk about where they've gone and what they have seen there. Use a map to make this a geography lesson or create imaginary places.

Variations: Children may bend the knees in the pose. Gradually, work on straightening the limbs. If this is too challenging, the child can stretch out his arms and fly like an airplane without lifting. Elevating the torso on a bolster or cushion gives the child a lift in this posture.

Precautions: (See description above.) Prevent shoulder tension by keeping arms below shoulder level while lifting. Avoid with children who are extremely high or low toned.

Counterpose: Follow with Baby; Folded Leaf

Sequencing: Works well with Snake or after Stretching Dog

33. HALF SUPERMAN

Starting Position: Belly

Benefits: Bilateral coordination, sensory motor skills, cross patterning

Instructions for the Child: Stretch your arms in front. Wiggle your right fingers. Raise your right arm off the ground. And lower. Now wiggle your left

15-42 Half Superman

toes. Lift your left leg off the floor. And lower. Let's lift your head, right arm, and left leg all at the same time.

Points to Remember: To make this easier, let the child bend her knees and raise just the lower left leg and the opposite hand. Support the arm and leg as needed.

Variations: The child may lie on her back and touch her bent knee with the opposite hand for cross patterning.

Precautions: See description above. This is a very demanding posture. Avoid with low or very high toned children.

Counterpose: Baby, Folded Leaf

Sequencing: Works well with Snake or after Stretching Dog; good warm-up for Superman

34. SUPERMAN

Starting Position: Belly

Benefits: Strengthens shoulders, upper arms; deepens breathing; creative play, language skills

Instructions for the Child: Who is your favorite superhero? Let's fly like Superman or Supergirl. Stretch your arms in front and your legs in back. Take a deep breath, lift up, and FLY! Watch the ground so you'll know where to land. Okay, let's touch down. Superman, you saved the day!

15-43   Superman

Points to Remember: This is a demanding posture, but children love it. Prepare with Airplane and Half Superman. Talk about superheroes, what they do, and how it might feel to fly. Even children who cannot do the full pose enjoy pretending.

Variations: Use bolsters as in Airplane. Children in chairs can fly, too. Stretch the arms up overhead and lean from side to side. If appropriate, let the child sit or stand in front of a fan. How does that feel? Can he make the sound of the wind?

Precautions: See description above. Avoid with shoulder injuries or instability and with children who are hypertoned in the postural muscles.

Counterpose: Baby

Sequencing: Works well with Airplane and after Half Superman

Foundational Posture 4: Supine

Most children are happy whenever they have a chance to lie down on their backs! If it's not a comfortable pose, keeping the knees bent relieves tight hamstrings or low backs.

SUPINE BACKBENDS

Backbends are energizing, activating the sympathetic nervous system. These poses open the chest and rib cage and stretch the front of the shoulders. Strengthening the muscles in the back of the body improves the ability to sit and stand upright. Backbending is not recommended for children with spinal, neck, or back injuries or hiatal hernia. Prevent the neck from overextending; avoid hanging the head back.

35. HALF FISH

Starting Position: Back; seated on floor or chair; standing

Benefits: Deepens breathing; improves proprioception, visual and vestibular senses

Instructions for the Child: A fish has gills to take in lots of oxygen. Let's open up the front of your body and breathe like a fish. Prop up on your elbows, lifting your back off the ground. Take a deep breath and open your chest.

15-44   Half Fish

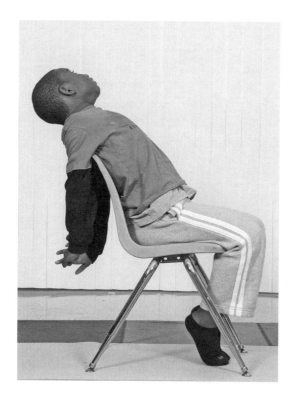

15-45   Half Fish in Chair

Look up with the next breath in, but don't let your head hang back. Breathe out and look down. Can you make a fish face?

Points to Remember: The primary emphasis of this posture is deep breathing. Some children may collapse the upper body after the effort, so have them take one deep breath and then release back to the ground. Repeat with rests in between until it becomes comfortable, or support the back with bolsters. Omit the eye motion if it is distracting.

Variations: In a chair, the child clasps his hands behind his back. Inhaling, he opens his chest; exhaling, he releases. You may combine this with Folded Leaf. If children cannot reach the hands, hold onto the back or sides of the chair. To make this an exercise for the eyes only, the child looks up and down without moving his head. Standing Half Fish opens the chest with hands clasped behind the back.

Precautions: See description above. If the child is very tight, work first with Elbow Circles to loosen the shoulder girdle before attempting this or the next posture.

Counterpose: Folded Leaf, Knee Hugs, Bug on Its Back

Sequencing: Works well with Bellows Breath, Elbow Circles; after Folded Leaf, Candle

36. CRAB

Starting Position: Half Fish

Benefits: Stretches pelvis, hips; strengthens legs, buttocks, arms, wrists, core body; creative play, language skills; cross patterning, motor planning, bilateral coordination

Instructions for the Child: Have you seen a crab walking on the beach? He seems to be going backwards! From Half Fish, straighten your arms. Bend your knees with your feet on the ground. Push into your hands and feet and lift up your hips. Walk backwards by leading with your hands. You look just like a crab! Walk forward by leading with your feet. Can you walk sideways?

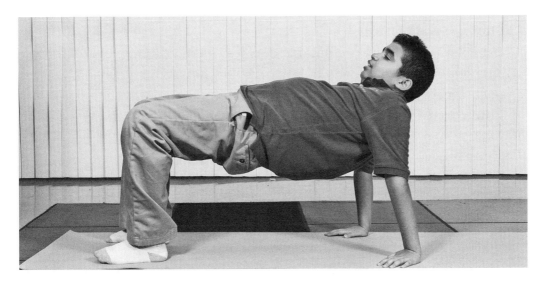

15-46   Crab

Points to Remember: This posture requires a great deal of arm strength and shoulder flexibility. If the child cannot get his hands on the floor behind him, do not attempt the hip lift. Instead, work on Drawbridge to increase core body strength. Practice Elbow Circles and Bellows Breath to increase shoulder flexibility.

Variations: Some wrists are more comfortable with the fingers pointing forward; other prefer backward. Before walking forward, backward, or sideways in Crab, try those positions from hands and knees to clarify direction of movements.

Precautions: See description above. Avoid with shoulder, elbow, wrist, hip injury, knee problems, or hyperextend elbows.

Counterpose: Baby, Folded Leaf

Sequencing: Works well with Half Fish, Drawbridge

SUPINE INVERSIONS

Supine inversions require strength, flexibility, and balance. When the body is upside down, the organs (stomach, heart, lungs) are stretched and massaged. Inversions change the direction of the blood flow in the body, improving circulation. Pelvic lifts and neck flexion promote calm. See contraindication for inversions.

37. DRAWBRIDGE

Starting Position: Back

Benefits: This posture is a backbend as well as an inversion. Stretches hips; strengthens lower back and buttocks; mindfulness; proprioception, gravitational security, motor planning

Instructions for the Child: How does a drawbridge make way for boats to pass beneath it? It lifts up! Bend your knees and press your feet down. Take a deep breath and lift up your hips so the boats can go beneath. Sound the drawbridge horn—honk! Lower slowly and wait for the next boat.

Points to Remember: Hold the child's feet, grounding him so he feels the downward push in the pose. Use your knees outside his feet to keep his toes aligned. Lifting the child by the trouser pockets gives him a sense of the upward motion. Use the breath in this calming pose—inhaling up, exhaling to sound the horn; inhaling up, exhaling down. To play in the posture, pretend your hand is a boat traveling beneath his drawbridge.

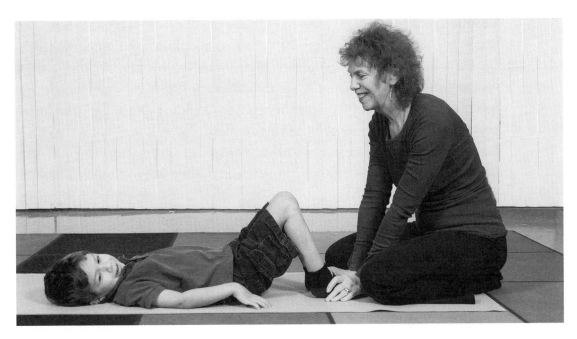

15-47   Drawbridge—Grounding Feet

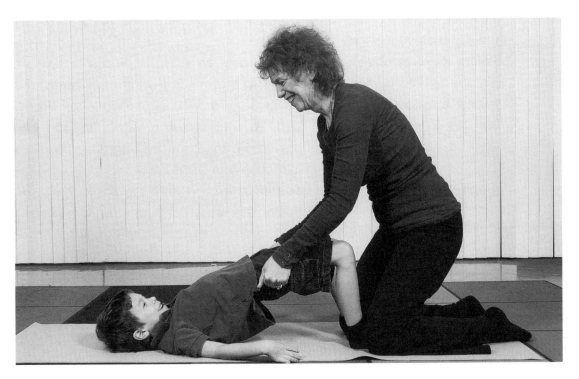

15-48   Drawbridge

Variations: Children may remain in drawbridge or move up and down. You can sing (see songs in Chapter 20) as you move up and down. For gravitational insecurity, work on grounding hands and feet without lift.

Precautions: This is a slight inversion, with the chest elevated above the heart. Please note contraindications above. Avoid with neck injury or instability, foot, ankle, hip, low back or spine injuries.

Counterpose: Folded Leaf, Knee Hugs, Seated Egg

Sequencing: Works well with Bug on Its Back, Knee Hugs; after Candle

38. ROCKING CHAIR

Starting Position: Seated with soles of the feet on ground, knees bent; on back

Benefits: Energizing, fun; touch pressure, massages back muscles; motor planning; provides momentum for leg lift in Candle

Instructions for the Child: Sit up and bend your knees with your feet on the floor. Reach underneath your knees and interlace your fingers. Look behind you to make sure you have enough room for your head. Take a deep breath and rock and roll on your back. Use your legs to rock your chair. Doesn't that feel good on your back?

Points to Remember: This exercise is best on a carpet or cushioned mat. Sit sideways to demonstrate threading the hands beneath the knees and interlacing fingers. A child with low tone may need assistance to start rocking or keep his hands together. Support him beneath the knees and mid-back until he feels the momentum of his body rocking itself.

15-49   Rocking Chair

Variations: A child may remain on his back, hugging his knees, and rock slightly forward and back for less demand on the neck or core body.

Precautions: Not recommended with neck, spine, or back injuries. Avoid on a hard floor. Vigorously rocking back will put the body in a partially inverted posture. Please note contraindications.

Counterpose: Drawbridge, Crab

Sequencing: Works well before Candle, with Knee Hugs

SUPPORTED SUPINE INVERSIONS

Please note that the back remains on the floor in these inversions. Supine inversions improve circulation by allowing blood flow from the extremities back toward the heart. The calming effect of elevating the legs and tucking the chin into the throat notch slows respiration. The back of the body receives a good stretch.

Although the head is not below the heart as in a true inversion, the gravitational effect of elevating the legs higher than the heart "increases the amount of blood entering and leaving the heart on each beat" (Roger Cole, personal communication, October 21, 2012) and may not be recommended for some individuals.

39. CANDLE

Starting Position: Rocking Chair, back

Benefits: Quieting; creative play, social interaction; strengthens abdominals, core

Instructions for the Child: When your legs are up in the air, it's refreshing for

15-50   Candle

your body and restful for your mind. From Rocking Chair, rock your legs up into Candle. Let your back rest on the ground like a candle holder. Hold onto your legs for support, and I'll come light your candle. Wiggle your toes like a candle flame twinkling until I blow out your candle. Hug your knees.

Points to Remember: Elevating the legs requires balance and core body strength. Help the child support the back of his thighs with his hands. Most children will join in Candle. It may be only a foot or one leg that is offered when you arrive to light his candle, but take every opportunity to engage the child in this playful posture.

Variations: Sing "Happy Birthday" after the candles have been lit. For children with very tight hamstrings, rest the legs over a chair seat. Help children lift their legs alternately to stretch tight muscles. Some children will rock up into Full Candle, with their backs off the ground. If they are comfortable in the posture, with no neck limitations, be certain they support their backs. Full Candle is a true inversion, so note contraindications. Follow this variation with Half Fish.

Precautions: Check contraindications for inversions. Avoid with neck injury or instability, back or shoulder pain, or extremely tight hamstrings.

Counterpose: Half Fish, Drawbridge, Snake

Sequencing: Works well after Rocking Chair; follow with Knee Hugs, Half Fish

40. WALL INVERSIONS: WALL CANDLE, WALL BUTTERFLY, WALL X

Starting Position: Back on the floor, with legs and buttocks on the wall

Benefits: Mindfulness; social interaction; motor planning

Instructions for the Child: Let's decorate the wall with candles today. Sit sideways very close to the wall and rock your legs up onto the wall. Rest your back fully on the floor.

Points to Remember: Using the wall for supported Candle is very relaxing; the hardest part is getting up the wall. If the child has difficulty, rest her calves and ankles on a chair. To keep the neck comfortably flexed, place a thin pillow beneath her head. For a child with tight hamstrings, move slightly away from the wall or place a bolster behind her knees. Resting alongside a child or group in this posture creates a sense of community.

Variations: For Wall Butterfly, bring the soles of the feet together and allow

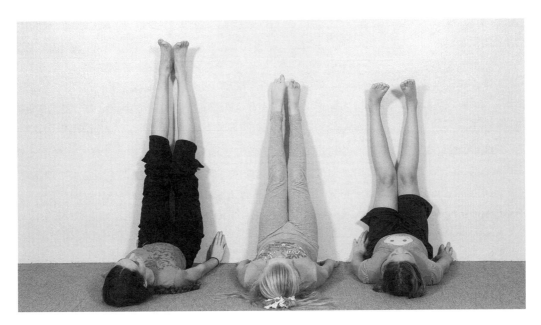

15-51   Wall Candle

15-52   Wall Butterfly

15-53   Wall X

the knees to relax in the direction of the wall without force. For Wall X, each child straightens her legs and crosses over or under her neighbor. Stronger children go underneath, where they get a deeper hamstring stretch.

Precautions: Check precautions for inversions. Not for children with neck injury or instability, back or shoulder pain, or extremely tight hamstrings. Contraindicated for knee or hip injuries or instability.

Counterpose: Half Fish, Knee Hugs, Drawbridge, Snake

Sequencing: Works well with Candle

SUPINE COUNTERPOSES

These stress-relieving postures follow supine postures and are useful whenever the child needs a "breather." These may be done with knees bent, feet elevated or on the floor. Pillows beneath the head are optional.

41. BUG ON ITS BACK

Starting Position: Back

Benefits: Stress relief; energizing, creative play; proprioception

Instructions for the Child: A bug on its back wiggles its arms and legs all

15-54   Bug on its Back

around. Pick up your feet and kick, kick, kick. Lift up your arms and shake, shake, shake.

Points to Remember: No kicking or flailing too close to a neighbor.

Variations: This variation of Shake It Out can be done seated on the floor or in a chair, or supine with arms and legs close to the ground. See song in Chapter 20.

Precautions: Do not encourage a child to kick or flail if he is highly agitated or having a tantrum. Use this posture for a controlled release.

Counterpose: Knee Hugs, Seated Egg

Sequencing: Works well after Drawbridge and with Knee Hugs

41. KNEE HUGS/NECK ROLLS

Starting Position: Back

Benefits: Soothing; mindfulness, self-regulating; massages back, neck; stretches spine, back of body; abdominal pressure aids digestion, relieves gas

Instructions for the Child: Lie down on your back and hug your knees. Wrap your arms around them like you're hugging a friend. Roll your head to one side, and then the other. Now gently rock from side to side, side to side.

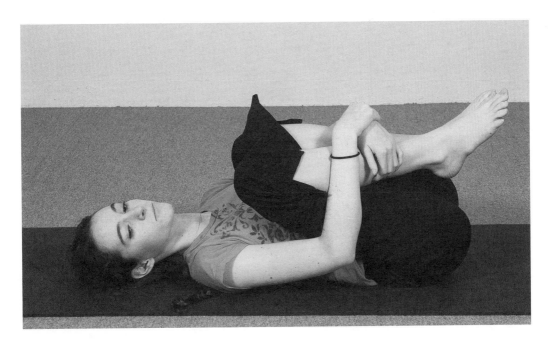

15-55   Knee Hugs/ Neck rolls

Points to Remember: Create a rhythm with your voice by repeating the soothing chant "side to side." If children have difficulty reaching their arms around their legs, they may hold their knees. Sit alongside and gently rock the child with your hands just below her knees.

Variations: The child may do neck rolls with her feet on the floor, knees bent. Or simply hug and rock sideways.

Precautions: Avoid with neck instability, knee, hip, or lower-back injuries. The gas-relieving element of this pose may cause embarrassment for children when working in groups. Avoid after eating.

Counterpose: Drawbridge

Sequencing: Works well as relaxation between supine postures or as a yoga break

43. SUPINE TWIST

Starting Position: Knee Hugs

Benefits: Same as seated twists, Knee Hugs/Neck Rolls; strengthens core body; stabilizes pelvis

15-56   Supine Twist

Instructions for the Child: Rock your knees over to your right side. Turn your head to look left. Release your hug and open both arms sideways, resting palms up on the ground. Turn your head and look at your left hand. Breathe and relax.

Points to Remember: You may need to assist the child by gently moving her head and opening her arms into position. Don't hold for long unless the child appears comfortable. Just getting there is an accomplishment!

Variations: Some children will be resistant to any effort to open their arms away from the body. This protective posture should not be challenged. Instead, have them hug the knees in position and roll their head from side to side. Then they may begin rocking knees to one side and head only to the other.

Precautions: Injuries to the nerves, disks, or abdominal organs contraindicate twists. Avoid with neck instability, knee, hip, lower-back, or shoulder injuries.

Counterpose: Drawbridge, Airplane

Sequencing: Works well with Knee Hugs, Bug on Its Back

Foundational Posture 5: Standing

Standing poses are strengthening. They require awareness in all parts of the body, increasing proprioception, balance, and bilateral coordination. They increase muscle tone in the legs, pelvis, abdomen, and back. For optimal balance, avoid thick gym mats or cushions. Standard yoga mats or towels, bare floors, or thin carpeting works well.

Standing poses may aggravate inguinal hernia (Coulter, 2001). Children with very low tone, unregulated high blood pressure, or heart disease should use seated variations of the more rigorous of these postures.

44. TREE HANDS

Starting Position: Standing; seated on floor or chair, supine

Benefits: Calming, mindfulness, self-regulation; focus

Instructions for the Child: A tree never gets tired of standing, because it has huge roots in the ground for support. Stand on both feet, tall and straight as a tree. Imagine your feet growing roots into the earth beneath you. Press the palms of your hands together at the center of your chest. How strong you are!

15-57   Tree Hands

Points to Remember: This posture increases awareness to the feet, legs, and pelvis and provides a focal point to improve concentration. It prepares the child for balancing and standing postures. Pressing the palms together helps turn the child's attention and energy inward, improving self-regulation.

Variations: Use to signal quiet throughout a child's day or for yoga breaks. Visual props help children position their feet and find a point of focus for their eyes.

Precautions: For mobility challenges, use seated or supine variation.

Counterpose: Shake It Out, Butterfly Hands

Sequencing: Works well as a calming posture between poses

45. TREE BREATHING

Starting Position: Tree Hands—standing, seated, supine

Benefits: Mindfulness, self-regulation, breathing, focus; visual tracking; language skills

Instructions for the Child: Stand tall and straight. Keep your palms together like branches of your tree. Breathing in, reach your branches up toward the sun. Breathing out, lower your branches back down. Watch your hands as your branches grow up; watch them coming back down.

Points to Remember: Have children keep their hands at heart level or above. Tree Breathing is a moving meditation, useful as a yoga break for self-regulation or to transition between activities. This pose prepares the child for standing and balancing postures.

Variations: The posture can be done seated or supine. Make this a playful posture: "A little bird

15-58   Tree Breathing

lands on your highest branch. Be very quiet so it will stay. The wind blows [exhale mouth], and the bird flies off. Lower your branches down."

Precautions: Avoid breath holding or straining. Match your instructions to the child's rate of respiration.

Counterpose: Rag Doll, Shake It Out

Sequencing: Works well before standing poses or as yoga break

46. TREE BALANCE

Starting Position: Tree Hands standing, seated, supine

Benefits: Mindfulness, self-regulation, breathing; concentration, focus; vestibular sense, cross patterning; creative play

Instructions for the Child: Stand in Tree Hands, your roots deep, holding you steady. Keep your eyes on your focus circle as you wiggle your right toes. Lift your right foot an inch and tuck it behind your left. Take a deep breath in and out. Place your foot back on the ground.

15-59 Tree Balance

Points to Remember: Balance poses require mental focus, a challenge for many children. By fixing the eyes on one point, most children improve their balance. Progress is motivating. While he is leaning against a wall, guide the child in shifting his weight from foot to foot. In time, he can do this without the wall. For further challenge, press the sole of the lifted foot against the shin or thigh of the standing foot.

Variations: The child may do this posture in a chair, using a focus circle for the eyes. While he is supine, you or the child may position one foot inside the opposite shin or thigh.

Precautions: Provide support for children with visual limitations, gravitational insecurity, or very low tone. Avoid with hip, knee, or ankle injuries.

Counterpose: Shake It Out, Rag Doll

Sequencing: Works well with Tree Hands, Willow Tree

15-60   Partner Tree

47. PARTNER TREE

Starting Position: Standing shoulder to shoulder with partner

Benefits: Same as Tree Balance; social interaction, building trust, language skills

Instructions for the Child: Stand next to your partner, holding hands. Breathe into the extra-large roots you two are growing deep into the ground. Wiggle the toes on your outside foot. Lift it into Tree position. When you are ready, bring your outside hands together. Raise your tree hands up toward the sky. Slowly lower your hand and foot.

Points to Remember: Balancing can be easier with a partner's help. Communication and trust are required. Start with their backs on a wall to learn the steps. The lifted foot should be placed as high as is comfortable on the shin or thigh. Standing too close to a partner creates difficulty in lifting the outer foot; too far apart provides insufficient support.

Variations: Let one child be the tree with a strong trunk (both feet on the floor) while her partner goes into the balance position. The hand positions are as described. Then switch roles.

Precautions: Same as Tree Balance

Counterpose: Shake It Out, Standing Twister

Sequencing: Works well with Tree Balance

48. TALL TREE

Starting Position: Tree Hands

Benefits: Creative play, language skills; mindfulness, breathing

Instructions for the Child: What is the tallest tree in your neighborhood? Start with Tree Hands. Feel your feet like roots in the ground. Take a deep breath and come up on your tip toes. Breathe out and come down on your heels. This time, stretch your branches up high. Breathe in, up on your toes; breathe out, down on your heels.

Points to Remember: For some children, lifting the heels is unnerving or even frightening. Use visual props to provide a point of focus and a wall for support. Emphasize the downward movement for toe walkers, increasing time to walk or stand on the full foot after briefly coming up on the toes. Create a lesson about tree sizes, shapes, and names.

Variations: If maintaining balance is a challenge, try these variations: While standing, keep the palms together in Tree Hands, or lift the arms only without the heel lift. If seated in a chair, the child may lift and lower his heels and arms. From a position on the ground seated on his heels, the child lifts up onto his knees for Tall Tree.

Precautions: Avoid with children who have injury to the shoulders, hips, legs, ankles, or feet; neck instability; vision problems; or extreme vestibular challenges.

Counterpose: Rag Doll, Shake It Out

Sequencing: Works well with Willow Tree, Tree Breathing

15-61   Tall Tree

49. WARRIOR 1

Starting Position: Standing

Benefits: Energizing, increases physical and mental stamina; pelvic stability; builds self-esteem; creative play

Instructions for the Child: You are a warrior standing guard outside of a grand castle. Be ready for any challenge that may come your way. Stand at the back of your mat. Take a giant step forward with your right foot, and stretch both arms up high. Can you see any danger ahead? Bend your right knee so you can see even farther. You are strong!

Points to Remember: This is a very challenging posture because so many parts of the body are moving in different ways: one leg straight, one bent;

15-62   Warrior 1

back foot grounded; arms overhead without leaning forward or hiking up the shoulders. For many children, this is just too much detail. Keep your emphasis on the fun of the warrior's quest in this posture. "When in your day do you need to stand like a warrior?" Work alongside the child to provide support.

Variations: From a chair, the child sits sideways with one foot forward, knee bent, and the back leg straight behind. Keep the palms facing inward to maintain inner focus. Or use Tree Hands to relax the shoulders. Warrior 1 walking strengthens knees and thighs: With Tree Hands, children march around the room, taking giant steps forward into Warrior 1.

Precautions: Use a chair for low-toned children. Avoid with shoulder, neck, back, hip, or leg injury. Assist children with balance challenges.

Counterpose: Shake It Out, Rag Doll

Sequencing: Works well with Warrior 2, Tree

50. WARRIOR LUNGE

Starting Position: Warrior 1; Table

Benefits: Energizing; pelvic flexibility

Instructions for the Child: From Warrior 1, lower your fingertips or palms down to the floor near your front foot, bringing your chest toward your thigh. Feel the big stretch in your back leg. Lower your back knee in Half Table. Press your toes into the floor.

Points to Remember: Like Warrior 1, this takes great strength and even more flexibility. If the child cannot balance or the stretch is too great, have her bring the back foot closer to her hands. Partially straighten the front knee.

Variations: Children may find it easier to step forward into the Warrior Lunge from Table. For Warrior Lunge backward, take a giant step back with the right foot. Lower the hands to the floor near the left foot.

15-63   Warrior Lunge

Precautions: Avoid with shoulder, wrist, neck, back, hip, or leg injury. Assist children with balance challenges.

Counterpose: Shake It Out, Rag Doll

Sequencing: Works well with Warrior 1, Stretching Dog, Rag Doll; useful transitional posture in flows

51. WARRIOR 2

Starting Position: Standing

Benefits: Energizing; hip flexibility, stability; builds self-esteem

Instructions for the Child: You are a brave warrior searching the seas for invading ships. Stand with your legs wide apart. Stretch your arms out wide. With your chest and hips facing front, turn the toes of both feet toward the right. Turn your head to look right. Bend your right knee so you can see farther out to sea. You are strong and fearless.

Points to Remember: Combines strength, balance, and flexibility. Use cues to identify right and left. You may make this a playful posture. "What do you see out in the water? What actions shall we take?"

15-64   Warrior 2

Variations: Combine with a history lesson on war or warriors. From a chair, sit on the edge of the seat with arms and legs out to the sides, one knee bent and the other leg straight.

Precautions: For standing challenges, sit on the floor with legs apart and arms out to the sides. Avoid if the complexities of the posture frustrate the child.

Counterpose: Shake It Out, Rag Doll

Sequencing: Works well with Triangle, Half Moon

52. TRIANGLE

Starting Position: Standing

Benefits: Lateral stretch, pelvic stability, flexibility

Instructions for the Child: Stand with your legs apart and your arms open wide. Turn both feet to the right, but keep your body facing front as in Warrior 2. Lower your right hand toward your right knee and reach up high with your left. Your feet and hips form a triangle, like a great pyramid. Pyramids have stood for thousands of years. Do you feel strong and steady in this triangle shape?

Points to Remember: The upper arm provides the lift and helps support the back. Use a wall or your own body for support behind the child. Holding his head level relieves neck strain and improves balance.

Variations: If separating the feet destabilizes the child, narrow the stance. The child can practice positioning the feet while seated on the edge of a chair. Keeping the back foot perpendicular may mitigate balance challenges.

Precautions: Support children with balance and gravitational insecurities. Avoid with neck instabil-

15-65   Triangle

ity or injury; with leg, back, or shoulder injuries. Don't let the head hang.

Counterpose: Shake It Out

Sequencing: Works well with Warrior 2

53. HALF MOON

Starting Position: Standing; seated

Benefits: Lateral flexion; creative play; language skills

Instructions for the Child: The moon changes shape throughout the month, from full to slight. Let's make our bodies into the shape of a half moon. Standing straight and tall, reach up with both arms. Lean your whole body right. Then lean left.

Points to Remember: If you are teaching directionality, use right and left cues and mirror the child. To ease tension in shoulders and neck, children may keep their arms at their sides, or lift the right arm only to lean left, and reverse.

15-66   Half Moon

Variations: Standing with her back against a wall, a child is less likely to rotate her spine or exaggerate a convexity from scoliosis. Guide a child with a right thoracic scoliosis to "bend from the right ribs" when leaning right. This stretches the compressed ribs on her left side. Before leaning to the left, help her "shift her hips to the right" (Miller, 2003) to lengthen both sides of her back equally.

Precautions: Avoid with neck or shoulder injuries or instability. Do the pose seated with low tone or vestibular challenges.

Counterpose: Tree Hands, Rag Doll

Sequencing: Works well with Standing Twister, Willow Tree, Fruit Picking

54. WILLOW TREE UPWARD/WILLOW TREE BACKBEND

Starting Position: Standing

Benefits: Spinal extension, shoulder and arm flexibility and strength; creative play; energizing, breathing; motor planning

Instructions for the Child: Willow trees have long branches that sweep up and back. Stretch your arms way up high, reaching your branches toward the sun. Can you touch the sky? This is upward willow tree. A big wind starts to blow your branches backward. Breathe in as you lean back into the wind in willow tree backbend. Breathe out and float your arms down.

Points to Remember: Keep the child's head in line with the neck. Avoid overly arching the cervical or lumbar spine. Many children lack the flexibility in the shoulders and upper back for the full backbend. Have them reach up high,

15-67   Willow Tree Upward

15-68   Willow Tree Backbend

arms close to their ears, palms facing in. To avoid hiked up shoulders, bend the elbows or drop the arms.

Variations: For some children, backbending creates anxiety, especially without support. Use supine backbends instead. If standing is a challenge, have the child do this posture seated.

Precautions: Avoid with shoulder, neck, back, or spine injuries or instability. To minimize swayback posture, use Willow Tree Upward.

Counterpose: Shake It Out, Rag Doll

Sequencing: Works well with Tall Tree, Rag Doll, Half Moon

55. RAG DOLL (STANDING INVERSION)

Starting Position: Standing

Benefits: Stretches the back, shoulders, arms and legs; stress relief, mindfulness, self-regulation; creative play

Instructions for the Child: Now it's time to let all the effort go. Take a deep breath in; breathing out, hang your arms down toward the ground, like a rag doll. If it feels good, let your head and upper body hang down, too. Sway to the right and sway to the left.

Points to Remember: Keeping the knees slightly bent may prevent hyperextension in the knees or increased tension in the upper back. To keep the pelvis relaxed, shift the weight from foot to foot in the swaying position. If a child has vestibular challenges, use a chair or wall.

Variations: Place a bolster or blocks under the child's head or hands so she will feel grounded in the position. Seated Folded Leaf with full release in the upper body has many of the same benefits of the pose.

Precautions: This is an inversion. See contraindications, p. 170.

Counterpose: Shake It Out, Tree Breathing

Sequencing: Works well with Tall Tree, Half Moon, Willow Tree

15-69   Rag Doll

15-70   Fruit Picking

56. FRUIT PICKING

Starting Position: Standing or seated

Benefits: Flexibility; creative play; language skills, social interaction; cross patterning

Instructions for the Child: What's your favorite fruit? Stretch up high to pick five apples from the top of the tree. Reach to each side to pick two ripe bananas. Stretch down low to pick six strawberries. Let's eat up our fruit!

Points to Remember: This posture offers many opportunities for learning. Children identify fruits by name and where they grow. You can add questions about how the fruit tastes, its color and size. Children count with you while picking fruit. They stretch their limbs and spine in all directions.

Variations: Fruit can be picked from a chair or a seat on the floor, stretching the spine and shoulders. Children may lead the pose, selecting a fruit, location (high, low), and how many to pick. Make fruit jam by stomping (running in place) on your fruit, and then make a jam sandwich (see Sandwich pose).

Precautions: Avoid with spinal or shoulder limitations.

Counterpose: Shake It Out, Willow Tree Backbend

Sequencing: Works well with Tree Hands, Tall Tree, Sandwich

57. SHAKE IT OUT

Starting Position: Standing or seated

Benefits: Stress relief; energizing; creative play, language skills

Instructions for the Child: Shake out all the tension from your arms and legs, your fingers and toes. Shake it out, shake it out, shake it out!

Points to Remember: Model this pose by hopping up and down or shifting the weight from foot to foot as if running in place. This is a favorite of many children, triggering participation, smiles, and laughter. The simple refrain is easily repeated. For children who are very active, make this a vigorous pose, used at frequent intervals. To quiet things down, wait to use this pose after a series of standing postures. To motivate or reengage a child, let her know that she'll have one more posture before Shake It Out.

Variations: Shake out the arms and legs while remaining seated on the ground or in a chair. This pose can be used as a transitional tool after very stimulating activities. Signal quiet with Tree Hands to conclude the pose.

Precautions: Very active children may fling arms and legs dangerously in this pose. Maintain a safe distance between children. Avoid with a child who has joint instability or extreme ligament laxity.

Counterpose: Tree Hands, Rag Doll

Sequencing: Works well after any standing posture

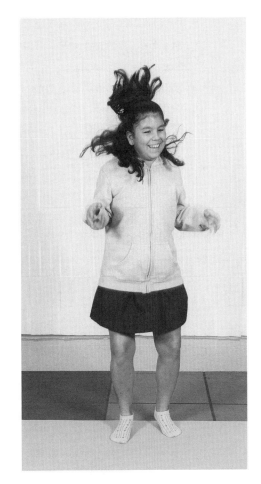

15-71   Shake it Out

Final Relaxation—Your Special Place

Ideally, the child will experience slower respiration and inner contemplation during this quiet period. But the most important element of this posture is experiencing comfort. Help each child find a position where he or she can truly relax for a moment.

58. FLOATING ON A CLOUD

Starting Position: Supine

Benefits: Relaxation, mindfulness

Instructions for the Child: See script for Floating on a Cloud in Chapter 18.

Points to Remember: Some children will deepen their relaxation with eye bags or by draping their arms across their brows to shut out the light and increase ocular pressure. They may use a pillow or their arms beneath their head. Conclude the relaxation before children become fidgety. For some it will last just a moment; for others, this posture may last 5–10 minutes, as long as you have their attention.

Variations: Some children are anxious about closing their eyes. Suggest they focus their eyes on a spot on the ceiling. If resting on the back is not comfortable, help the child find an alternative position, as in the photo.

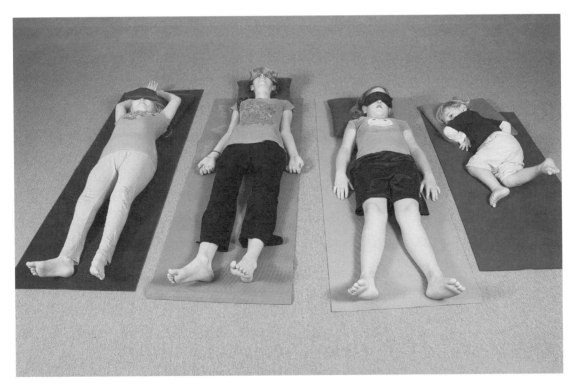

15-72   Floating on a Cloud

Precautions: Very high toned or anxious children may use pillows beneath their heads and knees to keep their bodies partially flexed.

59. MINDFUL PRACTICE: SHARING THOUGHTS

Starting Position: Seated on floor or chair

Benefits: Mindfulness, connection with others, self-calming

Instructions: Bring your hands to your heart for Namaste. Send a kind thought to a friend. [Pause]. Your light and my light are one. Take a deep breath in. Breathe out and say, "Namaste." (See script for mindfulness practice, Chapter 18.)

Points to Remember: You may suggest a caring thought. Children can name someone they like or are thinking about: "Get better, Grandma." Or make the caring thoughts general: "Sending a smile." Take this time to convey a loving thought of your own to the child.

15-73 Mindful Practice   Namaste

15-74   Mindful Practice

Variations: If you are in a public school or institution, you may end with hands on knees to turn inward. Ask the children to send a kind thought to someone special. Or suggest they plant an imaginary garden with seeds of love, friendship, laughter.

60. HUH

End each session with three huh breaths, just as you began, and a big smile!

15-75   Huh breath and Smile

CHAPTER 16

YOGA THERAPY FOR CLASSROOMS AND SCHOOLS

TEACHING YOGA THERAPY in a school presents special challenges. The stresses, noise, and demands of a school environment can be tempered by energizing or calming postures and breathing exercises. Whether children are sitting on the floor or at a desk, standing in a line, or preparing for high-stakes tests, yoga therapy fits easily into their day.

Throughout this book you have encountered examples of the effective use of yoga therapy in classrooms. Still, there are several special considerations when implementing it into a school setting. These also apply to libraries, hospitals, churches, temples, community camps, or other public institutions.

Once you have adjusted to these few differences, yoga therapy in school can be taught just as in any other program. If you have the space to clear a corner of your classroom or an empty area somewhere else in the school, you may use any of the postures and lessons presented in this book. (See Chapter 10 for suggestions about creating a sacred space.)

Working Within Your Space

When teaching in a classroom or office, your room may not be suited for a full yoga practice. You will find lessons below that can be done either seated at or standing by the children's desks, without reorganizing your classroom. The posture catalog and many of the lessons in the following chapters include adaptations for small spaces.

If the school floor is hard, provide adequate cushioning. Otherwise, adjust the routine to exclude postures that put excessive weight on the neck, spine, hips, knees, pelvis, or chest. Most seated and standing postures can be done on any surface, as can the breathing routines and many of the flows and activities you will find in Chapters 19–20.

Public Schools and Spiritual Practices

Yoga is *not* a religion. It is practiced by people of all faiths and philosophies. The effectiveness of yoga therapy is not dependent upon chants or prayers. Its emphasis on posture and breath to enhance mindful focus makes it especially useful for children in schools. "More than 250 medical centers worldwide now offer mindfulness-based therapies for mood and other disorders. . . . Mindfulness training works, at least in part, by strengthening the brain's ability to pay attention" (Jha, 2013, p. 28).

In the United States, public schools maintain the separation of church and state. For this reason, I do not recommend chanting "OM" or any other Sanskrit words or prayers; alternative sounds are listed in the final chapter that can be used for calming. You have probably noticed the absence of Sanskrit names for postures in this book. Identifying poses with animals and objects from daily life makes them easier for children to remember and eliminates unnecessary concerns among school staff and families. Using common names demystifies yoga.

Teaching the philosophy of yoga is not advisable in public schools. But this does not mean that you leave it at home when you enter a school. You can adhere to these principles in your own demeanor and your standards for students' behavior. Creating an atmosphere of cooperation and acceptance enhances learning and builds connections among children; this is a sensible educational philosophy.

Permission and Touch

Because of issues regarding touch, it's especially important to send home permission slips for parents to sign that stipulate that you will be touching and assisting children into positions. I do not recommend partnering children for massage in public school classes, although you may give massage to children while they rest in Baby pose with parental and the child's permission. Here, as previously discussed, is an excellent opportunity to teach children that they have the authority to refuse touch at any time. It behooves adults to empower children to say no to touch, as well as to invite appropriate touch.

Implementing a Program

Yoga therapy may be implemented by yoga therapists, classroom teachers, exceptional student educators, autism specialists, school psychologists, physical or occupational therapists, behavior specialists or counselors, PE teachers, or other trained staff members or parents. You can start with one class, one school, or an entire district. An advantage of working in schools is the access you have to staff who know the children and their individual needs.

Appendix 3 outlines a simple model for the development and assessment of a yoga therapy program in your school. It is often beneficial to set up one or two model classrooms in each school so that faculty can observe and be trained on site, once they have the curriculum materials needed to carry on the program.

Lessons Adapted For Classrooms

You may use postures and routines between other activities in your day, without adjusting your classroom arrangement. Follow the entire sequence or select one or two postures to use as yoga breaks throughout your day.

In addition to the routines below, you will find abbreviated lessons, more seated and standing sequences, and transitional postures for classroom use in Chapters 18–20.

POSTURES ROUTINE SEATED IN A CHAIR

Many of the floor postures can be adapted to chairs. Work the arms and upper body in these poses:

1. Huh Breath
2. Elbow Circles
3. Bellows Breath
4. Tense And Relax
5. Butterfly Hands
6. Finger Stretch
7. Pretzel (neck rotations or full twist)
8. Happy Cat (hands on knees, stretch chest through arms, look up)
9. Angry Cat (hands on knees, round back, tuck chin)
10. Volcano seated (scrunch up in seat, rumble, throw arms up for erupting volcano)
11. Airplane with arms out to sides (follow with Butterfly Hands)
12. Half Fish
13. Folded Leaf
14. Tree Hands
15. Tree Breathing
16. Half Moon
17. Fruit Picking
18. Shake It Out
19. Butterfly Meditation
20. Mindful Practice
21. Floating on a Cloud (seated progressive muscle relaxation)

STANDING POSTURES FOR SMALL SPACES

How much time do children spend standing in lines? Imagine if, instead of just waiting to leave a room or begin an activity, they practiced yoga therapy. What a difference their experience would be!

The following standing postures can be performed by children standing by their desks or in a room with limited space:

1. Huh Breath
2. Elbows Circles

3. Tense and Relax

4. Bellows Breath

5. Butterfly Hands

6. Finger Stretch

7. Twister

8. Volcano

9. Neck Rotations

10. Tree Hands

11. Tree Breathing

12. Tall Tree

13. Half Moon

14. Willow Tree Upward /Backbend

15. Rag Doll

16. Fruit Picking—all directions

17. Shake It Out

18. Mindful Practice

Yoga Therapy After Lunch

It's best to practice postures before lunch or an hour after eating. Sometimes school schedules rotate, however, requiring yoga directly after lunch. In such cases, avoid inversions and postures with abdominal pressure. Here's a suggested lesson:

Posture Routine for After Lunch

1. Huh Breath

2. Yoga singing—chanting vowel sounds, words

3. Soft Belly Breaths

4. Elbow Circles

5. Seated Circles

6. Bellows Breath

7. Tense and Relax

8. Finger Stretch

9. Butterfly Hands

10. Butterfly Meditation

11. Pretzel (neck rotations only)

12. Tree Hands
13. Tree Breathing
14. Tree Balance
15. Fruit Picking (no hanging down)
16. Floating on a Cloud
17. Mindful Practice
18. Huh Breath

GUIDED RELAXATION AFTER LUNCH

One teacher of fourth- and fifth-graders on the autism spectrum has a revolving schedule. On the days that yoga therapy falls directly after lunch, she uses a CD with my voice guiding children through Belly Breathing and Floating on a Cloud. I observed one day and saw seven children arrive from lunch at full volume. Pressed into a very small space, they quickly lay down on their mats. Within two minutes, every child was engaged, with the exception of the occasional poking of one's neighbor.

By the end of the 8-minute session, all but one child appeared serene and calm. Even the agitated child remained on his mat. Upon the completion of relaxation, the children moved in an orderly fashion to their first afternoon activity. I was full of praise, but the teacher was disappointed. She explained that most days every child in the group had fully settled down by the end of the relaxation session.

Test Anxiety

Students today are inundated with tests. Taking or anticipating tests may cause a wide range of physical symptoms, from nausea, heart palpitations, and shortness of breath to full-blown panic attacks.

Children who are easily distracted or who lack confidence in their ability to succeed are especially vulnerable. The University of Texas at Dallas Counseling Center (2012) suggests reducing test anxiety by learning how to relax, something that is most effectively practiced before test taking.

The Anxiety and Depression Association of America (2012) recommends slow deep breathing and progressive muscle relaxation to combat stress during tests and to improve focus during exams. This, of course, is exactly what we teach in yoga therapy for children.

Observing the increased levels of stress as test days approached during my son's early years in school, I began teaching relaxation techniques to his class. The program expanded into several schools. Some schools used a voice recording of the relaxation exercises. At others, we videotaped a small group of children doing the series. The audio or video was used each morning for two weeks before high-stake tests, with students participating with their teachers in their own classrooms.

Many teachers observed their students using the calming techniques independently on test days. Parents noted the easing of anxiety levels for some children. These anecdotal data speak to the need for further research on the impact of yoga-based relaxation techniques for easing test anxiety.

CREATIVE RELAXATION: EASING TEST ANXIETY

The following sequences have been used successfully with regular education and special-needs students from elementary school through college for easing test anxiety. The program includes scripts to read to the students prior to and following testing, in addition to movement routines to implement on test days.

If possible, guide children through the exercises during test preparatory activities. By generalizing the relaxation techniques in the context of test taking, they are more likely to implement the methods independently prior to and during the testing situation. Begin practice at least two weeks prior to the tests for general education and six weeks before for exceptional education students.

Before Test: Mental Rehearsal

In your imagination, pretend you are watching yourself on TV. Picture yourself going to school on the day of the test. Notice that you walk calmly down the hall and into your classroom to take your seat. Your breathing is easy, flowing in and out through your nose. You take a few deep breaths while waiting for the testing to begin. Scanning your jaws, forehead, neck, and fingers, you tense and then relax these muscles. You breathe deeply into those places.

Once you begin the test, notice that your breathing remains even and steady. The muscles in your face, shoulders, and fingers feel loose. You feel awake, alert, and comfortable. You work through the entire test calmly, confidently, knowing that you are doing the best you can.

After the test, you take a few deep breaths and let go all concerns about the test. You imagine the best outcome. You are ready to go home and have some fun!

During Test: Calming Tools

Remain quiet, without disturbing your neighbor. If your mind starts to wander or you feel anxious, do one of these techniques for a count of three seconds. Then return immediately to your work:

1. Mentally suggest that you are calm and relaxed; you are prepared to do well
2. Silent Huh
3. Posture check—feet on floor, back straight, belly relaxed
4. Am I breathing? Soft belly breaths
5. Shoulder Circles without hands
6. Finger Stretch—interlace fingers and turn the palms out, keeping hands in lap
7. Gently press bones around eyes
8. Smooth out eyebrows and forehead
9. Open chest by leaning into the back of the chair—no arms for this one
10. Wiggle feet and toes

Between Tests: Shake It Out!

STANDING IF POSSIBLE:

1. Half Moon: lean right, lean left
2. Finger Stretch: forward and overhead
3. Warrior 2 arms: stretch arms to sides
4. Twister
5. Shake It Out: especially fingers, hands, wrists and arms
6. Tree Breathing

FROM SEAT:

1. Folded Leaf: Hang Low
2. Half Fish with arms around back of chair
3. Bellows Breath
4. Pretzel
5. Neck Rotations
6. Massage face, neck, shoulders

7. Palm eyes: rub palms together until warm; cup them over eyes to shut out all light
8. Tense and relax arms and hands
9. Tense and relax legs and feet
10. Tense and relax face: yawn and stretch face; relax face

After Test: What's Done Is Done!

1. Shake It Out.
2. Visualize the best outcome.
3. Whenever you think about the test, take a Huh Breath. Remind yourself that you have done all you can for now.
4. Go home and take a brisk walk or jog around the neighborhood.

Relaxation Routine for School

This routine combines breathing, posture, and self-massage. It is effective for stress relief in classrooms before tests or for relaxation breaks. This sequence may also be used to begin or end any therapeutic session.

Begin with a reminder not to do anything that hurts or feels uncomfortable. Use this lesson in full or select exercises from within the categories, depending on the time available and needs and attention of the child.

Huh Breath
(Repeat three times. This is the only breath through the mouth.)

Breathing
All through the nose:
- Belly Breaths—if not breathing this way, a good gauge of tension.
- Power breath—imagine the breath coming in through the soles of the feet and traveling up through the legs, up the torso, through the face, up to the top of the head. Exhale fully with breath moving out like electrical sparks, energizing your whole body.
- Centering breath—Count to three as you inhale. Count to three as you exhale. Make a positive statement, such as "feeling calm."

Tired Hands

- Fling fingers (squeeze fists and then "throw" fingers) five to ten times fast
- Finger Stretch
- Rotate wrists
- Finger gymnastics: Starting with middle finger over index finger, cross each finger over the next. Then open hands wide, separating fingers. Rotate each finger; reverse
- Hand massage (guide children through simple routine to relax hands)

Pain in the Neck

- Rotate head with the breath—inhale right, exhale left. Inhale, look up (do not drop head back), exhale, look down.
- Hold the scruff of the neck (where a cat holds her kittens) and gently nod "yes"; gently shake "no" (Bertherat & Bernstein, 1977).
- Elevate the right shoulder. Grasp the right trapezius muscle with the left hand and let the shoulder gently drop. Allow the head to lean ever so slightly to the left. Release. Repeat on opposite side.
- Circle shoulders. Reverse.

Facing It

(For headaches, eyestrain, sinus pressure)
- Sinus points— apply gentle pressure with flats of fingers to smooth out eyebrows.
- Eye exercises—move the eyes in each direction four times with rests in between: up and down; right and left; diagonal upper right, diagonal lower left; reverse diagonal.
- Palming eyes—rub the palms together. Cup the warm palms over the closed eyes to block out all the light. Breathe.
- Jaw points—gently press fingers into temples and around jaw.
- Smooth out forehead.

Wet Noodle

- Progressive muscle relaxation

Huh Breath (three)

CHAPTER 17

CURRICULUM FOR YOGA THERAPY: CHALLENGES AND CAPABILITIES

THE LESSONS BELOW are designed to create a sequential approach to instruction. Each routine adds more challenging poses and complex sequences, while repeating some favorites as well as counterposes for continuity and comfort. These lessons may be augmented with routines, songs, and games from Chapters 18–20.

After assessing the child (Appendix 2, Part III), begin yoga therapy with Level 1. If this level is too elementary, choose Level 2 or any subsequent level. Remain on each level as long as is useful. You may use the complete routine, several postures from each starting position, or all the poses from one starting position. Work with those starting positions that the child can perform comfortably.

Keep the basic structure for lessons and then add and subtract. For example, if the child has mastered the seated postures from Level 1, introduce seated postures from Level 2 while continuing to work with the other Level 1 postures. You may also select postures from other categories that have been adapted as seated poses. Drop back down a level if advancing creates too great a challenge.

You may introduce free choice or questions at the end of lessons at any time.

If the child participates as directed, let him know that you will save time for one posture request or question of his choice. Postponing requests develops impulse control and rewards children for appropriate choices. This system mitigates the child's disappointment when you omit or alter familiar poses.

Repeat several of the child's favorites and at least one challenging posture in each routine. On days when a child is struggling or inattentive, avoid new or difficult poses; choose an abbreviated or familiar routine. If the child is uncomfortable supine, he can float on a cloud in Baby pose, on his side, or seated.

Level 1 Posture Routine
SEATED
1. Huh Breath
2. Seated Circles
3. Butterfly Hands
4. Folded Leaf prep: legs straight

HANDS AND KNEES
5. Table
6. Happy Cat

PRONE
7. Snake, elbows bent
8. Airplane prep: arms by sides, knees bent

SUPINE
9. Knee Hugs
10. Drawbridge prep: knees bent, feet on floor

STANDING
11. Tree hands
12. Shake It Out

RELAXATION
13. Floating on a Cloud: A child may spend just a few moments getting onto his back before repositioning onto his side or into Baby pose—any posture that feels restful and safe. Keep cloud brief, 1–2 minutes or less.

SEATED

14. Huh Breath

Level 2 Posture Routine

SEATED

1. Huh Breath
2. Seated Circles
3. Butterfly Knees
4. Finger Stretch
5. Tense and Relax
6. Butterfly Hands

HANDS AND KNEES

7. Table
8. Happy Cat
9. Angry Cat

PRONE

10. Snake, elbows bent
11. Superman prep: wiggle fingers and toes
12. Airplane prep: arms straight at side, knees straight

SUPINE

13. Drawbridge prep: ground feet
14. Neck Rolls
15. Knee Hugs

STANDING

16. Tree Hands
17. Tree Breathing
18. Willow Tree Upward
19. Shake It Out

RELAXATION

20. Floating on a Cloud: very brief in any comfortable variation

SEATED

21. Huh Breath

Level 3 Posture Routine

SEATED

  1. Huh Breath

  2. Seated Circles

  3. Back-to-Back Breathing

  4. Folded Leaf prep: legs straight, arms reaching up

  5. Rock the Baby prep: hold foot or leg

HANDS AND KNEES

  6. Table

  7. Balance Beam prep: straighten one leg, toes on ground; then other

  8. Happy Cat

  9. Angry Cat

PRONE

10. Bent Elbow Snake

 11. Airplane prep: Lift one arm only, then other

12. Airplane prep: Lift one leg only, then other

SUPINE

13. Drawbridge prep: hands and feet grounded

14. Rocking Chair with assist

15. Neck Rolls

16. Knee Hugs

STANDING

 17. Tree Hands

18. Half Moon: with Tree Hands

19. Fruit Picking

20. Shake It Out

 21. Free choice/questions: one question or posture request for each child

RELAXATION

22. Floating on a Cloud—very brief

SEATED

23. Huh Breath

Level 4 Posture Routine

SEATED

1. Huh Breath

2. Seated Circles

3. Bellows Breath

4. Butterfly Hands

5. Pretzel prep: sit cross-legged, rotate head only

6. Rock the Baby

7. Folded Leaf

HANDS AND KNEES

8. Table

9. Happy Cat

10. Angry Cat

11. Stretching Dog prep: grounding hands and feet

12. Baby

13. Hi, World

PRONE

14. Bent Elbow Snake

15. Half Superman with assist—head and each arm

16. Baby

SUPINE

17. Rocking Chair

18. Candle prep: single leg lifts

19. Drawbridge: position feet and hands, assisted hip lifts

20. Knee Hugs

STANDING

21. Tree Hands

22. Tree Breathing

23. Tall Tree with assist

24. Fruit Picking, high, to sides, low

25. Shake It Out

26. Free choice/questions

RELAXATION

27. Floating on a Cloud

SEATED

28. Huh Breath

Level 5 Posture Routine

SEATED

1. Huh Breath

2. Seated Circles

3. Butterfly Knees fast and slow

4. Elbow Circles

5. Butterfly Hands

6. Twister

7. Rock the Baby

8. Folded Leaf

HANDS AND KNEES

9. Table

10. Stretching Dog with assist

PRONE

11. Snake

12. Airplane arms and legs

13. Baby

SUPINE

14. Rocking Chair

15. Candle: rock up; light the candle

16. Drawbridge

17. Bug on Its Back

18. Knee Hugs

STANDING

19. Tree Breathing

20. Tall Tree

21. Half Moon

22. Rag Doll

23. Shake It Out
24. Fruit Picking

SEATED

25. Sandwich
26. Free choice/questions

RELAXATION

27. Floating on a Cloud: begin to lengthen time, encourage students to assume pose on back. Curl up on their sides at the end

SEATED

28. Sharing thoughts
29. Huh breath

Level 6 Posture Routine

SEATED

1. Huh Breath
2. Seated Circles
3. Butterfly Knees
4. Tense and Relax
5. Butterfly Hands
6. Pretzel
7. Rock the Baby
8. Folded Leaf

HANDS AND KNEES

9. Table
10. Frog
11. Stretching Dog
12. Snake
13. Baby

PRONE

14. Half Superman
15. Airplane
16. Baby

SUPINE
17. Rocking Chair
18. Candle—light the candle
19. Half Fish
20. Crab
21. Bug on Its Back
22. Supine Twist

STANDING
23. Tree Balance
24. Warrior 1
25. Half Moon
26. Willow Tree Backbend (or Upward)
27. Rag Doll
28. Shake It Out
29. Fruit Picking

SEATED
30. Sandwich
31. Free choice/questions

RELAXATION
32. Floating on a Cloud

SEATED
33. Sharing Thoughts
34. Huh Breath

Level 7 Posture Routine
SEATED
1. Huh Breath
2. Seated Circles
3. Bellows Breath
4. Tense and Relax
5. Butterfly Hands
6. Rock the Baby

7. Twister

8. Seesaw

9. Lounge Chair

HANDS AND KNEES

10. Table

11. Stretching Dog

12. Snake

13. Stretching Dog to Snake; repeat

14. Balance Beam—one arm, then other

15. Baby

PRONE

16. Airplane

17. Superman

18. Baby

19. Hi, World!

SUPINE

20. Drawbridge

21. Wall Candle

22. Wall Butterfly

23. Bug on Its Back

24. Knee Hugs

STANDING

25. Partner Tree

26. Warrior 2

27. Triangle

28. Shake It Out

29. Fruit Picking

SEATED

30. Sandwich

31. Free choice/questions

RELAXATION

32. Floating on a Cloud

SEATED

33. Mindful Practice
34. Huh Breath

Level 8 Posture Routine
SEATED

1. Huh Breath
2. Seated Circles
3. Butterfly Knees
4. Sandwich
5. Bellows Breath
6. Tense and Relax
7. Butterfly Hands
8. Seesaw
9. Flying Bats

HANDS AND KNEES

10. Table
11. Balance Beam: one leg, other
12. Happy Cat
13. Angry Cat
14. Stretching Dog to Snake to Dog
15. Walking Dog
16. Baby

PRONE

17. Airplane
18. Half Superman
19. Superman
20. Baby

SUPINE

21. Walking Crab
22. Wall Candle and Wall X
23. Half Fish
24. Drawbridge
25. Bug on Its Back
26. Supine Twist

STANDING
27. Willow Tree Backbend
28. Rag Doll
29. Warrior 2
30. Triangle
31. Shake It Out
32. Free choice/questions

RELAXATION
33. Floating on a Cloud

SEATED
34. Sharing thoughts
35. Huh Breath

Level 9 Posture Routine
SEATED
 1. Huh Breath
 2. Seated Circles
 3. Slow Butterflies
 4. Sandwich
 5. Finger Stretch
 6. Tense and Relax
 7. Seesaw
 8. Flying Bats
 9. Rock the Baby
10. Folded Leaf
11. Frog
12. Volcano

HANDS AND KNEES
13. Table
14. Happy Cat
15. Angry Cat
16. Balance Beam
17. Stretching Dog
18. Snake (Stretching Dog to Snake, 3–4 fast repetitions)
19. Baby

PRONE
20. Half Superman
21. Airplane
22. Superman
23. Baby

SUPINE
24. Walking Crab
25. Rocking chair
26. Candle—light the candle
27. Half Fish
28. Drawbridge
29. Bug on Its Back
30. Supine Twist

STANDING
31. Partner Tree
32. Warrior 1
33. Warrior Lunge
34. Warrior 2
35. Triangle
36. Half Moon
37. Willow Tree Backbend
38. Rag Doll
39. Shake It Out
40. Fruit Picking

SEATED
41. Sandwich
42. Free choice/questions

RELAXATION
43. Floating on a Cloud

SEATED
44. Mindful Practice
45. Huh Breath

CHAPTER 18

POSTURES AND LESSONS FOR SPECIFIC BENEFITS

THE FIRST PART of this chapter organizes postures according to their benefits. The second portion provides lesson plans and routines categorized by purpose and duration.

Postures to Deepen and Regulate Breathing

You will find more about breathing in Chapter 19.

Yoga Singing (see Chapter 20)	Back-to-Back Breathing
Huh Breath	Lawn Chair
Belly Breaths	Seated Half Fish
Blowing Bubbles	Folded Leaf
Bee Breath	Happy Cat
Cooling Breath	Snake
Slow Butterfly	Tree Breathing
Bellows Breath	Cloud

Postures for Balance

Sandwich with feet lifted

Seated Egg with feet lifted

Rock the Baby

Seesaw

Seated Bats

Stretching Dog

Rocking Chair

Candle

Frog

Table

Balance Beam

Tree Breathing

Tree Balance

Partner Tree

Tall Tree

Warrior 1

Warrior Lunge

Triangle

Half Moon

Willow Tree Backbend

Postures for Tension Release

Elbow Circles

Seated Circles

Tense and Relax

Butterfly Hands

Twister

Baby

Crown pose

Wall Candle

Half Fish

Knee Hugs

Supine Twist

Bug on Its Back

Rag Doll

Shake It Out

Neck Rolls

Postures for Flexibility

Note: Strength in one area of the body often requires flexibility in the opposing set of muscles. Thus, many of the exercises fall into both the strength and flexibility categories.

Seated Circles

Butterfly Knees

Elbow Circles

Rock the Baby

Finger Stretch

Bellows Breath

Pretzel

Twister

Seesaw

Folded Leaf

Frog

Happy Cat

Angry Cat

Drawbridge

Supine Twist

Rocking Chair

Wall Candle

Stretching Dog

Snake

Bug on Its Back

Half Moon

Willow Tree Upward

Rag Doll

Fruit Picking

Shake It Out

Sandwich

Postures for Strength

Flying Bats

Table

Balance Beam

Crab

Drawbridge

Rocking Chair

Candle

Half Fish

Stretching Dog

Walking Dog

Crown pose

Snake

Airplane

Half Superman

Superman

Volcano

Tree Balance

Half Moon

Warrior Lunge

Warrior 1

Warrior 2

Willow Tree Backbend

Postures for Vagal Stimulation

Seated Circles

Bellows Breath

Folded Leaf

Seated Egg

Twister

Rock the Baby

Seesaw

Lawn Chair

Stretching Dog

Crown pose

Crab

Drawbridge

Rocking Chair

Candle

Wall Candle and variations

Knee Hugs

Supine Twists

Tree Breathing

Rag Doll

Floating on a Cloud

Breathing routines (see Chapter 19)

Postures for Sensory Processing Skills

Motor skills, including proprioception, bilateral movements, balance, and motor planning, are often challenging for children with ASD and other special needs. Yoga therapy addresses many of these challenges while triggering the imagination, improving imitation skills, and fostering creative play.

PROPRIOCEPTION

Proprioception is experienced through the muscles, tendons, and joints.

SUGGESTED POSES:

1. Pushing and pulling: Seesaw
2. Extension with traction: Half Superman, Superman, Airplane, Snake
3. Flexion with compression: Seated Egg, Baby, Candle, Sandwich
4. Deep flexion and extension: Drawbridge
5. Strength in standing: Warrior 1, Warrior 2, Triangle, Half Moon, Willow Tree
6. Weight of body against ground: Stretching Dog, Walking Dog, Table

MOTOR PLANNING

Motor planning involves organizing body movements in a specific sequence. Imitating animals by crawling, sliding, squatting and hopping and "Simon Says"-type games promote motor planning.

SUGGESTED POSES:

1. Crawling on hands and knees in Cat
2. Walking inverted in Crab
3. Sliding on belly in Snake
4. Squatting in Frog
5. Hopping in Frog
6. Walking Dog
7. Follow the Leader Games
    a. Yoga Freeze
    b. Follow Me
8. Bilateral movements

BILATERAL COORDINATION

Bilateral coordination is required to use both sides of the body in an action. You may start with arm work first before combining arm and leg movements.

SUGGESTED POSES:

 1. Butterfly Hands
 2. Rock the Baby
 3. Twister
 4. Pretzel
 5. Folded Leaf
 6. Warrior 1
 7. Warrior 2
 8. Triangle
 9. Walk, march and skip in Yoga Freeze (see Chapter 20)
10. Supine Twist
11. Balance Beam
12. Walking Crab

MOTOR PLANNING AND BILATERAL COORDINATION: SMALL STEPS

To develop motor-planning skills, break each posture down to its smallest components. Teach each step individually before adding it to the next. If the child is unable to perform a motion, simplify it further.

A visual learner will often replicate a pose by seeing it illustrated but may not be able to perform individual phases of the posture. In such cases, reverse the method to develop motor-planning skills: Practice the full posture first, and then the separate steps. Here's an example of teaching a bilateral balance posture through sequential steps:

Balance Beam Pose

Start by practicing Table pose on hands and knees. Next instruct the child to wiggle the fingers of her right hand. Once she has mastered that, cue her to lift her right hand off the ground. You may use visual cue cards for right hand, or gentle prompting by touching or pointing to the hand that she will be moving.

Repeat on the left. Next ask her to lift her right arm out straight. If she is comfortable with your assist, you may hold her wrist or elbow in the pose. Repeat on the left. With practice, most children are able to hold each arm straight in front independently or with your assistance.

When the student is ready for an additional challenge, instruct her to wiggle her left toes. This may require additional prompting, as she cannot see her toes. Model or tap the toes to bring her awareness to this part of her body. The process for lifting her legs will proceed as above, until she can stretch each leg out behind her independently or with assistance. After this has become familiar, combine it with another action. With your support or the use of a wall for her hand and a chair for her foot, she will lift her left leg and right arm in Balance Beam. Repeat on the other side.

In all phases of this posture, offer praise for her effort and encouragement as she works through each small step. If she is unable to go beyond any of these steps, work there. Whatever she can do successfully will become her variation of the posture.

Use the same method from the supine position in Half Superman pose.

VESTIBULAR SYSTEM

Movements that stimulate the vestibular system include rolling, rocking, spinning, jogging, elevating the head from a prone position, shifting the weight from side to side, and balancing.

SUGGESTED POSES:

1. Rolling: From Tree Balance pose, "chop" down the trees and roll the logs to one side of the room and back. After Balance Beam, roll the beam along the floor.
2. Rocking: Seesaw
3. Spinning: Twister seated or standing
4. Jogging between postures in Yoga Freeze
5. Jog or skip in Follow Me
6. Prone with head up: Half Superman, Superman, Airplane
7. Shifting weight: Half Moon, Balance Beam, Tree Balance prep, Fruit Picking
8. Balancing: Tree Balance, Tall Tree, Warrior 1 and 2, Willow Tree Backbend

VISUAL SYSTEM

The vestibular sense and hand-eye coordination can be improved by following an object with the eyes. You may use objects such as scarves or balls, the movements of your body, or the child's own hands for visual tracking. Here are some examples:

Scarf Watching in Posture

Instruct the child to use his eyes to follow the motion of a scarf while you move it simultaneously with his upward and downward motion in Folded Leaf pose. The child may hold the scarf himself to improve his visual awareness in poses such as Butterfly Hands or Tree Breathing. In Warrior poses, he or you can use the scarf to help him direct his eyes correctly. With practice, he can watch his own hands moving up and down in Tree Breathing pose without a prop.

Visual Tracking in Pretzel

While a child is sitting on his heels for Pretzel, stand directly in front of him. Catch his attention and instruct him to watch you; walk slightly to the child's right and tell him to turn his head toward you. (You may use the directional terms right and left if the child recognizes these terms.) Then walk to the left, being certain that he follows your movements with his eyes. If following your movements is difficult, sit directly in front of the child and use your hand or a brightly colored scarf for him to follow instead.

After the child is comfortable with this exercise, he may begin practice in using just his eyes to follow your motion, without moving his head. Stay close to the child and limit your movements so he can more easily follow you.

After consistent practice in using *your* body for the child to follow movement, substitute visual cues such as left and right cards, Focus Circles, and Footprints to increase his independence.

Meditative Eye Exercises

1. Tree Hands: following the hands, move eyes up, down.
2. Follow your thumb: Following one thumb (yours or the child's own), move the eyes right; then left. Move them in a circle clockwise and counterclockwise.

3. Butterfly Meditation—look at open palm, turning head right and left.
   4. Eye exercises: move the eyes slowly in six directions with rests in between—vertical, horizontal; diagonal each way; clockwise; counterclockwise.
   5. Supine Twist: gaze at the open palm on each side.
   6. Bellows Breath: look up with inhalation, down with exhalation.
   7. Palming: Rub the palms together to make them warm. Cup them over the closed eyes.

Postures for Transitions

Change, whether unexpected or predictable, is often disturbing for children with special needs. Try using yoga postures that deepen breathing and focus the mind to signal transitions. Choose a pose that is energizing when it's time to get up and move, and one that is calming when it's time to settle down. Or, you may use the child's favorite pose each time to create continuity despite changes in his schedule. Creating a ritual for transitioning between activities can ease stressful periods in the child's day.

SINGLE POSTURE TRANSITIONS

- From seated to standing: Seated Pretzel before getting up
- From standing to seated: Rag Doll before sitting
- While waiting in line: Tree Breathing, Half Moon right and left, Shake It Out
- Unexpected change in schedule: three Huh Breaths before new activity
- After recess: Folded Leaf—in seat, standing, or on floor
- Before lunch: Half Fish—from seat or floor
- Between subjects: Butterfly Hands

ROUTINE FOR STANDING-TO-SEATED TRANSITION

Both playful and soothing, this sequence can be used as a transition when moving from standing to seated activities:

1. Tree Hands
2. Willow Tree Backbend (or Upward)
3. Half Moon right
4. Half Moon left
5. Rag Doll sway side to side
6. Stretching Dog

7. Table
8. Happy Cat
9. Angry Cat
10. Baby
11. Hi, World
12. Seated Tree Hands

Language Development and Creative Interaction

Yoga therapy motivates children to interact in a natural environment. Playful postures serve as a starting point for discussion; partner work promotes cooperation and communication. (Also see songs and games in Chapter 20.)

POSTURES TO PROMOTE COMMUNICATION

1. Butterfly Hands: What color is your butterfly?
2. Sandwich: favorite sandwich
3. Rock the Baby: how to hold a baby (includes singing)
4. Happy Cat: meow, purr
5. Baby: optional touch, sharing touch
6. Hi, World!
7. Walking Dog: bark
8. Half Fish: fish face; deepens breathing
9. Snake: hiss
10. Drawbridge: boats underneath; sounding horn
11. Candle: light flame; blow it out; counting candles; singing "Happy Birthday"
12. Wall Butterfly: Which flower does your butterfly like best?
13. Bug on Its Back: How many legs? How does it move?
14. Warrior: What do you see? helping others
15. Mindful Practice: sharing kind thoughts or words

PARTNER POSES TO ENHANCE SOCIAL INTERACTION

You may partner with the child in any posture, but these are poses specifically created to work in pairs. Partnering requires cooperation and language development. Remind children to thank their partners upon concluding the pose.

1. Seesaw (with singing)
2. Flying Bats

3. Back-to-Back Breathing
4. Lawn Chair
5. Partner Tree
6. Wall X (from wall candle)

Noisy and Quiet Lesson

Just as yoga therapy provides opportunities for communication and interaction, it offers tools for children to manage their noise levels,

If children are having trouble settling down, don't demand silence. Let them make some noise! But retain control by making the noise an acceptable outlet; contrast it with silence. During any class, you may insert a combination of noisy poses followed by quiet poses. Or vary noise and quiet within a posture.

YOGA SINGING

1. Start with the Namaste or "Hello Friend" song.
2. Chant "OM" repeatedly—establish Tree Hands (with a hand clap, if needed) as a signal to end the chants. When students are restless or noisy, this works well to release errant energy and refocus. You may interject this chant anywhere in the class. (In public schools or institutions, use "AH," "OH," or "HUM," or sing "There's no place like HOME!")

BUZZING BEE BREATH

3. Inhale through the nose. Exhale with a buzz or low humming sound with mouth closed.

SEATED

4. Huh Breath: For the first three, exhale with a loud HUH as the shoulders drop. Repeat with three silent Huhs.
5. Twister: Make a "whoosh" like the wind with each rotation. Start slowly, then go faster. End slowly and silently.

HANDS AND KNEES (TABLE)

6. Happy Cat: Meow
7. Angry Cat: Don't make a sound
8. Walking Dog: Bark like a friendly dog. Wag your tail!

9. Snake: Slither and HISSSSSSS

10. Baby: Rest quietly

BELLY

11. Airplane: Make the noise of a roaring jet when you fly!

12. Superman: Let the world know you are on your way!

13. Child's pose: Rest quietly

WALL INVERSIONS

14. Wall Candle: With legs up the wall, pretend you are the candles on a big birthday cake. Sing "Happy birthday."

15. Wall Butterfly: Blow out all the candles; become silent as a butterfly.

BACK

16. Crab: First you are a chatty crab, walking forward. Then walk backward without saying a word!

17. Drawbridge: Lifting, sound the horn to let ships come through. Lower silently.

STANDING

18. Tree Hands: Can you sing like a bird as it rests in your tree?

19. Tree Balance without a sound

20. Shake It Out: "Shake it out, shake it out, shake it out!"

21. Rag Doll: Hang down like a weeping willow tree, with your branches drooping low. There's not a sound; all the birds have flown away.

SUPINE RELAXATION: Include a short period of silence

SEATED CONCLUSION: Three Huh Breaths as above

Creating a Pace

As discussed in previous chapters, you create a rhythm for the class through your choice of postures and the speed at which you teach them. In addition, you can help children maintain a calmer pace throughout their day by interjecting quick stress-relieving postures as needed.

It's important to observe the child in order to determine a suitable pace. Some children need to move slowly, while others respond better to rapid, continuous motion. A slow pace is a good place to start with a child who is low toned or lethargic, or to redirect an anxious, distracted child. Choose calming, mindful variations of postures and keep the rhythm of instruction slow and steady. You may start with this slow pace and gradually move into more energizing postures. Or use this sequence after a 10-minute energizing flow.

SLOWING DOWN SEQUENCE (20–30 MINUTES)
1. Huh Breath
2. Yoga singing: Chant "AH" softly three times
3. Seated Circles
4. Slow Butterfly
5. Pretzel
6. Sandwich
7. Rock the Baby humming only
8. Back-to-Back Breathing
9. Lawn Chair
10. Folded Leaf
11. Drawbridge
12. Wall Candle
13. Half Fish
14. Knee Hugs
15. Tree Balance
16. Rag Doll
17. Baby
18. Cloud
19. Huh Breath

Some children need to keep moving. If children come to class loud, hyperactive, or agitated, get them moving right away to release errant energy. Use playful variations of the postures, transition quickly from pose to pose, and put power into your voice. They may need a full session of active poses, or you may follow with a 10-minute calming sequence.

ENERGIZING SEQUENCE (20–30 MINUTES)

1. Huh Breath
2. Butterfly Hands
3. Tense and Relax
4. Seesaw
5. Rocking Chair
6. Happy Cat
7. Angry Cat
8. Balance Beam
9. Stretching Dog
10. Snake (Stretching Dog to Snake repeat 2–5 times)
11. Airplane
12. Half Superman
13. Superman
14. Baby
15. Warrior 1
16. Warrior 2
17. Willow Tree Backbend
18. Fruit Picker
19. Rag Doll
20. Shake It Out
21. Cloud
22. Huh Breath

TEN-MINUTE CALMING SEQUENCE

To lengthen this lesson, extend the time in Baby and Floating on a Cloud. Or abbreviate it by selecting just a few of the child's favorite calming postures.

1. Huh Breath
2. Seated Circles and reverse
3. Butterfly Knees—slowly with breathing
4. Seated Egg
5. Folded Leaf with breathing
6. Drawbridge slowly up and down
7. Knee Hugs/Neck Rolls

8. Supine Twist
9. Baby with optional back massage
10. Floating on Cloud—quiet body, quiet voice, quiet mind
11. Mindful Practice
12. Huh Breath

TEN-MINUTE ENERGIZING SEQUENCE

To lengthen this lesson, repeat a posture to create energetic flows. Or abbreviate it by selecting just a few of the child's favorite energizing postures.

1. Huh Breath
2. Namaste song
3. Butterfly Hands
4. Seesaw
5. Volcano
6. Walking Dog
7. Crab
8. Superman
9. Tree Balance
10. Warrior 1
11. Warrior 2
12. Willow Tree Backbend
13. Rag Doll
14. Floating on Cloud (brief)
15. Huh Breath

QUICK TENSION RELEASE

Five-minute (or less) stress relief seated in chair:

1. Huh Breath
2. Bellows Breath
3. Butterfly Hands
4. Butterfly Meditation
5. Half Fish
6. Chair Folded Leaf
7. Chair Pretzel
8. Huh Breath

Five-minute (or less) stress relief standing:

1. Huh Breath
2. Shake It Out
3. Twister Fast
4. Twister Slow
5. Tree Breathing
6. Half Moon
7. Willow Tree Backbend
8. Rag Doll
9. Huh Breath

Yoga Therapy for Limited Mobility

Children with very limited mobility can benefit from yoga therapy. Talk to them about relaxing an arm or a finger. Guide them to breathe with every movement. Explain that they can help make new pathways in their brains just by thinking about and imagining a movement.

The sequence that follows is recommended for children in wheelchairs, in a seat, or on the floor. The following postures may *not* be acceptable variations for all children. Some will be able to do much more, and some less. Safety first!

Thanks to my neighbor Maggie Weiss who helped me develop this routine from her wheelchair.

- *Never* leave a child unattended in the chair. With children in wheelchairs, be certain that they are fastened securely in their seats and that the wheels are locked.
- *Never* move any body parts of a child who has mobility limitations unless you are licensed and trained to do so. Instead, encourage children to move what they can independently.

WARM-UPS
1. Three Huh Breaths
2. Yoga singing: Namaste or "Hello Friend"
3. Belly Breathing
4. Single Elbow or Shoulder Circles

5. Pretzel Adaptation: How many ways can you cross one part of your body over another? Cross wrists or ankles. Cross two fingers; cross the arms at the elbows.

6. Finger Stretch

7. Butterfly Hands

8. Double Elbow or Shoulder circles

9. Neck rotations

BREATHING FLOWS

10. Cat Breath adaptation: Open your chest when you breathe in. Round your back slightly and give it a stretch when you breathe out. Inhale and look up. Exhaling, say, "Meow!"

11. Cat's Claws: Take a deep breath in. With the exhalation, stretch your fingers and hands like a cat stretches her claws.

12. Silent Scream: Take a deep breath in. Exhaling, stretch your mouth and eyes open wide. What a sight!

13. Bellows Breath: May pump arms with hands on shoulders, ribcage, or belly.

14. Airplane Adaptation: As you inhale, open your arms out to the sides like a jet flying through the sky. As you exhale, return them to their resting position.

15. Tree Breathing Adaptation: In Tree Hands, move the hands up slightly higher with each breath in. Follow the hands with your eyes. Rest with each exhalation.

16. Folded Leaf adaptation: Sit up as straight as you can in the chair, breathing in. Slide your hands down toward your knees as you breathe out. Inhaling, slide your hands up your legs to come back up. Variation: Folded Leaf arms only, stretching up with inhalation and down with exhalation.

UPPER BODY STRENGTH

17. Swimming (Twister variation): Reach your right arm straight forward, feeling the stretch through your fingertips. Relax that arm as you stretch your left arm forward. Alternate your arms slowly or quickly, like a swimmer.

18. Tall Tree adaptation: Raise your hands up high like branches on a tall tree reaching toward the sun. [Sometimes holding an object in the hands, like a block or ball, increases stability and range of motion.]

19. Half Moon: Form a half moon by reaching up and swaying your arms to one side and then to the other side. [Lateral flexion may also be facilitated by holding an object between the hands.]

20. Warrior 2 adaptation: Imagine yourself as a proud, strong warrior, sitting up straight and stretching your arms out to the sides. [Encourage children to present themselves in this way, using their arms, hands, facial expression, etc.]

21. Triangle adaptation: How many triangles can you form with your body? A triangle can be formed using the fingers, hands, or arms. Press the palms together in Tree Hands position while moving the elbows apart into a triangle shape.

22. Fruit Picking: Reach up high for apples and out to the side for bananas. Reach down near your knees to pick your favorite berries.

CONCLUSION

23. Mindful Practice: Begin turning your awareness inward. Lightly place your hands over your mouth. Notice how easy it is to be quiet in this way. Move your hands to cover your eyes. Feel the warmth of your hands as you shut out all the light from this room. You may keep your eyes closed as you cover your ears and close out all of the sound, even my voice. Now relax your hands in your lap. Take a moment to breathe quietly in this way. [You may continue with guided progressive muscle relaxation.] When you are ready, open your eyes.

24. Three Huh Breaths

Parent-Child Partnering

In yoga therapy you have a wonderful opportunity to assist parents in partnering with their children. Partner poses build trust, enhance communication, and promote playful interaction.

Parents sometimes find it challenging not to correct their own children's form in poses. Clarify your therapeutic objective— to increase the child's receptivity to interacting with a partner by making poses fun and pressure-free. Explain that you will be exploring many variations of the poses. Model encouragement, non-criticism, and respect for boundaries in your own teaching; avoid overcorrecting either parent or child.

Sometimes you may sense that what the parent expects is beyond or less than the child's capacity at any given moment. Adjust your lesson based on input from the parent as well as your own observations and experience.

Partnering is a challenge for many children with special needs. A child's intolerance to touch can be the source of great anguish for parents. Just imagine how you might feel if the child you loved recoiled at your touch. In yoga therapy, you can offer an opportunity to partner without direct physical contact.

You may avoid "touching" poses or introduce them with lots of options. For Partner Tree, have children lean on the wall first. Once they have mastered the pose independently, they may be more comfortable working with a partner. Children who resist being touched in Baby may be willing to try less intimate poses such as Seesaw or Back-to-Back breathing. Working up to these poses can be a thrilling experience for parents and create a sense of accomplishment and connection for children.

If a child appears threatened or anxious about giving up control or surrendering to a partner, start with each partner working independently. Children may enjoy mirroring their parents. Or they may prefer to work in tandem, lined up beside or behind them. They still partner, but without direct contact.

If partnering is awkward or uncomfortable for either parent or child, suggest the independent variation of the pose. Reassure them that it's always okay to skip a pose or partner in another way.

PARENT-CHILD SEQUENCE FOR SPECIAL NEEDS OF ALL AGES

1. Huh Breath
2. Butterfly Knees—Child sits inside the parent's knees, or face to face with the knees just barely touching, or not touching at all.
3. Back-to-Back Breathing—Touching or with space between.
4. Lawn Chair—May use pillows behind for support or in between partners or sit side by side.
5. Seesaw—May be done sitting facing without touching, as each rocks and sings.
6. Flying Bats—Alternative is to sit side by side, facing wall, elevating one foot at a time.
7. Partner Pretzel—Sit back to back, not touching. Twisting your upper body toward your partner, smile at your partner. Reverse.

8. Rock the Baby— The child sits inside the parent's knees and the parent rocks the child and sings. Or the parent holds the child's foot and rocks it. Or side by side.

9. Heart Opener—Parent sits with her knees together and soles of the feet on the floor. Child sits on or close to her feet with his back resting against her knees. He may reach back for parent's hands.

10. Balance Beam—Face to face. Each partner rests her right hand on her partner's shoulder for support. Or reach toward your partner without touching. Reverse hands.

11. Partner Stretching Dog—Parent and child do the pose side by side or face to face.

18-1 Partner Rock the Baby

12. Slithering Snake—Face to face. Who has the louder hiss?

13. Under Dog—The parent comes into Stretching Dog. The child slides underneath like a Snake and comes out the other side.

14. Airplane—Plan a trip—where will we go? Come into pose face to face or side by side.

15. Superman—Facing the child, parent uses her hands beneath the child's arms to assist her lift. Or side by side.

16. Crab Walk—Walk toward, then away from partner; then walk sideways and reverse.

17. Candle—Light partner's flame; blow it out.

18. Partner Tree—If the child does not feel comfortable holding hands or standing close, do it together on the wall, side by side.

19. Trading Massages—Baby pose side by side; both partners massage each other's back or parent massages child's back, if comfortable. Or parent and child may each rub their own backs, experiencing simultaneous and parallel

touch. *Demonstrating partner massage:* Invite the child to bring his hands close to the parent, without touching. You can talk about the transference of good feelings through the hands. Move your hands onto the parent's back. Rest there. If the child is watching, gently stroke the back and invite him to participate. Be sure his touch is gentle. Talk about sending kind thoughts through your hands. If the child's touch is rough, switch to hands close to without touching, or quickly conclude the massage. Ask the child if he wants a massage before moving to the next pose.

20. Floating on a Cloud—An opportunity to be at rest together, perhaps touching hands, sharing a pillow, or lying side by side.
21. Huh Breath

Final Relaxation and Mindfulness Practice

Following is a suggested script for the conclusion of any yoga therapy session. Lower the pitch of your voice and slow the cadence of your speech and breathing. Although some children may not relate to the images in this sequence, they will respond to your soothing tone of voice and the quiet rhythm of your breathing.

GUIDED RELAXATION: FLOATING ON A CLOUD

Now it's time to float on a cloud.

Imagine that your mat is a soft, fluffy cloud. It's just your size, made especially for you. It's strong enough to support you, and soft enough to feel really good. This cloud is just right for your body, so you are completely safe, completely secure. Imagine floating in the sky with the birds. Can you hear the gentle sound of the wind?

Slowly roll your head to the right. And to the left. Let it rest in between. Get really comfortable. Feel the tension melting away from your face and shoulders like ice melting in the warm sun.

Raise your right leg an inch off the ground. As you breathe out, drop it, relax. Raise your left leg an inch. Breathe out, drop it, relax. Lift your arms an inch; make tight fists. Drop and relax. Gently shake out your arms and legs and let them sink down, feeling heavy and relaxed.

You may close your eyes if it's comfortable, or look at a spot above your head. Whenever your eyes get tired, close them if you like. Feel your body very calm, very still. This is how it feels to be relaxed: comfortable, safe, and quiet. Remember this feeling. The next time someone tells you to relax, remember how you feel right now: comfortable, safe, quiet. This is relaxation. [pause]

Now it's time to float your cloud back to the ground. Begin to wiggle your toes and fingers. Gently stretch and yawn as if you were awakening from a nap. Hug your knees and rock from side to side.

Curl up on your side, like a seed, planted in the ground. Feel your feet like roots working into the earth. Sitting up, stretch your fingers, then your arms, reaching toward the sun. Open your arms wide and smile like a beautiful flower.

MINDFULNESS PRACTICE: YOUR SPECIAL PLACE

To conclude the yoga therapy session, create a personal mindfulness practice for the child. You may substitute lying on the beach, resting in a meadow, curled up under a tree—any peaceful image that creates a sense of safety for the child.

MINDFULNESS PRACTICE: YOUR OWN CLOUD

Sit comfortably. Close your eyes if you like and notice the quiet rhythm of your breathing. Feel your belly softly filling up as you breathe in, getting smaller as you breathe out. Your belly gets bigger as you breathe in, smaller as you breathe out.

What a wonderful feeling to float on your own special cloud. Wouldn't you like to have that feeling any time that you wanted? Before we end our class today, let's gather up your cloud and fold it up really small. Now tuck your cloud inside a pretend pocket, one that you can get to any time you want. At bedtime, you can take your cloud out of your pocket and relax before you fall asleep. If you have time in the morning, take out your cloud and rest for a moment before you start your day.

Your cloud is always there for you, your special place to relax and feel comfortable, safe, and quiet.

MINDFUL PRACTICE: SHARING BREATH

Let's take three big belly breaths. Notice how it feels to breathe in and out.

Breathe in, feeling strong; breathe out strength to all those around you.

Breathe in, feeling friendly; breathe out friendship to all those around you.

Breathe in, feeling peaceful; breathe out peace to all those around you.

Om Shanti, Shanti, Shanti, Om peace, peace, peace.

CHAPTER 19

BREATHING LESSONS

THERE ARE MANY natural ways to adjust the rate at which a child is breathing. You can set a pace for respiration with the speed and sequence of postures you teach and the rhythm of your voice. Yoga therapy helps children become aware of their breathing and its impact upon their bodies. The breath is a child's constant companion. When he learns to attend to and use it for self-regulation, he has a tool to address any challenge, throughout his life.

Connecting to the Breath

Encourage the child to breathe in and out through his nostrils at all times, unless specified otherwise. Encourage children who habitually mouth breathe to try nasal breathing during restful postures.

POSITIONS TO FEEL THE BREATH
1. Seated or supine with hands on belly
2. Supine with fingers interlaced at lower ribs, fingers separate with inhalation

3. Lying on the belly, body elevates with inhalation and descends with exhalation

MODELING AND PARTNERING

1. Sitting close, the child watches your breathing
2. Lying beside you, the child listens to your breathing

Extending Breathing

Most children will be successful in learning belly breathing through the nostrils. Some children will benefit from additional exercises to promote extended breathing, especially if they are chronically stressed.

Caution: Don't overemphasize breathing exercises or variations. For some children it's simply too much to think about or takes the fun out of postures. Visual learners may not process the imagery in these exercises; others may be distracted by props. In such cases, work with the postures that promote breathing, rather than isolating breathing practices.

EXTENDING BREATHING THROUGH THE NOSE

Belly Breathing (a relaxed, abdominal breath through the nostrils)
1. Inhalation: Your belly fills up like a balloon.
2. Exhalation: Your belly gets smaller.

Full Breath
1. Inhalation: Fill the belly, widen the rib cage, expand the upper chest.
2. Exhalation: The belly sinks, rib cage narrows, upper chest lowers.

Counting Breath
1. Count to three as you inhale.
2. Count to three as you exhale (gradually increase count if suitable).

Centering Breath with affirmation (adapt to the child)
1. Inhale: I am.
2. Exhale: calm.

Centering Breath with mantra (adapt to the child)
1. Inhale: SO.
2. Exhale: HUM.

Buzzing Bee (avoid with children who make odd sounds)
Move the exhalation down into the throat, creating a rumbling or buzzing sound

Sniffing Breath (avoid with children who breathe erratically)
1. Take one breath in by sniffing three times through the nose.
2. Exhale normally
3. Inhale normally
4. Breathe out by expelling three short puffs of air through nose.
5. Resume Belly Breathing.

EXTENDING EXHALATION THROUGH THE MOUTH

Power Breath
1. Inhalation: Imagine the breath coming in through the bottoms of the feet, traveling up through the legs, belly, chest, face, to the top of the head, energizing your whole body.
2. Exhalation: Gush the air out through your mouth, sweeping away tension and negative thoughts and feelings, letting go.

Dancing Breath
Blow scarves or feathers through the air.

Bubble Blowing
Make many small bubbles by exhaling short puffs. Make bigger bubbles with long, slow exhalations.

Straw Breathing
Inhale through the nose and exhale through the straw.

Cooling Breath
1. Inhale through pursed lips.
2. Exhale through pursed lips.

Hand Cooling

Purse your lips and blow into your palm, in a slow cooling breath; your palm feels dry.

Hand Warming

Open your mouth and exhale into your palm with a slow warming breath; your palm feels moist.

Silent Scream

Inhale through the nose; exhale with mouth open wide (avoid with children who make or imitate unusual facial expressions).

PLAYFUL POSTURES TO EXTEND EXHALATION THROUGH SOUND

1. Hissing Snake
2. Barking Walking Dog
3. Meowing Cat
4. Whistling birds in Tree poses
5. Whooshing wind in Airplane
6. Blowing out their Candle
7. Swish sound in Twister

Creating Smiles

In *Yoga Skills for Therapists*, Amy Weintraub describes the benefit of a simple smile. The body's biochemistry is altered by facial expression, and a smile can give your "feel good hormones . . . a boost" (2012, p. 72).

SMILE MEDITATION

With permission, I have adapted Amy's technique slightly for use with children with special needs. (All breathing is through the nose.)

1. Breathe in; breathe out and tuck your chin way down into your chest.
2. Breathe in and out, feeling a smile start at the corners of your mouth.
3. Breathe in and lift up your chin.
4. Breathe out and show me your beautiful smile!

SMILE CHANT

The Smile meditation appeals to most children, but it does require auditory processing and control of facial muscles. Another method for children with varying challenges is the smile chant. By making the vowel sound E, the child stretches his mouth open and wide at the sides, much like a smile.

Display a visual with a large letter E. Children listen to and repeat E. Help them notice their mouths when they make this sound: What is the shape? How does it feel? It's just like a smile!

1. Breathe in; breathe out E
2. Breathe in; breathe out EEEE
3. Breathe in; breathe out EEEEEEEEEE
4. Breathe in; breathe out EEEEEEEEEEEEEEEEEEEE
5. Feel your mouth stretched wide like a smile. What a beautiful smile!

Breathing Routine to Strengthen Muscles of the Mouth

1. Huh Breath
2. Cooling Breath with pursed lips
3. Bubble Blowing
4. Straw Breathing: inhale and exhale through the straw
5. Silent Scream
6. Vowel Chanting (See Yoga Singing, Chapter 20)

Breathing Flows

You may combine movement and breathing in a single posture or in a sequence containing several postures. Moving fluidly from pose to pose is called a *flow*. Moving quickly accelerates the respiration; moving slowly decelerates it. In this way, flows provide children with a natural form of breath control (pranayama).

PARTNER FLOWS

By partnering with the child, you can create a rhythm for breathing and moving.

1. Back-to-Back Breathing—Sit and breathe together. Even if your breathing is not matched, the child can experience the slow, steady rhythm of your breathing.

2. Lawn Chair—Pause and breathe in each phase of the pose. You will mirror, so inhale as the child begins the movement backward; exhale as he begins the movement forward.

3. Seesaw—Change this playful pose into an exercise in rhythmic breathing by slowing it down. The child's backward motion begins with an inhalation, and his forward motion begins with an exhalation.

SINGLE POSTURE BREATHING FLOWS

1. Bellows—Even without the breathing, this pumping motion expands and compresses the thoracic cavity.

2. Twister—Increase the speed or slow it down to modify respiration.

3. Folded Leaf—Float up with inhalation, down with exhalation.

4. Drawbridge—Inhale lift, exhale lower.

5. Airplane—Inhale lift, exhale lower.

6. Superman—Inhale lift, exhale lower.

MULTI-POSTURE FLOWS

1. Stretching Dog to Snake—Exhale Stretching Dog; inhale Snake.

2. Rocking Chair into Candle—Breathing accelerates in Rocking Chair, slows in Candle.

3. Half Fish to Folded Leaf—Inhale Half Fish, exhale Folded Leaf.

4. Willow Tree Backbend to Rag Doll—Inhale up and back in Willow Tree Backbend; exhale into Rag Doll.

5. Willow Tree upward to Half Moon—Inhale reach up; exhale lean right. Repeat to other side.

6. Warrior 2 to Triangle, both sides—Breathing accelerates with exertion in Warrior 2, slows in Triangle.

7. Warrior 1 to Warrior Lunge to Stretching Dog to Baby—Inhale and exhale in Warrior 1 right foot forward. Inhale into Warrior Lunge. Exhale into Stretching Dog, right foot back. Rest in Baby. Repeat on the other side.

EXTENDED FLOWS

You can combine complementary postures into lengthier sequences to form a story or rhythmic flow. These can be energizing or soothing, depending upon the speed and complexity of the postures used. If extended flows are too challenging for a child, continue with single or double posture flows.

Hello Sun

Without the sun, our earth would be cold and barren. Its heat and light are essential to all the plant and animal life we know. So, it seems only fitting to greet the sun each day, whether it's bright in the sky or hidden from view.

The yoga form of acknowledging the sun is called Surya Namaskar, Salutation to the Sun. With kids, I call it "Hello Sun!" It is a series of twelve postures that stretch and strengthen every area of the body. It can be used as a demanding workout, an overall body conditioner, a rhythmic breathing flow, or a playful adventure.

In Sonia Sumar's trainings, *Yoga for the Special Child*, yoga teacher Laurie Schaeffer discovered another benefit of the sun salutation. "As the children's movements become smoother, their ability to speak becomes smoother," she explains. In her own work with individuals with autism and cerebral palsy, Laurie has observed that the series "balances things out so that students can more effectively process thoughts and pay attention" (personal communication, September 24, 2012).

To make this series energizing, move quickly from posture to posture without a lot of explanation. Some children may enjoy hollering "Hello, Sun" when they reach up and whispering "Hello, Earth" when they reach down. Their hands and feet may be off position, but if they are smiling and breathing, the series will provide a beneficial workout for them.

To move slowly through the poses, guide the children to breathe in and out while pausing in each position. With more independent students, synchronize the breathing with the movements. Adjust your pace to their breathing so they won't get out of breath. Once breathing and postures are unified, children experience a form of moving meditation.

A complete round of Hello Sun is two sets of the twelve positions, changing the starting foot for each series. Remember, you have the choice to make this a meditative or playful sequence, with or without the breathing instructions.

POSITION 1: THE SALUTE—TREE HANDS (INHALE, EXHALE)

Look down at your feet. Throughout Hello Sun, either your hands or your feet will be just where your feet are right now, rooted to the earth. Take a deep breath in, breathe out, and say, "Hello, Sun!"

POSITION 2A: HELLO, SUN—WILLOW TREE UPWARD (INHALE)

Reach up with both hands and embrace the warmth of the sun. (If you are pausing in the position, the children may call out "Hello, Sun!")

POSITION 2B: EMBRACING THE SUN—WILLOW TREE BACKBEND

Stretch your whole back. (If students are very tight, stay with Position 2a.)

POSITION 3: HELLO, EARTH—RAG DOLL (EXHALE)

Bend your knees—a little or a lot—until you are comfortable hanging down. Press your palms down alongside your feet, rooting you to the earth.

POSITION 4: WARRIOR LUNGE BACK (INHALE)

Take a giant step back with your right foot.

POSITION 5: STRETCHING DOG (EXHALE)

POSITION 6: TABLE (INHALE, EXHALE)

POSITION 7: SNAKE (INHALE)

Like a slithery snake, you bask in the sun on the warm ground. (When taking an extra breath here, say "Hello, Sun!")

POSITION 8: STRETCHING DOG (EXHALE)

POSITION 9: WARRIOR LUNGE FORWARD (INHALE)

Step your right foot up in between your hands. If it doesn't quite reach, you can slide or wiggle your foot up. Look up and see the sun smiling down on you!

POSITION 10: HELLO EARTH—RAG DOLL (EXHALE)

Push off from the left foot and step between your hands into Rag Doll. With a deep, quiet voice, say "Hello, Earth!" Imagine your voice echoing down into the center of the earth.

POSITION 11: HELLO SUN—WILLOW TREE UPWARD AND BACKBEND (INHALE)

(Same as 2a and 2b)

POSITION 12: TREE HANDS (EXHALE)

Close your eyes and feel your connection to the sun above and the earth below. How grateful we are to the sun for making the earth a comfortable home for us all. "Thank you, Sun!"

BREATHING TREE FLOW

Coordinate the motions with the breath. To slow the pace, breathe in and out (or out and in) in each position. Heel lift is optional in Tall Tree. (Sequence may be done seated.)

1. Tree Hands inhale, exhale
2. Tall Tree inhale
3. Tree Hands exhale
4. Tall Tree inhale
5. Half Moon right exhale
6. Willow Tree upward inhale
7. Half Moon left exhale
8. Willow Tree upward inhale
9. Rag Doll (Folded Leaf seated) exhale and remain in pose for two full breaths

10. Tree Hands exhale
11. Willow Tree Backbend (Half Fish seated) inhale
12. Tree Hands exhale

CHEST OPENING SEATED FLOW

Seated on floor or in chair, deep breathing in each position:

1. Tree Hands
2. Tree Breathing
3. Half Moon left
4. Half Moon right
5. Half Fish
6. Folded Leaf
7. Half Fish
8. Folded Leaf
9. Pretzel right
10. Pretzel left
11. Twister fast
12. Tree Hands

Complete Lesson for Breathing (30 minutes)

Focus on breathing in each posture.

SEATED

1. Huh Breath
2. Belly Breathing
3. Pretzel—twist slowly with the breath
4. Hip rocks—hum quietly in position or be silent
5. Butterfly Knees—slowly with the breath
6. Sandwich

HANDS AND KNEES

7. Happy Cat (inhale)
8. Angry Cat (exhale)
9. Repeat Cat breathing
10. Stretching Dog—inhale, up on the toes, exhale, lower heels

PRONE
11. Snake, elbows bent—feel the motion of the belly with the breath
12. Baby—quietly or with back massage

SUPINE INVERSIONS
13. Rocking Chair—rock up with inhalation, back with exhalation
14. Candle or Wall Candle
15. Wall Butterfly

SUPINE
16. Half Fish

SEATED FORWARD BEND
17. Folded Leaf

STANDING
18. Tree Breathing
19. Tree Balance
20. Rag Doll

RELAXATION
21. Floating on a Cloud with soft belly breathing

MINDFUL PRACTICE
22. Butterfly Meditation
23. Send healing thoughts with each exhalation
24. Huh Breath

CHAPTER 20

CHANTS, SONGS, AND GAMES

This final chapter includes yoga chants, songs, and games to promote language development, social interaction, and motor skills. Songs and games may be used to initiate active play or to create a calming pace.

Yoga Singing

Children's responsiveness to rhythm and music is widely recognized. Music has been shown to promote healing, focus, and imaginative play (Campbell, 1997). Singing develops language skills and social interaction, and it's fun. When a child sings, he breathes.

VOWEL CHANTS

Most children enjoy hearing and repeating simple sounds. The following vowel sounds correspond to the body's energetic centers, or *chakras* (Paul, 2004). Chanting these sounds has a calming, balancing effect.

VOWEL SOUND	WORD
Oh	Home
Ooh	Too
Ah	Ma
Ay	Stay
Ee	Me
Mm	Yum
Ng	Sing

When teaching yoga singing to children, you may use visual cues, printed in large letters on card stock, slightly simplified:

Sound Cards

O
OO
AH
A
E
M
N

Syllable Cards

OM (alternative: HOME)
SO (alternative: HO)
HUM

Holding one card at a time, pronounce each sound for the children to repeat. Follow the sequence from O to E. Gradually include M and N.

After children have mastered these sounds, teach combinations. Practice singing O and Oo. Then combine O, Oo, and Ah, and so forth. Adding sounds increases the duration of the exhalation.

When singing all the sounds together, add a circular arm sweep. Begin with arms down at their sides for the sound O. Start to open the arms out to the sides with Oo. Sweep the arms in a large circle upward singing Ah, A, E. Elevate the arms overhead with M, bringing the palms together in Tree Hands. Singing N, lower the Tree Hands to the center of the chest. Lower and repeat. You may move slowly, pausing for a breath after each sound, or practice combining as many of the sounds as the child can repeat with a single exhalation.

To create syllables, begin by chanting O. Then M. Demonstrate the gradual closing of the mouth from O to M, a simplified version of the OM chant. For SO HUM, sing each portion separately, and then combine in a single exhalation.

Chanting Sanskrit Mantra

You may sing these to your students, or use a call and response approach. After each Sanskrit phrase, you will find an alternative for use in public education.

Steadying: OM (alternative: Home)

Turning inward: SO HUM (alternative: Ho Hum)

Overcoming challenge: Jaya Ganesha (alternative: I think I can)

Peace: Om Shanti, Shanti, Shanti (alternative: Peace, peace, peace)

Soothing: Sri Ram, Jaya Ram, Jaya, Jaya, Ram O (alternative: Rock-a-Bye or any lullaby)

Namaste Song

Use this to begin each session. Pronounced NAH MAH STAY, this Sanskrit greeting has many translations. My preference: "Your light and my light are one." In public institutions, you may substitute the phrase, "Friendship connects us all."

You may engage in a discussion about the connection among all beings or the concept of inner light. Or you may simply enjoy this sweet song with your students. If you are working in a school or public institution, use the same tune and instructions, but change the lyrics to "Hello, Friend."

Use the first, second, and final verses of "Three Blind Mice." Each verse is the same: "Namaste, Namaste." Or "Hello, friend, hello friend."

Students stand in a circle of four or more. To keep the numbers even in a group, either stand in the circle or stand behind a child and share his partner.

To begin, stand facing the person across from you with tree hands. Looking at your partner, sing "Namaste, Namaste" (verse 1). To sing Verse 2, turn to face a new partner next to you in your circle. (This will take planning so everyone knows who his next partner is.) For the final verse, face the person on your other side in the circle.

If there are just two participants, sing all three verses facing your partner. For larger groups, form two circles, one inside the other. The inner circle faces the outer circle for Verse 1. For each verse, the children in the inner circle move over one space for a new partner.

SINGING AND RHYMES IN POSTURE

Singing in posture combines language skills with body awareness. Using words, rhythm, and motion, you teach directionality, foster imitation, and keep the child engaged.

Seesaw

Seated cross-legged, face the child and hold hands. Coordinate the motion so that each time the child goes back you sing "back," and when he comes forward, you sing "forth" to reinforce the concept of these directional terms. Sing to the tune of "Row, Row, Row Your Boat."

Seesaw back and forth, back and forth we go.
Back and forth, and back and forth,
Back and forth we go!

Butterfly Song

Use any or all verses with Butterfly Hands pose. Chant or invent a simple melody for accompaniment.

Butterflies, butterflies all around
Flying up and flying down
Flying left and flying right,
Butterflies make a lovely sight!
Flying high and flying low
Where oh where did my butterfly go?
Fly in front and fly behind
Butterfly, butterfly, please be mine.

Folded Leaf Rhymes

Sing or chant these while the child imitates you.

Breathe in reach up high,
Breathe out reach your thigh.
Breathe in reach up to the trees,
Breathe out hold on to your knees.
Breathe in reach up to your nose,
Breathe out reach down to your toes.

Bug on Its Back

Sung to the tune of "Three Blind Mice," as in Namaste.

Bug on its back

Bug on its back.
So many legs. So many arms.
Can't get off its back! Still on its back!

Rock the Baby

To help the sleepy baby they are holding drift into peaceful slumber, children sing this lullaby. Notice that the final line has been changed.

Rock-a-bye baby on the tree top.
When the wind blows the cradle will rock.
When the bough breaks, the cradle will fall.
And I will catch baby, cradle and all.

Drawbridge

Sing this coming up; lower with the word "down."

London Bridge is falling down, falling down, falling down.
London Bridge is falling down, my fair lady!

Games in Yoga Therapy

Yoga games are noncompetitive and inclusive. Like the postures, they combine movement, body awareness, creative play, language development, and relaxation. They teach children to take turns and interact with others in a natural environment.

NAME GAMES

These games support self-esteem and help with language development, memory, and social interaction. Children may select silly names for themselves, but derogatory names are not acceptable. Select the game suitable for the language and cognitive skills of the child or group with whom you are working. You may use a different name game each time you meet.

Speaking Your Name

This is the simplest name game. Ask the child to say her or his name aloud. Making oneself heard and speaking before others is challenging for many children with special needs. If the child has difficulty saying his name, give him a moment and a cue. If nothing comes, say his name and wait for nonverbal confirmation.

When working with groups, wait for everyone to say his or her name. Then see how many names the others can recall. Who knows everyone in the class? This is especially helpful when meeting new groups or when new children join a class.

Descriptive Names

Select from one of the following categories. After explaining and giving examples, the child chooses a name. Provide assistance as needed.

1. Color: The name includes the color of one item of the child's clothing: David is wearing a red T-shirt: Red David.
2. Same Letter: Children choose names for themselves that begin with the same letter as their first name: Nice Nancy, Playful Peter, or Musical Mark.
3. Appearance: These are names that describe something interesting about the child's appearance: Tall Sarah, Smiling Rachel, or Rebecca with Big Brown Eyes.
4. Rhymes With or Sounds Like: Children choose descriptive words that sound like their name in some way: Sweet Jeannie, Friendly Brenda, or Ticklish Richard.
5. Interests: Children choose names that reveal their hobbies or interests: Michael Who Loves Snorkeling, Math Whiz Brian, or Interested-in-Presidents Julie.
6. Something Great About Me: As the title suggests, children select at least one exceptional quality about themselves and use it for their nickname that day. The name may be descriptive—Laughing Debby; positive—Loveable Mark; or informative—I Said Thank You Today Howard.

GAMES FOR LANGUAGE DEVELOPMENT

Temple Grandin (2006) explains that her way of perceiving the world is concrete and visual. When she is spoken to, she translates others' words into pictures. She describes her imagination as a "video library" collected from her experiences.

Like Grandin, many individuals with autism understand illustrations and images more easily than they do words and symbols. Unfortunately, there are many commonly used words that represent concepts. From Grandin's *Thinking in Pictures:* "Spatial words such as 'over' and 'under' had no meaning for me until I had a visual image to fix them in my memory. Even now, when I hear the word 'under,' . . . I picture myself getting under the cafeteria tables at school during an air raid drill" (2006, p. 14).

In Integrated Movement Therapy, Molly Lannon Kenny suggests using yoga postures to help children experience these concepts.

Preposition Games and Postures

These games increase the child's understanding of spatial and relational terms.

Pillow Talk

Pillows are a useful prop in yoga therapy sessions. Here's another way to use them:

Place the pillow UNDER your head.
Place the pillow ON TOP OF your belly.
Place the pillow NEAR your foot; move it AWAY from your foot.
Place the pillow BEHIND your back
Sit ON the pillow
Step OVER the pillow

Prepositions in Posture

UNDER and UP: In Drawbridge, the toy boat goes under your hips when the drawbridge goes up.
NEXT TO: Position two children side by side. Roberta is sitting next to Anita.
OVER: The frog hops over the lily pads.
IN FRONT: Stand in line in Tree Hands pose. Michael is in front of David.
IN BACK: In the same pose, Brenda is in back of Karen.
ABOVE: In Butterfly Hands, fly your hands above your head.
BELOW: In Butterfly Hands, fly your hands below your head.
AROUND: In Butterfly Hands, fly your hands all around.

Half Moon Pose for Language Development and Creative Play

You can use this posture to trigger the imagination. For an introspective dance-like sequence, ask children to form a full moon with their arms in a circle overhead and gradually change its shape to a half moon. They can flow between the various stages of the moon, prompting a discussion of the changing night sky, tides, and the earth's rotation.

To teach punctuation, two children form parentheses, leaning toward one another; the middle child is the parenthetical word or phrase. To experience the shape of the letter C, students lean right. To become a comma, they lean left.

FOLLOW THE LEADER GAMES

Imitation is an important skill for triggering mirror neurons and improving motor skills. These games are recommended for sensory processing and motor planning.

Yoga Freeze

Having fun with physical activity is an important element of yoga therapy. When playing Yoga Freeze, every child has a chance to imitate, lead, and play. This game improves listening skills and direction following and is suitable for private sessions or groups. By taking a turn yourself, you can introduce new variations in postures.

Children start on their mats. With your signal ("1-2-3, go!"), the children follow you around the room. You may walk, run, or do anything in between. When kids are full of energy, let them run for as long as you like. When you are ready, shout "Freeze," and call out a posture; every child takes that pose.

One yoga teacher uses a variety of music for this game. The children run, dance, or hop around, following the beat. As soon as she stops the CD, the kids run to their mats for the posture she has called. Other teachers use drumbeats or other percussive instruments for marching or dancing to the varied rhythms.

You may lead the entire session, especially if the group is very large or you are working with children who teeter on the verge of losing control. Ideally, though, every child will have a turn choosing a position. Each may select his favorite pose, make up a new name for a pose, or invent a posture.

Children enjoy playful variations of postures. One example is Log Rolling.

20-1 Follow the Leader

From Tree Balance, they sway while the wind blows, blows, and blows until their tree falls down. Now a log, they roll toward one end of the room, and reverse. This gives children a playful option when they "fall" out of tree pose, especially when balance is challenging.

Yoga therapy invites novelty within a familiar structure. One of my students created a relaxing alternative to Tree Balance. She stands with one hip and shoulder against a wall with a pillow nestled beneath her head. Lifting her outside foot into position, she balances in what she calls "Sleeping Tree." This posture is frequently requested by her classmates.

Children are often willing to try something new when they feel safe and prepared. A child who has difficulty calling out the name of a posture may participate by selecting a visual card depicting a pose. He (perhaps with your help) holds up the cue card when it's his turn. He's in the game!

One of my students loves to run and laugh with her peers, but each time she is called on to select a pose, she panics. Before we begin Yoga Freeze, I remind her to choose her pose and keep it in her head. When I call her name, she shouts, "Dog!" She relies on her favorite pose every time, and I congratulate her on her choice each time. Pleased with herself, she feels part of the group and is willing to try whatever poses her classmates invent or select.

To add a challenge to the game, ask verbal children to give instructions for the pose. Many children enjoy an opportunity to be the teacher. Or give children a chance to lead the group between postures. For this, you might want to use the next game.

Follow Me

This is a game that can be included in Yoga Freeze or played independently. Here the children set the pace for movement around the room. Each child chooses a speed and a particular gait for his classmates to imitate as he leads them. Children may use Warrior 1 Walk, Crab Walk, Dog Walk, or their own made-up silly walks (see Photo 20-1). They may walk fast or slow, skip, crawl, hop, or slither around the room. This, too, is a useful way to help active children release energy or to engage a sluggish child in movement.

Down by the Pond

Games such as Down by the Pond invite children to imitate animals through movement and sounds and invent or act out stories about these animals. Children swim like fish or hop like grasshoppers (from Frog pose). They glide along the edge of the pond like slithery snakes and surprise a group of barking dogs. Even those children who may not understand the subtlety of this kind of creative play usually enjoy watching or making some of the animal sounds. Each child participates in her own way.

Lily Pond

This game fits in well with Down by the Pond or can be played as a variation of Frog pose. To create lily pads for hopping frogs, one child lines up pillows (paper squares taped to the floor work, too). To make this a cooperative game, children line up in Frog pose behind the leader. Her goal is to keep everyone out of the pond, and she learns that some children require shorter distances

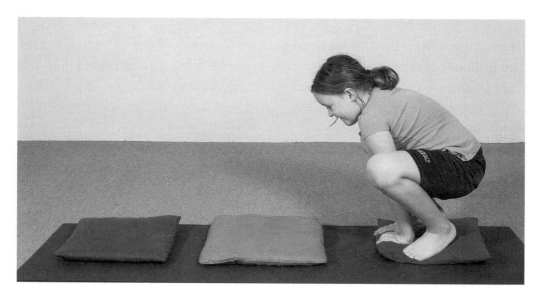

20-2   Frog on Lily Pad

between lily pads for hopping. By seeing how her choices affect her classmates, she learns to create the lily pond that keeps all the frogs out of the water. This kind of play helps children observe consequences and develop empathy in a natural setting.

Conclusion

In yoga philosophy, there is a concept called *sankalpa*, meaning resolve or intention. But unlike a goal or objective, this inner commitment is rooted in desire, belief, and acceptance.

When you teach yoga therapy to children with special needs, do so with full faith in your capacity to share this gift and in the child's capacity to receive it. Put aside the have to's and the should have's. Fuel your intention with knowledge and practice, but without judgment or expectation.

Be ever guided on your path by the message of the Bhagavad Gita (Eas-waran, 2007, p. 93):

"On this path effort never goes to waste,
and there is no failure."

PARENT QUESTIONNAIRE FOR YOGA THERAPY

NAME of CHILD _____

DATE of BIRTH _____

PARENT/GUARDIAN _____

ADDRESS _____

_____

PHONE _____ CELL _____ E-MAIL _____

EMERGENCY CONTACT TELEPHONE NUMBER AND NAMES _____

_____

PHYSICIAN'S NAME AND TELEPHONE _____

SPECIAL NEEDS DIAGNOSIS _____

PHYSICAL SYMPTOMS _____

_____

HISTORY OF CARDIAC CONDITIONS _____

HISTORY OF SEIZURES_____

INJURY TO JOINTS, SPINE, BONES _____

IS THE CHILD IN PAIN? RECENT ILLNESS OR SURGERY_____

_____

HISTORY OF RESPIRATORY PROBLEMS, ASTHMA, ALLERGIC REACTIONS

_____

MEDICATIONS TAKEN AT THIS TIME AND REASONS_____

_____

EXTREME SENSITIVITIES: SMELLS, SOUNDS, TOUCH, ETC. _____

_____

BEHAVIORAL PATTERNS: (AGGRESSIVE, SELF-STIMULATION, SELF-INJURY, FEARFUL, OPPOSITIONAL, ANXIOUS, WITHDRAWN, RESISTANT TO TOUCH)

_____

BEHAVIOR WITH OTHER CHILDREN _____

_____

BEHAVIOR WITH ADULTS _____

_____

ABLE TO FOLLOW INSTRUCTIONS: (CIRCLE)

    VERBAL

    VISUAL CUES

    TAPPING OR GESTURES

    DEMONSTRATION

    OTHER _____

ABLE TO REPLICATE TEACHER'S MOVEMENTS OR BODY POSITIONS INDE-

PENDENTLY OR WITH ASSISTANCE _____

DEVELOPMENTAL DELAYS: MOTOR, SPEECH, COGNITIVE, OTHER_____

_____

AREAS OF SPECIAL INTEREST_____

DESCRIBE ANY PRE-EXISTING CONDITIONS THAT CONTRAINDICATE YOGA

PRACTICE OR SPECIFIC POSITIONS _____

_____

PLEASE CONSULT YOUR PHYSICIAN BEFORE CHILD'S PARTICIPATION.

TO THE BEST OF MY KNOWLEDGE, MY CHILD IS IN GOOD HEALTH AND

ABLE TO PARTICIPATE IN YOGA THERAPY: YES / NO

I GIVE THE YOGA THERAPIST PERMISSION TO TOUCH AND ADJUST MY

CHILD IN POSTURE

SIGNATURE _____

PRINT NAME AND DATE _____

APPENDIX 2

Assessment Process for Yoga Therapy

I. Preliminary Assessment

    A. Parental permission (written)

    B. Medical history

    C. Cognitive, physical, and emotional challenges

    D. Learning style

    E. Behavioral challenges

II. Instructional Assessment

    A. Modality: Is the child responsive to

        1. Verbal instructions

        2. Visual cues and prompts

        3. Gestures

        4. Tactile cues

        5. Your movements or posture

            Can he imitate?

            Do you have to be close to child to gain his attention?

    B. Readiness

        1. Sits quietly

        2. Attends to instruction

        3. Easily distracted

        4. Aggressive or self-injurious behaviors

        5. Self-stimulation or repetitive behaviors

6. Areas of independence

7. Areas of dependence

8. Physical considerations

9. Contraindications based on medical history

10. Injury or limitation

11. Muscle tone

12. Environmental considerations

13. Sensitivities

14. Sources of distraction

15. Needs chair or wall for support

III. Assessment of Foundational Postures

	INDEPENDENTLY	WITH ASSISTANCE	NOT TODAY

A. Seated

   1. On floor

      a. Cross-legged

      b. On knees

      c. Legs straight

   2. In chair

   3. Other support

B. Hands and knees

C. Prone

   1. Arms by sides

   2. Arms overhead

   3. Legs on floor

D. Supine

   1. Knees bent

   2. Legs extended

   3. Head on floor

E. Standing

   1. Back on wall

   2. Other support

IV. Assessment of Breathing Patterns

A. Depth: Shallow or deep

B. Rhythm: Erratic or rhythmic

C. Location: Upper chest, thoracic, abdominal

D. Awareness: Able to attend to his breathing

E. Movement: Does movement alter his breathing?

    1. Accelerates with active postures

    2. Decelerates with soothing posture

V. Implementation

A. Mode of instruction

B. Duration of session

C. Frequency of instruction

D. Goals and objectives

E. Curriculum

F. Periodic reassessment

G. Measurement

Creative Relaxation: Yoga Therapy in School Autism Cluster

This excerpt[1] describes a pilot program to determine the efficacy of yoga therapy for children with autism spectrum disorder, which became the foundation of the S.T.O.P. and Relax curriculum.

The following pilot project was conducted in spring 2001 by Louise Goldberg, Sally Miller, Debra Collins, and Daniela Morales. The purpose was to teach yoga-based relaxation skills to children with autism so they could function more productively in stressful situations.

Participants were upper-elementary-school children with autism from self-contained classes and regular education with support. The six students were chosen because their teachers and parents documented overt signs of anxiety and dysfunction under stress. They would soon make the transition to middle school, and they lacked some or many of the skills needed to cope with changes in their routine. One or more of them were prone to violent outbursts. Students were divided into two groups, and they participated in 30-minute sessions three times a week for eight weeks.

The [S.T.O.P. and Relax Rev. 2010] program included yoga exercises and breathing, role playing, guided imagery, discussion, visual aids, rules, music, soft lighting, stories, and mnemonics. The staff and I made presentations to parents and teachers so they would be able to reinforce skills the children were learning.

Evaluation was by pre and post rating scales from teachers and parents; hand measurement of pulse rates before and after sessions; observation of students' breathing patterns and muscle tone before, during, and after exercises; teachers' observations of overt signs of stress vs. relaxation in target situations; and anecdotal reports from teachers, parents, and children who participated. Students were videotaped early and late in the training.

Evaluation results: Rating scales completed by parents and teachers demonstrated lower stress levels. Pulse rates taken at the end of class were over 90 percent lower than at the beginning of the sessions. The mean pulse rate (based on a 10-second reading) before class was 17.577, and the mean pulse rate after class was 14.954. Using the two-sample-t-test, the difference was found to be statistically significant ($p < 0.01$).

In addition, students demonstrated deeper breathing and increased stillness, as evidenced by video clips from early and late in the training. Improved muscle tone enabled students to do more challenging postures and sit straighter. They were successful at following more complex instructions. Students demonstrated increased awareness of the parts of their bodies and how to move them. Their ability to fix the eyes on one point and balance on one foot increased significantly. Students learned to respond to verbal cues such as "relax" and "breathe." Classroom teachers reported increased alertness after sessions and more self-monitoring; teachers were able to use the relaxation cues to help children de-escalate in volatile situations.

Parents observed children using relaxation techniques during stressful situations and before bed . . . Children shared scenarios of using the techniques to help calm themselves.

1   Excerpted from L. Goldberg (2004). Creative Relaxation: A yoga-based program for regular and exceptional student education. *The International Journal of Yoga Therapy. 14,* 74–77. Reprinted with permission of the publisher.

Conditions for Calm

Adapted from Roger Cole[1]

How Does Your Body Relax?

DUELING SYSTEMS

Activating systems: 8 major nervous systems inhibit quieting
- Rev up brain (accelerate brain waves to make decisions)
- Contract muscles (to carry out decisions)
- Mobilize support (activate respiration and circulation)
- Shut down nonessential functions (digestion, immune system)

Quieting systems: three major nervous systems inhibit activating

Relaxation-inducing conditions in wall-supported inversion

1. Get comfortable—pain stimulates reticular activating system (RAS)—rouses brain, turns on senses, readies muscles for action.
2. Muscle release—gentle prolonged stretching releases tension, desensitizes stretch reflex. Through stillness, no muscular effort is engaged.
3. Warmth—cold skin stimulates sympathetic nervous system (SNS), raising

blood pressure; warm skin stimulates anterior hypothalamus, the relaxation center that inhibits all known activating systems.

4. Reclined or inverted posture—lie down, legs up, hang upside down. Gravity pushes blood down from legs toward upper body; stimulates pressure sensors in neck and upper chest. This stimulates the solitary tract nucleus located in brain. Signals from this center strongly inhibit several activating centers and stimulate parasympathetic nervous system (PNS)—slower heart rate, reduced muscle tension, rest and restore.

5. Darkness—Cover eyes or darken room. Light that reaches eyes sets off nerve impulses that inhibit anterior hypothalamus.

6. Ocular pressure (with eye bag)—Light pressure on bones around eyes triggers reflex that stimulates PNS to slow down heartbeat.

7. Giving yourself permission to relax—if you are not feeling safe or that it's truly OK to let go, that feeling stimulates amygdala (anxiety-generating center in brain), which inhibits relaxation.

8. Taking time for body to release—chemical reactions such as breakdown of stress hormones need time; may require up to 10 minutes or longer. The more time you take, the deeper your relaxation.

1   R. Cole, Conditions for calm, *Yoga Journal 216* (2008), 87–90. Copyright 2008 by Roger Cole. All rights reserved. Reprinted with permission.

APPENDIX 5

Ten Ways to Become a Better Communicator

Adapted from Linda Hodgdon[1]

I. Get on the student's level (eye level)

II. Establish attention

    A Physically close to child, in child's line of vision

    B. Become animated

    C. Use visual props

III. Prepare child for what you are going to communicate

    A. Verbal signals to cue child

    B. Pair verbal signal with a gesture

    C. Use visual prop to help child shift attention to your topic

IV. Use gestures and body language meaningfully

    A. Purposeful movements can enhance your interaction

    B. Exaggerate your movements

V. Support your communication visually

    A. Your body is a visual tool; use it!

VI. Speak slowly and clearly

    A. Choose your words carefully

    B. Avoid mumbling, run-on sentences, interjecting nonsequential information

VII. Limit verbalization

    A. More talk is NOT better; talking less may be best

B. Match your verbal output to the child's (single words, phrases, short sentences)

VIII. Include "wait time" in your interactions

  A. Count to five (or twenty)

  B. Wait expectantly; stay engaged

  C. Determine when to repeat a request (if child looks distracted)

IX. Guide or prompt child to respond (if needed)

  A. Physical guides (move an object)

  B. Point to the place he needs to look

  C. Turn his head a bit if acceptable; touch his hand or arm gently to move it in the direction of the action he needs to take

  D. Prompt the child by beginning the sentence or activity

  E. WAIT FIRST—do not guide or prompt too much too soon

X. Stay with the interaction until you attain a desired response

  A. Immediately correct errors by showing the child the correct response

  B. Modify YOUR communication as needed

  C. Enlist visual (and physical) supports to help the child be successful

  D. Give "closure" to the interaction so both you and the child know it has ended successfully—a smile, a gesture, or verbal encouragement

Once you've identified how to be effective with a child, remember to use these techniques. Those things on this list that are most difficult for you to do may be the very strategies that will help your child/student the most.

1 L. Hodgdon, *Solving behavior problems in autism.* (1999). Troy, MI: QuirkRoberts Publishing, 89-93. © Linda Hodgdon. Used by permission of the author.

APPENDIX 6

My Yoga Time: My Feelings, My Poses

(Directions: Circle words that apply. Blanks may be filled in by student with assistance.)

SOMETIMES I FEEL TENSE IN

    My legs

    My arms

    My stomach

    My face

    My mind

    Other: _____

    When _____ happens, I feel tense

    When I am tense, I feel _____

SOMETIMES I FEEL RELAXED IN

    My legs

    My arms

    My stomach

    My face

    My mind

    Other:_____

    When _____ happens, I feel relaxed

    When I am relaxed, I feel _____

CHOOSE ONE POSE THAT HELPS YOU FEEL RELAXED:

Bellows Breath

Baby

Folded Leaf

Breathing Tree

Drawbridge

Huh Breath

Candle

Other:_____

MY FAVORITE POSTURE FOR HAVING FUN IS

Rock the Baby

Fruit Picker

Butterfly Hands

Seesaw

Other:_____

MY FAVORITE POSTURE FOR FEELING QUIET IS

Baby

Floating on a Cloud

Butterfly Knees

Folded Leaf

Other:_____

MY FAVORITE POSTURE FOR _____ IS

1.

2

WHEN THINGS ARE JUST NOT GOING RIGHT, THERE IS ONE POSE THAT I CAN COUNT ON TO MAKE ME FEEL BETTER. THIS IS MY YOGA TIME—MY TIME.

MY Time pose is _____

Training Resources

Budding Yogi's mission is to impart mindfulness and yoga to children and teenagers. Therapeutic yoga classes for children with varied special needs are available on a private session basis. www.buddingyogis.com

Creative Relaxation with Louise Goldberg provides trainings for yoga teachers, educators, therapists, and parents in yoga therapy for children with special needs, including autism spectrum disorders, emotional behavioral disorder, ADHD, and sensory processing disorders. Curriculum adapts postures, breathing, and mindfulness for use in public school education and varied therapeutic settings. Course includes the book *Yoga Therapy for Children with Autism and Special Needs*. www.creativerelaxation.net

Every Kid's Yoga Teacher Training explores the many ways that yoga supports other therapeutic modalities in addressing difficulties with attention, self-regulation, speech and language, learning, and motor skills for children ages 4–12. It is appropriate for anyone with prior yoga experience. www.everykidsyoga.com

Get Ready to Learn is a researched classroom yoga curriculum designed to prepare students (and staff) to achieve optimal states for learning. The program series provides a foundation for all ages and stages of development and across the range of student challenges from mild to severe. www.getreadytolearn.net

Global Family Yoga offers introductory workshops in addition to an advanced course on therapeutic yoga for children. Regardless of where an individual falls on the spectrum of health or disease, yoga is a life-affirming practice that promotes wellness on all levels. www.globalfamilyyoga.com

GreenTREE Yoga offers trainings and materials to bring the benefits of yoga to people of all ages and abilities and to those who work with them. Programs include yoga for trauma, autism, schools, caregivers, and compassion fatigue. www.greentreeyoga.org

Honoring the Child with Developmental Challenges teaches children to connect to breath, movement, meditation, and mindfulness. It offers training to utilize yoga with children with ADHD, ASD, PDD, sensory processing disorders, anxiety and stress-related disorders, learning disabilities, cerebral palsy, Down syndrome, and developmental delays. www.zensationalkids .com

The International Association for School Yoga & Mindfulness (k-12yoga.org) facilitates implementation of sustainable, evidence-based programs to improve health, positive behavior, and achievement in school communities. As a coalition, K-12YOGA.ORG promotes collaboration among schools, colleges/universities, researchers, healthcare, business, and the diverse community of school yoga and mindfulness trainers. www.k-12yoga.org

The International Association of Yoga Therapists supports research and education in yoga and serves as a professional organization for yoga teachers and yoga therapists worldwide, as well as yoga practitioners, yoga researchers and health-care practitioners who utilize yoga in their practices. IAYT serves members, the media, and the general public as a comprehensive source of information about contemporary yoga education, research, and statistics. www.iayt.org

Integrated Movement Therapy was developed to meet the challenges of all phases of life. While empirically grounded, IMT nurtures the very heart of yoga through its focus on divinity rather than pathology. Working with a variety of developmental challenges, IMT draws extensively on best practices for children with autism spectrum and related disorders. www.samarya center.org

Next Generation Yoga Teacher Training focuses on typically developing children. Trainers have a background in special education, and the training does include a module on yoga for kids with special needs. www.nextgenerationyoga.com

OMazing Kids LLC promotes inclusive wellness activities for kids of all abilities. The blog and social media pages share information about books, DVDs, CDs, games, and products designed for kids' wellness, mindfulness, and relaxation;

product reviews; lesson plans and activities; research; and kids' wellness in the news. A connection corner provides listings of adapted yoga programs and trainings. www.omazingkidsllc.com

Pediatric Yoga provides training for hospital staff in yoga-based tools to help children manage pain; recover more quickly from surgery; decrease anxiety, stress, pain, and suffering due to hospitalization and medical procedures; and increase the healing process. www.colormeyoga.com

S.M.Art Kids Adaptive Yoga (ages 3–11) uses a multifaceted approach that incorporates story, movement, and art to support health, explore the body, engage the senses, and improve inner calm and focus. www.bodylogique.com

The SMILY (Sensory Motor Integration & Learning with Yoga) program is designed to enhance learning and brain development by blending stories, songs, yoga postures, breathing, and relaxation. It can be adapted for children with special needs such as autism, cerebral palsy, Down syndrome, and ADHD. www.kidslearnyoga.com

The Special Yoga Centre in the UK offers trainings in Yoga for the Special Child as well as Special Yoga for Children with Developmental Challenges for children and adolescents with special needs including ASD, PDD, anxiety disorder, learning difficulties, motor planning issues, ADD, ADHD, and general developmental delays. www.specialyoga.org.uk

S.T.O.P. and Relax, Your Special-Needs Toolbox, provides self-calming skills to children whose language development, self-regulation, and social interactions are impaired by disorders such as autism. The visual curriculum integrates evidence-based practices in yoga, psychology, and special education. Techniques for breathing and posture instruction, music, lesson plans, and guided relaxation facilitate implementation by teachers, therapists, and parents. www.stopandrelax.net

STRIPES: Systematic Training in Relaxation; Inner Peace for Every Student is a brain/body fitness training for adults who work with children, K–12. www.stripesyoga.com

Yoga Calm reduces stress and optimizes learning. A blend of the traditional yoga practices of mindfulness, physical activity and nervous system regulation with social skills, Yoga Calm works with a wide range of students, including those struggling with ADHD, anxiety, and other behavioral and emotional challenges. www.yogacalm.org

Yoga 4 Classrooms is a model of yoga and mindfulness education geared to the general school population, conducted seated or standing by the children's desks. The program includes staff and parent education and a ten-week classroom residency of half-hour weekly sessions. Families receive practices for home follow-up. www.yoga4classrooms.com

Yoga for Autism, ADHD, and Differently Abled Children teaches participants to effectively integrate yoga into their therapeutic treatment of children with learning and developmental challenges such as ADD/ADHD, autism, and sensory processing disorders. Through lecture, videotape, and experiential labs, participants learn to apply breath, movement, and meditation/relaxation. www.childrensyoga.com

Yoga for Children with Developmental Challenges training program targets varied needs, including autism. Training includes creating the yogic environment, breath control, therapeutic postures, and deep relaxation, as well as techniques/postures to calm the senses, energize, focus, organize, and self-regulate, using props and modifications. www.peacefulpathwaysyoga.com

Yoga for the Special Child, Sonia Sumar's training, offers a comprehensive program of Yoga techniques to enhance the natural development of children with special needs. Gentle and therapeutic, it's safe for babies and children with Down syndrome, cerebral palsy, microcephaly, autism, and other developmental disabilities, and it provides an effective treatment for children diagnosed with ADD, ADHD, and learning disabilities. www.specialyoga.org

Yoga Therapy for Every Special Child—Meeting Needs in a Natural Setting, by Nancy Williams, offers products, courses, and an informational blog. www.yogatherapy4children.com

Yoga Wonderland participants learn to adapt classes for "differently abled" children, including those with neurological, physical and cognitive impairments, such as cerebral palsy, muscular dystrophy, Down's syndrome, spina bifida, mental retardation, and autism. Trainings include music to choreograph yoga sequences. www.yogawonderland.org

Yoga-Yingo offers trainings on integrating yoga into OT and pediatric practices. Yoga-Yingo games for home, school, therapy, or studio use adapt poses for different challenges and developmental levels. www.yoga-yingo.com

Yoga4Karma Practitioner Training, developed by an occupational therapist and yoga teacher, is offered to health-care providers and teachers. Training focuses on the development, health promotion, and potential of every child regardless of special needs. Be the change you want to see in the world. www.yoga4karma.com

YogaKids Tools for Schools program combines yoga, multiple intelligences theory, curriculum integration techniques, and character education in a fun, engaging, and developmentally appropriate manner, K–5. www.yogakids.com

YogAutism is a one-on-one yoga program specially designed to meet the challenges of those on the autism spectrum, including individuals with sensory processing disorder, Asperger's syndrome, PDD, high-functioning autism, and classic autism. www.yogautism.org

References

A.D.A.M. Medical Encyclopedia. (2012). Retrieved from http://www.ncbi.nlm.nih.gov/pubmedhealth/PMH0001992/

Ahmed-Ullah, N. S. (2011). Schools face new challenge: Return of recess. *Chicago Tribune*. Retrieved from http://articles.chicagotribune.com/2011-10-25/news/ct-met-cps-playground-20111013_1_recess-middle-schools-school-day

American Psychiatric Association. (2000). *Diagnostic and statistical manual of mental disorders* (4th ed.). Washington, DC: American Psychiatric Association.

Anxiety Disorders Association of America. (2012). Test anxiety. Retrieved from http://adaa.org/living-with-anxiety/children/test-anxiety

Autism Society of America. (2012). About autism. Retrieved from http://www.autism-society.org/about-autism/

Ayres, A. J. (1995.) *Sensory integration and the child*. Los Angeles, CA: Western Psychological Services.

Baptiste, B. (2004). *My daddy is a pretzel*. Cambridge, MA: Barefoot Books.

Barker, R. (2009). A yoga and mindfulness study: The case of Henry. *The Educational Therapist, 30,* 10–12.

Barnes, P. M., Bloom, B., & Nahin, R. (2008). *Complementary and alternative medicine use among adults and children: United States, 2007* (CDC National Health Statistics Report No. 12). Hyattsville, MD: National Center for Health Statistics.

Baron-Cohen, S., Leslie, A. M., & Frith, U. (1985). Does the autistic child have a "theory of mind"? *Cognition, 21,* 37–46.

Bensen, H. (1975). *The relaxation response*. New York, NY: Avon Books.

Bertherat, T., & Bernstein, C. (1977). *The body has its reasons*. New York, NY: Avon Books.

Betts, D. E.,. & Betts, S. W. (2006). *Yoga for children with autism spectrum disorders*. London, UK: Jessica Kingsley.

Birdee, G., Yeh, G., Wayne, P., Phillips, R. S., Davis, R., & Gardiner, P. (2009). Clinical applications of yoga for the pediatric population: A systematic review. *Academic Pediatrics*. 9(4): 212–220.

Bremner, J., Elzinga, B., Schmahl, C., & Vermetten, E. (2008). Structural and functional plasticity of the human brain in posttraumatic stress disorder. *Progressive Brain Research, 167,* 171–186.

Brown, R., Gerbarg, P., & Muskin, P. (2009) *How to use herbs, nutrients, and yoga in mental health care*. New York, NY: Norton.

Brown, S., & Vaughan, C. (2009). *Play: How it shapes the brain, opens the imagination, and invigorates the soul*. New York, NY: Avery.

Buckley-Reen, A. (2009). Get ready to learn: Yoga therapy in the classroom. Retrieved from http://getreadytolearn.net/GRTL/Home.html

Cabral, P., Meyer, H. & Ames, D. (2011). Effectiveness of yoga therapy as a complementary treatment for major psychiatric disorders: A meta-analysis. *Primary Care Companion CNS Disorders*, *13.* doi:10.4088/PCC.10r01068

Campbell, D. (1997). *The Mozart effect*. New York, NY: Avon Books.

Centers for Disease Control and Prevention. (2012a). Press release: CDC estimates 1 in 88 children in United States has been identified as having an autism spectrum disorder. Retrieved from http://www.cdc.gov/media/releases/2012/p0329_autism_disorder.html

Centers for Disease Control and Prevention (2012b). A growing problem. Retrieved from http://www.cdc.gov/obesity/childhood/problem.html

Chessen, E. (2010). Finding fitness. *Autism Advocate, 59,* 42–47.

Chronis-Tuscano, A., Molina, B., Pelham W., Applegate, B., Dahlke A., Overmyer, M., & Lahey, B. (2010). Very early predictors of adolescent depression and suicide attempts in children with attention deficit hyperactivity disorder. *Archives of General Psychiatry, 67,* 1044–1051.

Collins, D., & Goldberg, L. (2012, Winter). Evidenced-based practices in teaching self-calming to special needs children. Learning & the Brain 31st Conference. San Francisco, CA.

Cole, R. (2005). Nonpharmacologic techniques for promoting sleep. *Clinics in Sports Medicine, 24,* 343–353.

Cole, R. (2008) Conditions for calm. *Yoga Journal. 216,* 87–90.

Cole, R. (2012). High blood pressure and inversions. *Yoga Journal.* Retrieved from http://www.yogajournal.com/practice/594

Cottingham, J., Porges, S., & Lyon, T. (1988). Effects of soft tissue mobilization (Rolfing pelvic lift) on parasympathetic tone in two age groups. *Physical Therapy, 68,* 352–356.

Coulter, D. (2001). *Anatomy of hatha yoga.* Honesdale, PA: Body & Breath.

Council for Exceptional Children. (2011). Behavior disorders/emotional disturbances. Retrieved from http://www.cec.sped.org/AM/Template.cfm?Section=Behavior_Disorders_Emotional_Disturbance

Daichman, J, Cueli-Dutil, T., & Tuchman, R. (2010). Motor deficits in children with autism and related disorders. In J. Redlich (Ed.), *Autism spectrum disorders.* Retrieved from http://kidpt.com/2010/04/18/motor-deficits-in-children-with-autism-and-related-disorders/

Dennison, P., & Dennison, G. (1986). *Brain gym.* Glendale, CA: Edu-Kinesthetics, Inc.

Desikachar, T. K. V. (1995). *The heart of yoga.* Rochester, VT: Inner Traditions International.

Doidge, N. (2007). *The brain that changes itself.* London: Penguin.

Easwaran, E. (2007). *The Bhagavad Gita.* Berkeley, CA: Nilgiri Press.

Faherty, C. (2000). *Asperger's: What does it mean to me?* Arlington, TX: Future Horizons.

Feuerstein, G. (1998). *Yoga tradition.* Prescott, AZ: Hohm Press.

Feuerstein, G. (1997). *The Shambala encyclopedia of yoga.* Boston: Shambala.

Feuerstein, G. (2002). Reflections on yoga, yoga therapy, and psychotherapy. *Yoga Studies.* Retrieved from http://www.iayt.org/Publications_Vx2/news/news2.aspx#hypo

Field, T., Sanders, C., & Nadel, J. (2001). Children with autism display more social behaviors after repeated imitation sessions. *Autism, 5,* 17–23.

Fishman, L, & Saltonstall, E. (2008). *Yoga for arthritis.* New York, NY: Norton.

Foss, R. (2002). *Music for Dreaming* (CD). Margate, FL: Relaxation Now. www.relaxationnow.net.

Gage, F. (2003). Brain, repair yourself. *Scientific American. 289,* 46–53.

Goldberg, L. (2004a). Creative Relaxation. A yoga-based program for regular and exceptional student education. *The International Journal of Yoga Therapy, 14*, 68-78.

Goldberg, L. (2004b). *Creative Relaxation: Yoga for children* DVD. Margate, FL: Relaxation Now LLC. www.relaxationnow.net

Goldberg, L. (2011). *Creative Relaxation: Yoga therapy for children with autism and special needs manual* (rev. ed.). Margate, FL: Relaxation Now LLC.

Goldberg, L., Miller, S., Collins, D., & Morales, D. (2006, Revised 2010). *S.T.O.P. and Relax* Instructor's Manual. Margate, FL: STOP and Relax LLC.

Gordon N., Burke S., Akil H., Watson S., & Panksepp J. (2003). Socially-induced brain "fertilization": play promotes brain derived neurotrophic factor transcription in the amygdala and dorsolateral frontal cortex in juvenile rats. *Neuroscience Letters, 24,* 17–20.

Grandin, T. (2005). *Animals in translation.* Orlando, FL: Harcourt.

Grandin, T. (2006). *Thinking in pictures.* New York, NY: Vintage Books.

Gray, C. (2002). What are social stories™? The Gray Center for Social Learning and Understanding. Retrieved from http://www.thegraycenter.org

Groden, J., Cautela, J., Prince, S., & Berryman, P. (1994). The impact of stress and anxiety on individuals with autism and developmental disabilities. In E. Schopler and G. B. Mesibov (Eds.), *Behavioral issues in autism.* New York, NY: Plenum Press.

Gutstein, S. (2000). *Autism Aspergers: Solving the relationship puzzle.* Arlington, TX: Future Horizons.

Gutstein, S. (2005, Winter). Relationship development intervention. *Autism Spectrum Quarterly*, 8–12.

Hagins, M., Moore, W., & Rundle, A. (2007). Does practicing hatha yoga satisfy recommendations for intensity of physical activity which improves and maintains health and cardiovascular fitness? *BMC Complementary and Alternative Medicine, 7.* doi:10.1186/1472-6882-7-40

Harada T., Okagawa S., Kubota K. (2004). Jogging improved performance of a behavioral branching task: Implications for prefrontal activation. *Neuroscience Research, 49,* 325-337.

Hillman, C., Buck, S., Themanson, J., Pontifex, M., & Castelli, D. (2009). Aerobic fitness and cognitive development: Event-related brain potential and task performance indices of executive control in preadolescent children. *Developmental Psychology, 45,* 114–129.

Hillman, C., Erickson, K., & Kramer, A. (2008). Be smart, exercise your heart: Exercise effects on brain and cognition. *Nature Reviews Neuroscience, 9,* 58-65.

Hillman, C., Motl, R., Pontifex, M., Posthuma, D., Stubbe, J., Boomsma, D., & de Geus, E. (2006). Exercise appears to improve brain function among younger people. *Health Psychology, 25,* 678–687.

Hodgdon, L. (1999). *Solving behavior problems in autism.* Troy, MI: Quirk Roberts.

Iacoboni, M. (2008). *Mirroring people.* New York, NY: Farrar, Straus & Giroux.

Ingersoll, B., & Schreibman, L. (2007). Teaching reciprocal imitation skills to young children with autism using a naturalistic behavioral approach: Effects on language, pretend play, and joint attention. *Journal of Autism and Developmental Disorders, 36.* doi:10.1007/s10803-006-0089-y

International Association of Yoga Therapists. (2012). Educational Standards for the Training of Yoga Therapists. Retrieved from http://www.iayt.org/development_Vx2/IAYT_Standards_7%201%2012%20.pdf

Iyengar, B. K. S. (2001). *Yoga, the path to holistic health.* London, UK: Dorling Kindersley.

Jacobson, E. (1934). *You must relax.* New York, NY: Whittlesey House.

Janzen, J. (1996). *Understanding the nature of autism.* San Antonio, TX: Therapy Skill Builders.

Janzen, J. (2009) *Autism handbook for parents.* Waco, TX: Prufrock Press.

Jha, A. (2013). Being in the Now. *Scientific American Mind, 24,* 26–33.

Jotika, U., & Dhamminda, U. (1986). *The greater discourse on steadfast mindfulness of the Buddha.* Maymyo, Burma: Migadavun Monastery.

Keedle, J. (2012). How music saves your soul. Retrieved from http://www.healthylifect.com/home/article/How-Music-Saves-Your-Soul-3600125.php

Keltner, D. (2009). *Born to be good.* New York. NY: Norton.

Kemper, K., Vohra, S., & Walls, R. (2008). The use of complementary and alternative medicine in pediatrics. *Pediatrics, 122,* 1374. doi:10.1542/peds.2008-2173

Khalsa, S. B., Hickey-Schultz L., Cohen, D., Steiner, N., & Cope, S. (2012). Evaluation of the mental health benefits of yoga in a secondary school: A preliminary randomized controlled trial. *Journal of Behavioral Health Services & Research, 39,* 80–90.

Khalsa, S. B., Shorter, S. M., Cope, S., Wyshak, G., & Sklar. E. (2009). Yoga ameliorates performance anxiety and mood disturbance in young professional musicians. *Applied Psychophysiology and Biofeedback, 34,* 279–89.

Koegel, L,. & LaZebnik, C. (2004). *Overcoming autism.* New York, NY: Viking Press.

Koenig, K. P., Buckley-Reen, A., & Garg, S. (2012). Efficacy of the Get Ready to Learn yoga program among children with autism spectrum disorders: A pretest–posttest control group design. *American Journal of Occupational Therapy, 66,* 538–546.

Kraftsaw, G. (1999). *Yoga for wellness.* New York, NY: Penguin.

Kranowitz, C. S. (2005). *The out-of-sync child.* New York, NY: Penguin.

Lupien, S. J., McEwen, B. S., Gunnar, M. R., & Heim, C. (2009). Effects of stress throughout the lifespan on the brain, behaviour and cognition. *Nature Reviews Neuroscience 10,* 434–445.

Madigan, J. B. (2009). *Action based learning.* Murphy, TX: Building Better Brains through Movement.

McCall, T. (2007). *Yoga as medicine.* New York, NY: Bantam-Dell.

McEwen, B. (2001). *The end of stress as we know it.* New York, NY: Dana Press.

McGonigal, K. (2008). Tame your stress. *Yoga Journal, 215,* 82.

McGuire, E. A. (2000). Navigation-related structural change in the hippocampus of taxidrivers. *Proceedings of the National Academy of Sciences, 97,* 4398–4403.

Medina, J. (2008). *Brain rules; 12 principles for surviving and thriving at work, home, and school.* Seattle, WA: Pear Press.

Medina, J. (2012). Brain rules: Exercise. Seattle, WA: Pear Press. Retrieved from http://www.brainrules.net/exercise

Mendelson, T., Greenberg, M., Dariotis J., Gould, L., Rhoades, B., & Leaf, P. (2010). Feasibility and preliminary outcomes of a school-based mindfulness intervention for urban youth. *Journal of Abnormal Child Psychology, 38,* 985–994. doi:10.1007/s10802-010-9418-x

Mesibov, G., Shea, V., & Schopler, E. (2004). *The TEACCH approach to autism spectrum disorders.* New York, NY: Springer Science + Business Media, Inc.

Miller, E. (2003). *Yoga for scoliosis* (Booklet). Palo Alto, CA: Shanti Productions.

Miller, L. (2006). *Sensational kids.* New York, NY: Penguin.

Ming X., Brimacombe, M., & Wagner, G. (2007). Prevalence of motor impairment in autism spectrum disorders. *Brain & Development, 29,* 565–570.

Muktibodhananda, S. (2001). *Hatha yoga pradipika*. Mungar, Bihar, India: Yoga Publications Trust.

National Institute of Mental Health. (2008). Attention deficit hyperactivity disorder. Retrieved from http://www.nimh.nih.gov/health/publications/attention-deficit-hyperactivity-disorder/complete-index.shtml

O'Connor, J., French, R., & Hendersen, H. (2000). Use of physical activity to improve behavior of children with autism: Two for one benefits. *Palaestra, 16,* 22–26.

Panksepp, J. (2008). Play, ADHD and the construction of the social brain: Should the first class each day be recess? *American Journal of Play, 1,* 55–79.

Paul, R. (2004). *The yoga of sound.* Novato, CA: New World Library.

Payne, K, & Ross, L. (2010). *Simplicity parenting.* New York, NY: Ballantine.

Petrus C., Adamson S., Block, L., Einarson, S., Sharifnejad, M., & Harris, S. (2008). Effects of exercise interventions on stereotypic behaviours in children with autism spectrum disorder. *Physiotherapy Canada, 60,* 134–145. doi:10.3138/physio.60.2.134

Philippot, P., Chapelle, G., & Blairy, S. (2002). Respiratory feedback in the generation of emotion. *Cognition and Emotion, 16,* 605–627.

Porges, S. (2005). The vagus: A mediator of behavioral and psychological features associated with autism. In M. Bauman & T. Kemper, (Eds.), *The neurobiology of autism* (pp. 65–78). Baltimore, MD: The Johns Hopkins University Press.

Prabhavananda & Isherwood, C. (1981). *How to know God: The yoga aphorisms of Patanjali.* Hollywood, CA: Vedanta Press.

Radhakrishna, S. (2010). Application of integrated yoga therapy to increase imitation skills in children with autism spectrum disorder. *International Journal of Yoga, 3,* 26–30.

Rately, J. (2008). *SPARK.* New York, NY: Little, Brown.

Robin, M. (2009). *A Handbook for Yogasana Teachers.* Tucson, AZ: Wheatmark.

Rosen, R. (2002, May–August). Q & A: Headstand and high blood pressure. *Yoga Studies.* Retrieved from http://www.iayt.org/Publications_Vx2/news/news2.aspx

Sanford, M. (2006). *Waking.* Chicago, IL: Rodale.

Sanford, M. (2008). Matthew's vision. Retrieved from http://matthewsanford.com/content/matthews-vision

Sapolsky, R. (2003). Taming stress. *Scientific American, 289*(3), 86–95.

Sattelmair, J., & Ratey, J. (2009). Physically active play and cognition: An academic matter? *American Journal of Play, 1*(3), 365–374.

Saraswati, S. (1990). *Yoga education for children.* Munger, Bihar, India: Bihar School of Yoga.

Saraswati, S. (1999). *Asana pranayama mudra bandha.* Munger, Bihar, India: Bihar School of Yoga.

Schilling, E., Aseltine, R., & Gore, S. (2007) Adverse childhood experiences and mental health in young adults: A longitudinal survey. *BMC Public Health 7.* Retrieved from http://www.ncbi.nlm.nih.gov/pmc/articles/PMC1832182/

Selye, H. (1974). *Stress without distress.* New York, NY: Signet.

Sensory Processing Disorder Foundation. (2012). About SPD. Retrieved from www.spdfoundation.net

Sequeira S., & Ahmed, M. (2012). Meditation as a potential therapy for autism: A review. *Autism Research and Treatment, 2012.* doi:10.1155/2012/835847

Shannahoff-Khalsa D. (2010). *Kundalini yoga meditation for complex psychiatric disorders: Techniques specific for treating the psychoses, personality, and pervasive developmental disorders.* New York, NY: Norton.

Siegel, D. J. (2007). *The mindful brain: Reflection and attunement in the cultivation of well-being.* New York, NY: Norton.

Siegel, D. J. (2011). *The whole-brain child: 12 revolutionary strategies to nurture your child's developing mind.* New York, NY: Delacorte Press.

Smith, D. (2007). *Introduction to special education: Making a difference.* New York, NY: Prentice-Hall.

Soosalu, G., & Oka, M. (2012). *mBraining: Using your multiple brains to do cool stuff.* Retrieved from http://www.amazon.com/mBraining-Using-multiple -brains-ebook/dp/B007SU4LBE

Sparrowe, L, & Walden, P. (2004). *Yoga for Healthy Bones: A Woman's Guide.* Boston, MA: Shambala Publications.

Streeter, C., Gerbarg, P. L., Saper, R. B., Ciraulo, D. A., & Brown, R. P. (2012). Effects of yoga on the autonomic nervous system, gamma-aminobutyric-acid, and allostasis in epilepsy, depression, and post-traumatic stress disorder. *Medical Hypotheses, 78,* 571–579.

Streeter, C., Whitfield, T. H., Owen, L., Rein, T., Karri, S. K., Yakhkind, A., . . . & Jensen, J. E. (2010). Effects of yoga versus walking on mood, anxiety, and brain

GABA levels: A randomized controlled MRS study. *The Journal of Alternative and Complementary Medicine, 16,* 1145–1152. doi:10.1089/acm.2010.0007.

Streeter, C., Jensen, J., Perlmutter, R., Cabral, H., Tian, H., Terhune, D., . . . & Renshaw, P. F. (2007). Yoga Asana sessions increase brain GABA levels: A pilot study. *Journal of Alternative and Complementary Medicine, 13,* 419–426.

Sumar, S. (1998). *Yoga for the special child.* Evanston, IL: Special Yoga Publications.

Taras, H. (2005). Physical activity and student performance at school. *Journal of School Health, 75,* 214–218.

Templin, S. (2012). Bio-energetic focusing. Retrieved from http://www.bio-energeticfocusing.com/.

Tortora, G., & Grabowski, S. (1996). *Principles of anatomy and physiology.* New York, NY: HarperCollins.

Tullis, P. (2011). The death of preschool. *Scientific American Mind, 22,* 36–41.

Tyrka, A., Price, L., Marsit, C., Walters, O., & Carpenter, L. (2012). Childhood adversity and epigenetic modulation of the leukocyte glucocorticoid receptor: Preliminary findings in healthy adults. *PLoS ONE, 7,* 1http://.

UNC TEACCH Autism Program. (2012). Structured teaching. Retrieved from http://teacch.com/educational-approaches/structured-teaching-teacch-staff

University of Texas at Dallas Counseling Center. (2012). Self-Help: Test Anxiety. Retrieved from http://www.utdallas.edu/counseling/testanxiety/

Vishnudevananda, S. (1960). *The complete illustrated book of yoga.* New York, NY: Harmony Books.

Vythilingam, M., Heim, C., Newport, J., Miller, A., Anderson, E,. Bronen, R. M., & Bremner, J. (2002). Childhood trauma associated with smaller hippocampi in women with major depression. *American Journal of Psychiatry, 159,* 2072–2080.

Walsh, D. (2011). *Smart parenting, smarter kids.* New York, NY: Free Press.

Walsh, D. (2012, Winter). The brain goes to school. Learning & the Brain 31st Conference. San Francisco, CA.

Weinstein, C. (1994). Cognitive remediation strategies. *Journal of Psychotherapy Practice and Research, 3,* 44–57.

Weintraub, A. (2004). *Yoga for depression.* New York, NY: Broadway Books.

Weintraub, A. (2012). *Yoga skills for therapists.* New York, NY: Norton.

Willis, J. (2008). *How your child learns best.* Naperville, IL: Sourcebooks.

Young, E. (2001). Balancing act. *New Scientist, 15,* 25.

Index

Note: Italicized page locators indicate photos.